2012 Enlightened

Gabriel Blows his Horn

SECOND EDITION

Order this book online at www.trafford.com
or email orders@trafford.com

Most Trafford titles are also available at major online book retailers.

Printed in Victoria, BC, Canada.

ISBN: 978-1-4269-3324-0 (sc)

Library of Congress Control Number: 2010906468

Our mission is to efficiently provide the world's finest, most comprehensive book publishing service, enabling every author to experience success. To find out how to publish your book, your way, and have it available worldwide, visit us online at www.trafford.com

Trafford rev. 5/4/2010

www.trafford.com

North America & international
toll-free: 1 888 232 4444 (USA & Canada)
phone: 250 383 6864 • fax: 812 355 4082

A Guide to Understanding 2012 & The Path to Enlightenment.

UNIVERSAL SCIENCE of DIVINE LIGHT

There is an abundance of universal knowledge, truth, techniques and mantras that can help attain a deeper connection to one's self and the universal consciousness. The teacher who evolves from a universal light brotherhood or a guru parampara is able to guide the seeker along the spiritual path into the divine light consciousness. However, this can only be accomplished with pure love and a desire to help others become their own guru and master. In truth, guiding another seeker along the journey to their enlightenment helps to build a solid foundation for the universal community of light consciousness to expand brick by loving brick. This is especially important as we journey through the changes of 2012 and into the "Golden Age".

It is with great humility and surrender that this book was created. It was inspired through the writings, wisdom and words of many great authors, teachers, masters and incarnates, as well as through a divine light connection to the Akashic. My intent is that those who read the contents of this book, see not my hand, but experience the wisdom of evolution and the beautiful universal truth shared by all. From the microcosm to the macrocosm, there is only one light of collective divine love.

Love and Blessings to All ...  ... Children of the Light

Introduction

We have chosen a beautiful time in our evolution to take our birth. Rather than approach the aspects of 2012 with doom and gloom, this book was written to present a clear understanding of the multi-leveled reality that existed historically and that will exist in the future. It sheds light on the 200,000 year history of evolution from the ape-man, to the human being, and into the spiritual being. Our journey becomes less daunting if we use common sense and the Akashic to allow a flow of information that weaves together a historical puzzle.

By integrating the past with 2012 and beyond, we may understand and prepare for the significant transformation about to take place. Evolution is inevitable and by putting the facts into perspective, we can prepare ourselves to meet the upcoming events that may affect us both on a physical and spiritual level. The bottom line is empowerment, because as we attain true understanding, we empower the choices that allow us to be free of the illusions that prevent lucid thoughts and clarity on the level to which they resonate. The truth is what it is, however, personal empowerment comes from being our own guru and taking responsibility for our spiritual and physical planning. When researching other views please remember the misinformation and fraudulent cover-ups created by the powers of church, state and global illuminati that have distorted the facts and truth about JFK, 911, Swine Flu, WTO, GMOs, Electric Cars, holistic Cancer cures—and the list goes on.

Truth, transformation and knowledge of how everything integrates into the reality of time-space and light consciousness can only be attained through trusting one's inner being and connecting to the place of peace and spiritual love that guides us. Be wise and search for this truth, as truth will not search for you. Personally and spiritually as I have grown in life, I have tried to find truth in places where truth does not exist, but through love all becomes clear.

What is Love

What is love, but the pure essence of the soul expanding into another form, as it allows two to become one and one to become formless with all that is, and all that will ever be.

Love is beyond this life, and yet it is all that we really are. Love knows no boundaries, no limits to its making or its sharing. It softly crosses the valleys, the oceans, up the mountains moving beyond the most distant stars. It is as gentle as the most beautiful dream, but is beyond thought. It has no form and no desire other than to be collective with all that can accept its magnificent radiance. Unconditionally it is and will always be, it is formless and mindless and fills the human heart with all it can handle, overflowing its limited capacity of self, ego and conditionings.

Love has no boundary on its pure compassion, nor does it understand self or can it be captured and horded. It is free flowing as the summer winds that blow though the mountain trees or like the forest streams that nourish all those that come to share it's refreshing essence.

Love is and will always be and never was there a time it did not exist, nor a time it will not be. The formless, mindless, thoughtless, all compassionate unconditional love is all there is, and all that will ever be.

Love is the spirit, the loyal friend that guides us through the emotional rains of life, with no desires or conditions. Love is all that we are and all we can ever be, there is no more and no less, everything else is just the illusion.

Love is all I have and all that I am ... *Brad C. Carrigan*

"This message of love was received in a dream and written down upon awakening."

Picture by Julie Hubbell

Table of Contents

Mother Earth

Mother Earth is the beautiful and immaculate giver and sustainer of life. As our true mother, she is both the macrocosm and our microcosm. She shares our Kundalini energy, Chakras, and is our civilization's beacon to the universe, and reflects our human discretion as the mother of our earthly family. There was a time when humankind was in resonance with this living, breathing integral part of our universal body. This dharma is to understand that we are part of her, just as she is part of us. We must live within sustainable boundaries that respect the balance and the laws of this living universe and stand up to those who deceive us by disrespecting and plundering our precious home.

Disrespecting Mother Earth is akin to denigrating the laws of "cause and effect" and the fundamental nature of "karma", which holds that for every action there is an equal and opposite reaction. If we collectively approach 2012 with sensitivity and responsible global actions, this along with collectivity of the spirit may help avert the devastation predicted, while allowing the transformation to the higher light consciousness.

Essene Brotherhood

Loving and respecting Mother Earth was a main part of the wisdom and culture of ancient times. As our current civilization became more "modernized", leaving our roots of the family farm, this connection, wisdom and natural understanding was lost. Many great spiritual masters, subcultures and indigenous peoples still carry on traditions that understand the power and gifts that Mother Earth supplies to us freely. There is a beautiful integration of all things from the microcosm of our body to the macrocosm of the universe, and Mother Earth is part of this intricate web woven gently through the cosmos.

The archaeological discovery of the Dead Sea Scrolls in 1946 revealed that two thousand years ago a commune brotherhood of spiritual people known as the Essenes lived together in a sacred community. They understood and executed basic alchemic earth and metaphysical connection principals and lived life according to the basic laws that govern the divine connection between humankind, Mother Earth and the universe.

Many great souls including Jesus, Joseph and Mary, John the Baptist, John the Evangelist, and others who changed the direction of our history and spiritual world have been associated with this community. Their spiritual life and knowledge of the metaphysical mysteries were unknown to the mainstream society of the times, resulting in controversy. Consequently, fearing persecution the Essenes withdrew and lived collectively far outside the cities. Some of the great souls of the brotherhood would leave to expand their wisdom and spiritual base, understanding their universal connection to the great teachings.

The Essenes were masters of the ancient arts, spiritual understanding and metaphysical sciences. They possessed advanced knowledge of the stars and light consciousness and worked collectively to advance their spiritual understanding and connection. They also felt they were decedents of a great ancient civilization that had perished ages before. The brotherhood of light was responsible for the spiritual knowledge and growth of Jesus and other masters as they journeyed into the metaphysical world seeking spiritual enlightenment through the door of the universal light consciousness. As workers in the realm of light consciousness, they also had direct access to the secrets of the Great Pyramid and its hall of the initiates. They understood alchemy with an aim of achieving ultimate wisdom as well as spiritual immortality. They believed this power of light could defeat the darkness inhibiting human assent.

Ancient scrolls reveal that after leaving the Essene community, Jesus spent seventeen years mostly in India, Tibet then Egypt before heading back to Jerusalem at 30 years of age. From age thirteen to age twenty-nine, he was both a student and teacher of Buddhist and Hindu holy men of India. From Jerusalem to Benares, Brahman historians recorded this beautiful journey, and even today they still know and love him as Saint Issa—their 'Buddha'.

The teachings of the Essenes were universal without boundaries or borders. Each day and evening the Essene collective would meditate and give thanks and love to Mother Earth, the heavenly father, the angels of light and the aspects (deities) of the divine that allowed their sustainable connection to Mother Earth and the universal divine light consciousness to continue and grow.

In the **evening** they would praise: The Heavenly Father and a different aspect each day of the week: The Angel of Sun, The Angel of Water, The Angel of Air, The Angel of Earth, The Angel of Live, The Angel of Joy.

In the **morning** they would praise: The Earthly Mother and a different aspect each day of the week: The Angel of Power, The Angel of Love, The Angel of Wisdom, The Angel of Eternal Life, The Angel of Work, The Angel of Peace.

Tree of Life

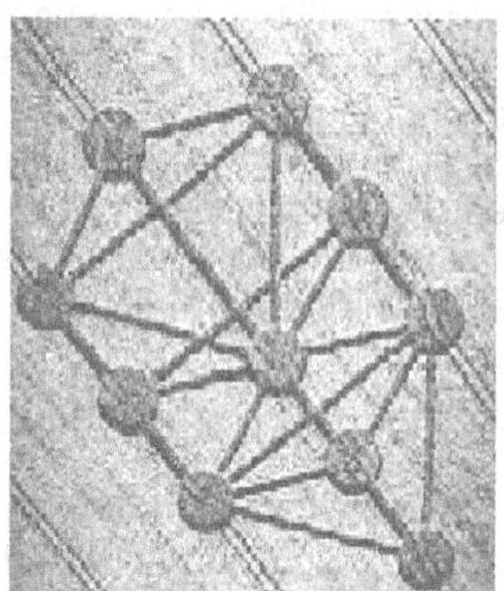

Barbury Castle Crop Circle - May 1997

The Tree of Life represents all living things including every culture and spiritual master of the light. With its branches reaching skyward toward the universal light consciousness, and its roots going deep in the mother earth seeking and creating the balance of all living things, it dwells in three worlds, of heaven, the earth, and the underworld, connecting all three. It represents both a feminine symbol, bearing nourishment, and a masculine symbol of strength. This wonderful Tree is mentioned many times in the Bible, from Genesis to the Book of Revelation. It is said; one who eats from the Tree is given "eternal life", because to eat from the Tree of Life is to drink the knowledge of the light consciousness. The Tree, imbibes the above ground or positive world, as well as the evil or negative below ground world. It is also three dimensional, and is the gateway to the light consciousness and the dark side.

The crop circle above (right) is a diagram of the Tree of Life from the ancient tradition "Kabbalah." This is a Hebrew occult philosophy said to be from the Middle Ages, and based on a mystical or metaphysical interpretation of the Scriptures. Some biblical scholars believe that origin in fact dates much further back to the ancient Sumerians, Egyptians, or even to the Atlantians, which is more probable given that the wisdom is universal and beyond the scope of one religious concept. According to the Kabbalah, a person must metaphorically and spiritually ascend the ten points of the Tree of Life to reunite with the Divine. As one increases his or her spiritual capabilities, one increases the capacity to contain more of the light pouring in through these ten branches, and so draws nearer to the universal divine light consciousness.

The Tree of Life has many symbolic spiritual meanings and reference points. The Tree sets out the wisdom or the 'map of the Universe'. Each branch or path and sphere has a specific relationship and meaning and represents the overall connection to the Universal Divine Light Consciousness or God.

The Tree of Life, in the Kabbalah consists of four worlds;

Atziluth, the highest of four worlds, it represents the fire and creative energy,

Briah, the second, "World of Creation" it represents the water and receptive energy,

Yetzirah, the third, "World of Formation" it represents air and formative power or energy,

Assiah, the forth, "World of Action" it represents the earth and material energy.

The Tree also represents the Chakra system within the human body as each Chakra rotates and vibrates at a specific frequency based on the harmonic patterns or frequency of our lives. The Chakra system also forms the energy grid within the human body that produces the color and field of the "Aura" and can be used in healing as well as evolving spiritually through meditation.

The empowering Kundalini Shakti energy is described as a coiled up serpent lying dormant near the base Chakra until being awakened. The purpose of awakening the Kundalini as mentioned later in the book, is to allow our connection to the power of creation. This energy will spiral, almost DNA like, up through the Chakra system around the Yin and Yang channel as it connects.

The action of this energy is also known as the **Caduceus** (above) shown as a double-helix serpent moving around the Tree of Life or spinal column and out through the Sahasrara (crown) Chakra, to where it connects to the universal light consciousness.

The Tree of Life also represents all the primordial masters, incarnations, great teachers and sages, as flowers on this divine Tree. They are translated as a fragrance of its truth into the human awareness, but the knowledge is not connected to the human ego, dogmas or conditionings, this is because humankind cannot alter or change its form. It is pure universal light consciousness manifested as "one" truth and represented by the different masters or flowers on it's branches. Historically, instead of enjoying the fragrance of this whole Tree the illusion of earthy power, money or control attracted the lower self of the human ego. In this illusion the beautiful flowers of Jesus, Buddha, Krishna etc, were picked from the Tree and put into the lapel promoting the dogmas of organized religion and false teachings. So the flowers slowly died and with them the wisdom and knowledge that connected them to the fragrant Tree. In today's world these beautiful teachings of the primordial masters are still divisible into sects and religious dogma.

The sheep are still being led by the blind, and do not recognize that we are our own guru and master, and alone are responsible for our assent into the divine light consciousness.

To be divisible is anti evolution, all are one light, one drop in the ocean of divine light consciousness.

All are "ONE" in the NEW **Golden Age.**

Over the ages of our spiritual evolution, the pure divine knowledge of light and solar occultism was horded by the dark forces, to control and divide humankind. We are "children of the light", and for too long our innocence was suppressed, oppressed and deceived as we followed, believed, worshiped, and were force fed anti-God dogmas in the name of spirituality.

We have learned our collective connection to the light consciousness is not divisible by religion, false gurus, self-proclaimed masters or any secret society. This connection starts within and no middle person is required for ascension to the divine. The reveling of 2012 will finally open the door to our evolutionary and spiritual truth, but beware of the great deceivers; they will not give up their domain over human kind easily or gently.

Time

We are leaving the Age of Pisces, a disparaging and oppressive period and moving into the Age of Aquarius, a period of revealing, peace and love. The earth is also transforming through a period of great change, and these changes are mirrored within us, our bodies, our DNA and our ascension to the 4th – 5th dimensions. As this happens, more than ever before, we are becoming consciously aware and drawn towards spirituality and personal development. It seems everything that is happening now, has been predicted in the Mayan Calendar.

As mentioned in other parts of the book, "Time" as we know it, is also speeding up—or collapsing. Mars polar ice caps are melting, there is a heat wave on other planets and the Sun is also heating up. This all equates to a massive galactic frequency change. To back this up, many years ago Scientists discovered that the earth gives off a pulse. This pulse or frequency that is similar to a heartbeat is called the *Schumann Resonance* or pulse (heartbeat) of the Earth. It has been stable at approximately 7.8 cycles per second for thousands of years, and was even used by the military because of it consistency. However, since 1980 this resonance has been slowly rising. It is now over 12 cycles per second! This mean there seems to be less than 16 hours per day instead of the old 24 hours. So "linear time" as I understand it, is measured in increments of astronomical or atomic motions, while "nonlinear" time is described in increments of free flowing progressions. Seems some scientists actually believe the earth will stop rotating for about three days when this pulse reaches 13 cycles per second—sometime around 2012.

So it stands to reason then, if time really is speeding up—flying faster than our calendars indicate: then our internal clocks will also be thrown off by whatever is happening. So its okay to be late for work!

Past Civilizations

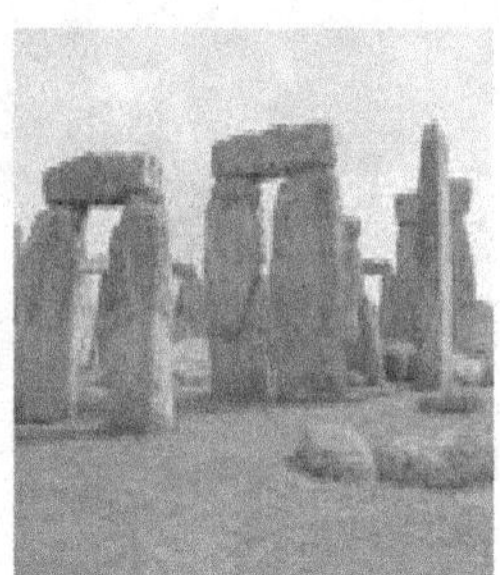

Atlantis

The ancient Greek philosopher Plato (360 BC) tells a legendary tale about a cataclysmic destruction of the ancient civilization of Atlantis which he said occurred around 9,000 BC. This numinous tale has captured our attention for years. Atlantis has shaped many aspects of the history of civilization, as the guiding architect of the Great Pyramids and the Mayan calendar. It is said the founders of Atlantis were half God and half human—similar to the Hindu mythology and folklore about Star Teachers from the star constellation *Pleiades.* Ancient Sumerian tablets also speak of planet Nibiru and the Anunnaki as having shaped our early civilizations by DNA modifications then enslaving people.

It is believed Atlantis was during a time of great power. With an abundance of rare, unusual minerals, they were able to harness solar power through the use of crystals. They also had the ability to move freely through land, water and air using aircraft and guided vessels.

The Atlantians not only enjoyed all of our "modern" advancements, but those that still remain undiscovered today. Machines and lasers were used for rejuvenation of the body and their technology assisted in developing their psychic abilities, including telepathy and astral traveling. According to Plato, the last civilization of Atlantis existed about 12,000 years ago. The surviving poets, priests, and others were able to pass along its legends of wealth and tales of a cataclysmic end. Plato's writings of Atlantis are the only known records of its existence other than in the Hall of Records that remain hidden in the Labyrinth or under the Sphinx in Egypt, as foreseen by the clairvoyant Edgar Cayce. In his trances Mr. Cayce also described Atlantians as thought-form beings—projecting pure white light energy—but gradually taking on a more material density of this Earth plane after engaging in acts of the lower self and self-indulgence. They then began to separate into two groups—the *Children of the Light* who followed the Laws of One, and those that chose to follow the Sons of Belial and their carnal pursuits.

According to Greek folklore, a change occurred in Atlantis after the fourth race of man had completed its pinnacle of development. A power struggle ensued after the humility, truth and dharma of the Children of Light ("spirit masters") was overcome by the transgression, treachery and dishonesty of the Sons of Belial. As this terminal condition festered, the universal divine authority was steadfast to destroy Atlantis in an attempt to revert back to where humankind would once again live a dharmic and evolving spiritual life. This resulted in destruction from the great floods, leaving little record. The fifth race of man then emerged into what is now our current modern civilization.

Interestingly, the early Christians have a similar story in Genesis about Noah and the great flood, where he was warned by the Gods through visions to prepare and build his Ark so he could escape the cataclysm and establish the new Earth civilization. Could Noah have been from Atlantis?

The survivors of Atlantis also spread into Africa and to Central America, establishing their knowledge and advancing the civilizations of the Maya, Egyptians and others. Even today the Mayan elders recognize their heritage as descendants of Atlantis, although most of those records were either lost or preserved in the great Hall of Records in Egypt and the Mayan calendar.

It is believed a few of the light and dark forces of the fourth race of the Atlantian civilization survived, building foundations within our current civilization, and setting the stage as we move into 2012 and the final battle of Armageddon.

According to the Aztec calendar, our modern civilization is in the 4th great cycle with the 5th starting after the great purification of 2011/2012. It appears that we are in a similar cycle of corruption that Atlantis experienced before its destruction.

Lemuria—Mu

According to many channeled sources, the ancient civilization of Mu was destroyed 26,000 years ago by earthquakes, subduction and submergence during a period of the Earth's last alignment to the dark rift (or end of the great cycle). It is also said that Queen Moo (a survivor from Mu) may have founded the ancient civilization of Egypt, and that other Mu survivors ventured to China and Central America, giving rise to their advanced civilizations of the time.

The Great Sphinx

It may be in the best interests of Egypt's history books and tourism to have their descendants take credit for building the Sphinx, but it is not their work or vision. Many top scientists assert that there is a pattern of erosion on the

Sphinx that indicates that it was created 12,000 years ago—closer to the end of the last Ice Age and during a period when heavy rains fell in the eastern Sahara. This is a major contrast with Egyptological dating that claims the Sphinx was created about 4,500 years ago.

Edgar Cayce, the famous clairvoyant of the 20th century, mentioned in a physic reading that survivors of Atlantis built the Sphinx around 10,500 BC, and left behind a "Hall of Records" that contained all the knowledge of their lost civilization and the true history of our past great civilizations. There are many cultures including the Mayans that link the sinking of Atlantis to the building of the Sphinx, claiming there is a chamber beneath the paws that contains the legendary "Hall of Records".

Cayce also prophesied that this Hall of Records would be discovered and opened by 1998. Unfortunately that did not happen, however in his favor there was a seismic survey done to the Sphinx that indicated the existence of several unexplored tunnels in the rock beneath, including a large rectangular chamber about 25 feet beneath its front paws. Curiously, they also discovered a massive underground labyrinth of large halls and rooms in the Gaza Plateau but the government has halted exploration until the year 2012. If the of Hall of Records were discovered before 2012, it would expose the truth about our history and behind the religious and political dogmas we have been forced to embrace for thousands of years. When 2012 does arrive it won't matter, since the world will be in the throes of a major chaotic transition! Edgar Cayce connected the opening of the Hall of Records to the second coming of Christ (or Shri Kalki) at the time of revelation—the Armageddon and 2012.

This is just another example of the politics and power preventing truth and progress and hindering the evolution process of humanity by re-defining our deeper historical heritage. So what would really happen if the records indicated that we have been misled and misinformed about our spiritual understanding, alien contacts, and galactic proof of the coming cataclysm?

Pyramids

There are beautiful metaphysical references of how the pyramids were built, but where did these ideas come from? The truth is, there are hundreds of pyramids around the world as well as on Mars and the Moon, and they all seem to stand on gateways of energy, vortex or power grid centers, that could represent a form of "star-gate" between planets. Many believe that the pyramids act as a portal to the inner world and another spiritual dimension connecting through time-space to the universal light consciousness. What we know for sure is they are scientifically designed instruments that harbor a complete detailed knowledge of the stars, galaxy, Sun, and planets, Earth's dimensions, rotating speed of magnetic field, gravity, time, space and energy, and the life force of body, mind and spirit. In ancient times the Great Pyramid was also known as the hall of the initiates, where the connection to the great forces of the 5th dimensional light consciousness was attained. The "Aquarian Gospel" states this is were Jesus achieved Christ consciousness.

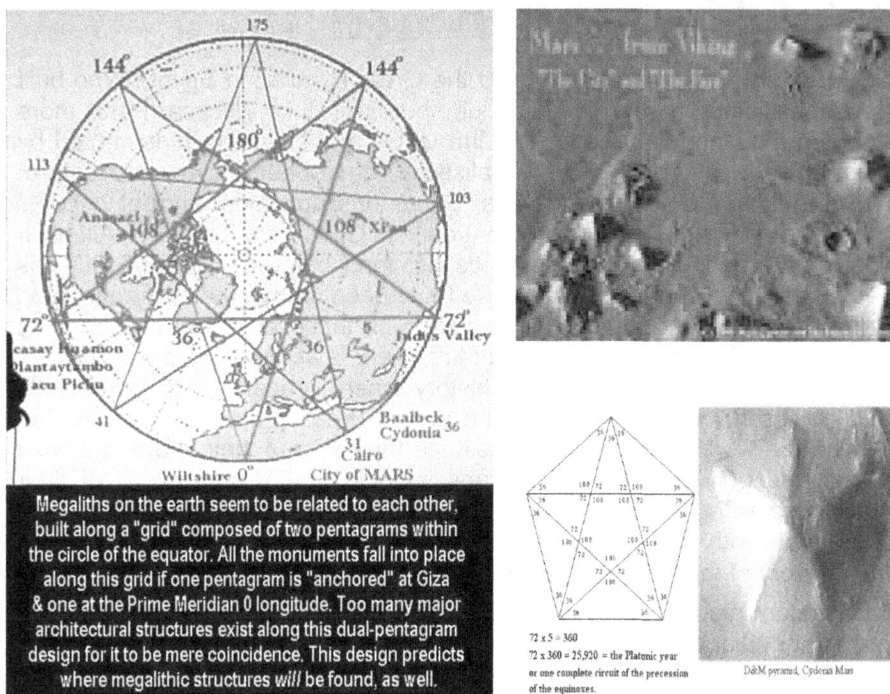

Megaliths on the earth seem to be related to each other, built along a "grid" composed of two pentagrams within the circle of the equator. All the monuments fall into place along this grid if one pentagram is "anchored" at Giza & one at the Prime Meridian 0 longitude. Too many major architectural structures exist along this dual-pentagram design for it to be mere coincidence. This design predicts where megalithic structures *will* be found, as well.

The four sides of the pyramid represent the four dimensions of time space, with the 5th side representing the 5th dimension or the totally liberated human being. It is said Atlantis was a top Earth connection with the pyramids as entrance portals to the center of the Earth—possibly a different dimension. The Hopi Indians say they knew of entrances to huge underground cities.

A properly aligned and constructed pyramid is a source of peaceful energy and can be helpful in all aspects of life—including curing disease and negativity. Harnessing this energy in the next age will be part of the building blocks of our outward connection to the stars.

Alien Presence

Hieroglyph *- Giza Plateau, at Abydos*

So, what advanced technology built the Great Pyramid in Egypt? Who built the sophisticated harbor city near the shores of Lake Titicaca (Peru) more than ten thousand years ago, and the UFOs and flying machines noted by most ancient cultures? Could it realistically have been the descendents of Mu or Atlantis? Since the Mayans, Sumerians and most ancient cultures have painted images or a history that depicts Gods from the sky or Aliens in spacecrafts dating back; in some cases; long before Atlantis or Mu, this seems unlikely. Could it be that there have been many great civilizations on Earth over the past 200,000 years, whereby these ancestral descendants were the forefathers of Atlantis and Mu? There is a strong historical connection to aliens throughout ancient history where renderings of spacecrafts and beings from the stars were the norm. These renderings are charted around the world and it is fair to assume they shared their knowledge with inhabitants of Mu and the Atlantians. who in turn shared some of their knowledge with the Mayans and Egyptians. Sumerian stone tablets also show visits with the Anunnaki from planet Nibiru over 6,000 years ago but their history of these aliens goes back 200,000 years.

Our modern global society is the first civilization that has been subjected to constant denial by the religious and political powers that control the media, our thoughts, and our history. If the mass population were to relate to a higher life form, it would de-stabilize their dominance, so they hide the truth to maintain control as the "highest authority". Consequently, all information about alien presence has been kept TOP Secret, along with creating multi-million dollar misinformation strategies. This was clearly evidenced during Roswell, and later with crop circle sightings, where misinformation to the media reduced these warnings and messages to nothing more than an elaborate hoax created by a few drunken English men in the dark of night. Yet, the fact is aliens have been part of this world since the beginning of civilization and may even walk among us. The powers that control us are surely aware of this, and most likely using the aliens to access advance technologies to increase their power base.

There is a plethora of information on the internet: some of it fiction—but also diligent research about alien abductions, NASA, and a 2012 government conspiracy that will reveal some truths—one being how the ancient Sumerian history is connected to a strong alien presence.

To staunchly deny that life exists on other planets of the solar system and galaxy is the epitome of arrogance and control. Government and religious interests have done a good job keeping our attention on terrorists and flu vaccines instead of 2012 and the reality of alien presence.

These highly evolved alien life forms dwell in both our 3rd and higher 5th dimensional planes. Those residing in the lower frequencies may be considered lower evolved and not so friendly toward humankind but technologically advanced. While those in the higher dimensions of pure light consciousness guide our evolution and promote our spiritual assent to the light consciousness. This would easily explain some of our ancient history that describes Avatars, Gods and Deities that radiate pure love and share divine wisdom through the Vedas and similar historical books of wisdom and, Meta science.

These evolved alien spiritual beings have attempted to guide us using the frequency of their evolved spiritual communication, but our conduit opening is very weak on Earth. So due to our inability to tune in to the higher frequencies of the light, some higher evolved aliens are using crop circles to communicate with us, through an advanced form of Cymatics. However, as we transform into the higher consciousness of the 5th dimension though 2012, and the morphing of our respective DNA, and channels of light awakened, the use of symbolic messages through crop circles will no longer be required.

The Maya are known for their Serpent Gods.

Pleiades—Star Teachers

Pleiades in the constellation of Taurus

Shri Agni Devi

The Pleiades are known as a cluster of stars in the constellation Taurus. In Sanskrit this group of stars is known as Krittika, ruled by Shri Agni Devi—the God of Fire. Kritikka is known as the star of fire where power is born. In Indian mythology it is believed the Deity Lord Karttikeya, the second son of Lord Shiva, and Goddess Parvati originated from there before coming to the planet Earth.

Legends and stories about this star cluster can be found in almost every culture. Aztecs, Australian Aboriginals, Chinese, Columbian Amazons, Egyptians, Greeks, Hebrews, Hindus, Incas, Japanese, Maori, Mayans, Native Americans, Old Europeans, Persians, Romans, and South African tribal cultures all have storytelling legends about the Pleiades.

The star cluster of Pleiades is "the connection to our higher light consciousness" our galactic family. It is this region of space that has signaled to Earth through their crop circle messages that a higher light consciousness is watching and helping us understand what is occurring during the ascension of 2012. Pleiades is the gateway bringing centering and balance to the higher self. Throughout the ages, these masters of light have helped us understand our connection to the living library of the Akashic and universal light consciousness in our spiritual evolution, and they will appear before 2012 to support us during our forthcoming transformation.

Many legends of Pleiades are found around the world, and all seem to point to their protection and ultimate help during our evolution and transformation. This assistance, in part, has encouraged humankind to elevate and reprogram via DNA transformational upgrade to the higher realm of the collective light consciousness.

The roots of Hinduism date back to 3000 BC. This ancient and complex religion has no clearly defined religious associations, but rather a family of faiths that extended from the monistic triad, (Brahma, the Creator, Vishnu, the Preserver, and Shiva, the Destroyer) to a pluralistic Hindu theism (the Supreme Being or collective light consciousness manifesting qualities as many Deities or Gods and Goddesses).

The mentors and benefactors of ancient Hinduism were Pleiadian and Orion's star teachers. It is said the myths and spoken traditions such as storytelling arose from Pleiadian traditions and spiritual teachings. Many of the immortal or spiritually evolved Goddesses and Gods described in the folklore of the Vedas as Deities, were in fact beings of Pleiadian ancestry in human form that came to Earth during ancient times and past civilizations. For example: the Lemurians of Mu were descendants of Pleiadian star teachers on the continent of LEMURIA, but before LEMURIA was destroyed they acted as the mentors for those living in India. The spoken traditions, tales and spiritual protocols of the Chakras and Kundalini evolved from the ancient Pleiadian and Shamanic ancestry into the early traditions of ancient Hinduism.

The Vedas—ancient Hindu scriptures created in the form of mantras or hymns, were the timeless and eternal religion of dharma, and shruti "cosmic sound of truth". All were handed down directly from the Deities or Pleiadian. They also taught how to align to the universal light consciousness through Kundalini awakening. However, as time passed the knowledge became clouded and lost through, dogmas, greed and ego of those seeking control

Mayans

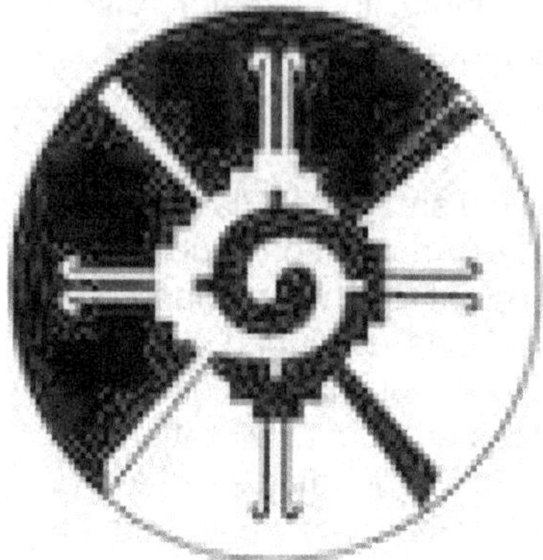

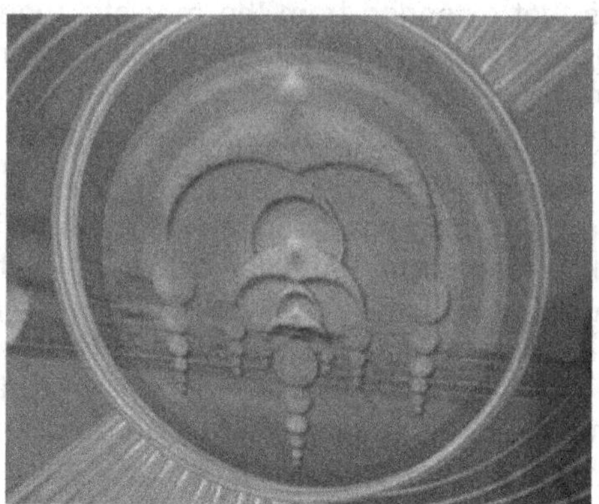

The Mayan civilization was very advanced in many ways—especially with their "time-science" intelligence. Their calendar is reputed to be the most accurate in the world: off by merely 2 seconds every 100 years. This calendar also refers to this period in our history as the "Apocalypse". This means all will be revealed—the history of civilization, our true connection with the stars, and all things relevant to our transformation into the light consciousness. During this Apocalypse (or time "between worlds") many of us will experience personal transformation and changes—all of which are part of our journey and the reason we chose to be here during this period of great conversion. The Mayan believe this is the time to work through the karmic residue of our collective civilization, and individually to attain a higher atonement. Hence, by 2012 and just beyond we will have transcended to the 5th dimension and our planet Earth and the solar system will finally come into galactic synchronization with the rest of the universe. As a result the earthly quarantine will be lifted. This transformation is occurring now into and beyond 2012 and our DNA is being reprogrammed from a double helix to eventually a 12-strand "upgrade". This evolution of our DNA will correspond with the 12 Chakras—7 in the physical plane and 5 outside or above the crown or Sahasrara chakra.

The Mayan say we are evolving into the sixth world, which is actually "blank". This means as co-architects, it is our responsibility to immediately start implementing the new world and civilization of peace and attunement, while becoming the spiritual change we want to experience in this new era.

Mayan Calendar

The creators of the Mayan calendar gave birth to a system capable of tracking both astronomical and non-astronomical cycles of nature, and calculate eclipses, galactic alignment and conjunctions. With these complex math equations and time scales of lunar solar and planetary systems they could even chart future events such as the solar eclipses a thousand years in advance. The length of their calendar's sub-cycles even matched natural cycles such as human growth and the snakes shedding their teeth. They also could see the orbits of the observable planets and calculate the length of the journey around the sun. The Mayan calendar is much more complex and accurate than our current annual calendar. It is actually an astronomical computer that predicts the ages, solar and galactic events. Referring to the Mayan calendar, Dr. Jose Arguelles wrote in "Time and the Techno-sphere" that the date of August 13, 3113 BC is as precise and accurate as one can get for a beginning of history. The first Egyptian dynasty is dated to ca 3100 BC; the first "city"—Uruk in Mesopotamia, also ca 3100 BC; the Hindu Kali Yuga, 3102 BC; and most interestingly, the division of time into 24 hours of 60 minutes each and each minute into 60 seconds (and the division of the circle into 360 degrees), also around 3100 BC in Samaria. Given the fact that this data documenting the beginning of history was so accurately placed, it must be concluded that the end of history on December 21st 2012 be deemed equally accurate.

So how did the Mayan people create a calendar that is the world's most accurate calendar ever, off by only 2 seconds every 100 years, or did they?

All research shows that the Mayan calendar has two circles that interact as one. They are the TZOL KIN (sacred calendar) and the TUN calendars. This calendar created by the Mayans started recording time in 3,114 BC and the calendar abruptly ends in 2012 AD—"The End of Times".

The calendar known as TZOL KIN has a cycle of precisely 5,125 days. It is based on the 26,000-year cycle of the star cluster Pleiades. This is mirrored by 260 days, pairing the numbers one through thirteen with a sequence of twenty (name) days. A Mayan baby's first name is assigned based on the day they were born, (260 names). This was done primarily for vibrational reasons that corresponded to the universal vibration and astrological correspondence. The Mayan believe that thirteen is the vibrational universal force found in all things, the source of all knowledge, and representative of galactic movement.

The twenty is derived from the number four, representing Measure, and five is the number of the structure's primary matrix (the center and four cardinal points). The calendar also predicts a combination of several cosmic cycles within the movement of the Sun, Moon and Venus. The days on this calendar are made up of 13 intentions (energies) and 20 aspects of creation x 13 = 260 days.

The TUN (divine) calendar is 360 days, where the two circles line up every 52 rotations. Beyond the physical aspects this calendar also maps out astrological events within our galaxy and beyond. By contrast the western calendar is 30 days/12 months but the Mayan uses the numbers 20/13. No inaccuracies have ever been found in the Mayan calendar.

According to the Mayan calendar we are experiencing the climax of an evolutionary stage—the last few years of this 26,000 year cycle! This cycle will end December 21st 2012, with a rare celestial alignment, aligning the galactic and solar planes. Here the winter solstice Sun will conjunct with our Milky Way galaxy, creating a "sky portal or entrance" into the "dark rift" of the Milky Way galaxy. This will create a morphogenetic genesis. This means, DNA transformation and its connection with the universal light consciousness.

Dr. Jose Arguelles, a historian of the United States, has devoted his life studying the Maya civilization. In his book *"The Mayan Factor: Path Beyond Technology"*, he explains the Mayan calendar with great knowledge and detail. The Mayan calendar states in our solar system "The Great Cycle" of 5,200 years, (3113 BC to 2012 AD) is ending. In The Great Cycle, our Earth and our solar system are racing across the "Galactic Beam", which originated within the core of the galaxy. The diameter of this Galactic Beam is 5,125 Earth years across, so it has taken 5,125 Earth years to cross through this Galactic Beam. In the Mayan prophecy it states after crossing through this Galactic Beam, our solar system will experience a fundamental and spiritual change—one that we are currently starting to experience on many levels.

It is also believed the transition leading up to 2012 is a very important period before this "Galactic Synchronization", called the purification or "Earth Regeneration Period". In many different scriptures it has been called the End of Time, Armageddon or the time that will ultimately renew and evolve humankind and the universal consciousness into the next phase of our spiritual evolution. This is consistent with the dawning of the new Age of Aquarius as the age of enlightenment, and the translation of the Bible's Lord's Prayer *"Thy will be done on Earth as it is in heaven"* could be easily interpreted as the coming new age.

The Mayans believe they are direct descendants of Atlantis and other great pre-civilizations, all of which lived on the Earth but were destroyed by cataclysms when the powers of their societies were misused and the connection with the mother Earth was lost. Because they have been through it, they understand how the changes will manifest, and that the build-up we are experiencing is in fact the beginning of the purification period or end of times as we know them.

Aztec

The sacred Aztec calendar is known as the Eagle Bowl and it represents their solar deity Tonatiuh. According to Aztec mythology, the first age (Ice Age) of mankind ended when animals devoured humans. The second age was ended by the winds, the third by great fire, and the fourth ended by water of flood (Noah). The present or fifth age is called Nahui-Olin (Sun of Earthquake). Hmm! I wonder what that means? It began in 3113 BC and ends December 24th 2011.

"After Thirteen Heavens of Decreasing Choice, and Nine Hells of Increasing Doom, the Tree of Life shall blossom with a fruit never before known in the creation, and that fruit shall be the New Spirit of Men."—*Prophecy on the Eagle bowl.*

On the other hand, the Mayan calendar is divided into Seven Ages of Man. The fourth age ended in August 1987. The Mayan calendar comes to an end on Friday, December 21st 2012. It is said few will survive the devastation that results. Then as the fifth age manifests, humanity will finally realize its spiritual destiny.

With the advent of yoga and meditation coming to the west over the past few years, this awareness is beginning to manifest—although mostly still in the intellectual domain of understanding. The "Yoga business" seems to resonate with past dogmas and attachment to money. Even so, modern western Yoga is still a stepping-stone that will allow many to begin the process of finding the path to their spiritual awareness, and then through pure meditation, finding the path to enlightenment.

Who Are We?

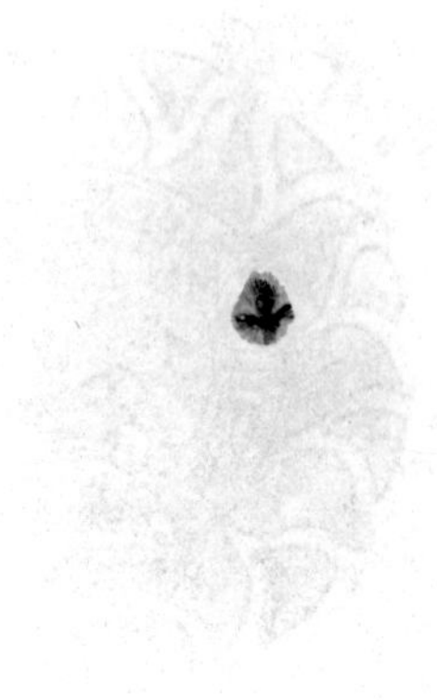

Darwin's theory of evolution seems to have run its course. We have evolved past the old "world is flat" doctrine and the fantasy our moon is made of cheese. It seems there are those who still sell us the fantasy, keeping us in the dark, uninformed so as not to unravel or rattle the power structures that benefit from the farce that UFOs do not exist. UFOs don't exist only because the political and/or religious media and dogma doesn't want them to exist. So maybe it is time common sense evolves, and modern thinking discards out dated 1950's concepts about UFOs and moon cheese.

Lets consider the billions of stars with planets just in our Galaxy, beaming eons longer than our Mother Earth and Solar Sun. It would be very illogical and egotistical to think that Mother Earth is the only planet with intelligent life in this universe, or that 200,000 years of human history makes us advanced! Maybe were advanced to the primates and ants but not to the vast intelligent life forms that inhabit the cosmos in multiple dimensions. It would also be naive to believe our governments, and the powers that truly run them are an honest bunch with our best interests in mind. So when we take off the blinders we can clearly see the universe is beaming with intelligent life. Our human history has piles of verified UFO contact, sightings and abductions. So why have we been misinformed and lied to time and again about the existence of Alien intelligence and their ongoing contact with some of our World Governments? Well for one, the aliens know our true history, and I would bet it does not coincide with the versions we have been fed by the Governments and religions. The other reality is, who ever controls this information and technology controls the world, and those that have this information do not want to hand it over to the democratic public, or the mainstream government for scrutiny. So it is classified "Top Secret" with many credible NASA and CIA insiders now coming forward exposing the truth, with some of them even being killed for doing so.

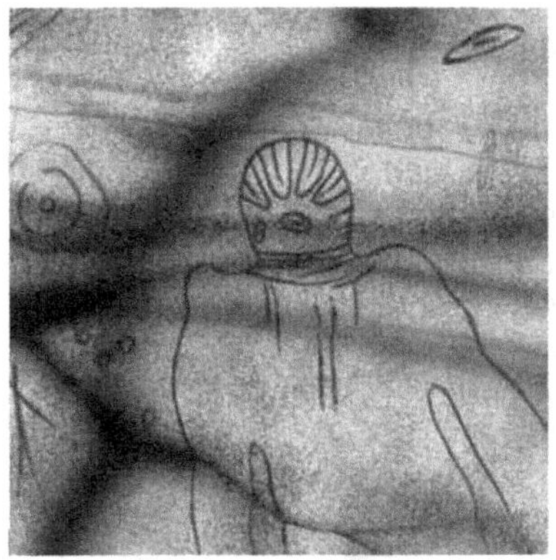

Sahara—North Africa

6000 BC Tassili Mountains

As we approach 2012 the frequency shift is changing life as we know it, and hundreds of researchers and insiders including Apollo and Space Shuttle astronauts have come forward. They have been telling stories about the dark side of the moon, alien sightings, abductions and contact since the 50's. They also speak about the ongoing contact our government has with the Gray Aliens (Grays) and trading UFO technology for looking the other way on the abductions of a small percentage of the population. Just think of the growing missing people lists, the war in Iraq, and the thousands of useless killings over oil before we say—our Government? Not possible! This information has been hidden since the 50's in small independent top-secret classified sections of the Government in Area 51 and others, with special outside interest groups benefiting.

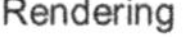

Rendering

Medieval painting with space craft clearly shown

It was not always this way, explains JFK researcher Professor Lawrence Merrick, author of the book: Killing the Messenger: *"It appears that some individuals within our government were determined to maintain the secrecy surrounding captured UFOs -- and decided to silence the President before he could speak."* He also goes on to say *"I was surprised to find that Kennedy handed Governor Connally the speech, which was on note cards, to look at, shortly before the motorcade set off at 12:55 p.m.,"* The Professor's research reveals that just days before JFK's trip to Dallas, he met with his predecessor President Dwight D. Eisenhower, *"I believe he was seeking advice on whether to go public with the facts about UFOs,"* Professor Merrick said. *"But other government insiders apparently felt the truth about UFOs would cause widespread panic, and they were willing to kill to keep the information secret."* Professor Merrick was staggered when he read the cards. He took them to five expert handwriting analysts, who all agreed that this speech was "95 percent certain" to be Kennedy's.

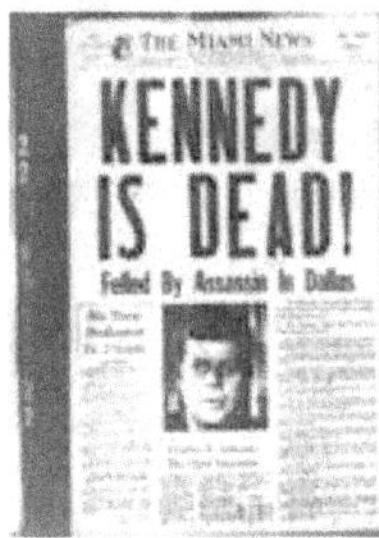
KENNEDY IS DEAD!

Felled By Assassin In Dallas

This is the speech that President John F. Kennedy was to give the day he was assassinated:

"My fellow Americans, people of the world, today we set forth on a journey into a new era. One age, the childhood of mankind, is ending and another age is about to begin.

The journey of which I speak is full of unknowable challenges, but I believe that all our yesterdays, all the struggles of the past, have uniquely prepared our generation to prevail.

Citizens of this Earth, we are not alone. God, in His infinite wisdom, has seen fit to populate His universe with other beings -- intelligent creatures such as ourselves. How can I state this with such authority? In the year 1947 our military forces recovered from the dry New Mexico desert the remains of an aircraft of unknown origin. Science soon determined that this vehicle came from the far reaches of outer space. Since that time our government has made contact with the creators of that spacecraft.

Though this news may sound fantastic -- and indeed, terrifying -- I ask that you not greet it with undue fear or pessimism. I assure you, as your President, that these beings mean us no harm.

Rather, they promise to help our nation overcome the common enemies of all mankind -- tyranny, poverty, disease, war. We have determined that they are not foes, but friends. Together with them we can create a better world. I cannot tell you that there will be no stumbling or missteps on the road ahead.

But I believe that we have found the true destiny of the people of this great land: To lead the world into a glorious future. In the coming days, weeks and months, you will learn more about these visitors, why they are here and why our leaders have kept their presence a secret from you for so long.

I ask you to look to the future not with timidity but with courage. Because we can achieve in our time the ancient vision of peace on Earth and prosperity for all humankind.

God bless you".

Whether we believe the JFK story or not, does not matter. What matters is that humankind has a long history of Alien contact, at least 200,000 years and probably much more. There are countless cave paintings, carvings, artist renderings, statues, historical lore, modern sightings, NASA and earth photos, videos and Crop Circles to support this reality. Yes! We have been, and are being visited almost daily. Seems as 2012 approaches sightings are getting much more common. Most governments have been making fools of their citizens for years, under the guise of "National Security" that allows the secret society that really controls policy to move far beyond the controls of the governments. They now have advanced technologies through reverse engineering of alien crafts as well as the information they have traded abductions for. This mess is beyond the scope of our innocent understanding, as there really are two different unelected powers controlling this information and our Governments. This was the leading concern of JFK and the reason he wanted to make the UFO speech public, and the main reason he was murdered.

Please Note: The special interests of the Government, and secret societies aligned with the Illuminati will continue to distort, and promote disinformation through controlled media. This is done to quiet and confuse the population as they have become very good at this, starting in 1947 with the Roswell UFO crash, then JFK's Warren Commission, on to 911 and the following oil wars of the arrogant Bush government.

Stone tablet records of the Sumerians tell stories that date back 200,000 years, where Aliens genetically altered the DNA of our primitive ancestors. This is not far fetched considering we are currently doing the same thing now, by manipulating the DNA of plants and animals to benefit our race of humanoids! DNA fusing ages ago by the Anunnaki does seem reasonable, and this would sensibly bridge the missing link in Darwin's theory of evolution. So if we let go of the conditionings set in motion and mainly created by government and religious dogma—it makes logical sense.

What we should remember when trying to figure out if our DNA was fused with a higher alien intelligence is that 3 or 4 primary races make up the modern human race. The Genome project research stated there is a 2 – 3 % discrepancy in the genetics of the 3-4 dominant human races. It was also stated these races had up to a 15% discrepancy in their reactions to things like a flu virus. It is also genetically unworkable for 3 or 4 different skin tones and features to have evolved naturally from the Homo sapiens over our 200,000 years of evolution. This is all off the charts when the modern science of genetics is applied to the old theory of human evolution.

If we move into **The Book of Enoch**, as well as **Jubilees**, it connects the origin of the Nephilim with the fallen angels, and in particular with the Grigori (watchers). Samyaza, who is depicted as an angel of high rank, is said to have led a rebel sect of angels descending to earth to have sexual intercourse with human females:

"And it came to pass when the children of men had multiplied that in those days were born unto them beautiful and comely daughters. And the angels, the children of the heaven, saw and lusted after them, and said to one another: 'Come, let us choose us wives from among the children of men and beget us children.' And Semjaza, who was their leader, said unto them: 'I fear ye will not indeed agree to do this deed, and I alone shall have to pay the penalty of a great sin.' And they all answered him and said: 'Let us all swear an oath, and all bind ourselves by mutual imprecations not to abandon this plan but to do this thing.' Then sware they all together and bound themselves by mutual imprecations upon it. And they were in all two hundred; who descended in the days of Jared on the summit of Mount Hermon, and they called it Mount Hermon, because they had sworn and bound themselves by mutual imprecations upon it."..

The fallen angels according to these texts, who *begat* the Nephilim were cast into Tartarus or Gehenna, the place of 'total darkness'. Jubilees also states "*God granted ten percent of the disembodied spirits of the Nephilim to remain after the flood, as demons, to try to lead the human race astray* (through idolatry, the occult, etc.) *Until the final Judgment*". This final judgment is coming in 2012.

Note the size difference humans—gods.

Remains of ancient giants, discovered in India
Note size of the man digging

So some how it does not resonate that angels would descend from heaven for sex? So lets put on our thinking caps and say they were Anunnaki descending from the sky on space ships via Planet Nibiru. Also a closer review of the Old Testament reveals two brothers, known as Enki, and Enlil. They are mentioned in many ancient, scrolls and texts, including the Bible, where they are referred to as giants.

However, in the original Hebrew version they were known as the Nephilim. The Nephilim do appear in the Bible:

> **Genesis 6:4-6**
>
> *"The Nephilim were on the Earth in those days, and also afterwards, when the sons of the Gods came in to the daughters of man and they bore children to them. These were the mighty men who were of old, the men of renown."*

Translated, it means that the Anunnaki or Nephilim bore children with our earth women, so it would seem we descended genetically from these higher evolved alien beings.

So given the beautiful and unique color, features and DNA discrepancies within the three or four distinct races of peoples evolving on our planet, it would be fair to say there have been many interplanetary visits. Because I am sure the science of genetics has and would prove we could not have evolved such a vast separation of skin tones and other differences in just 200,000 years.

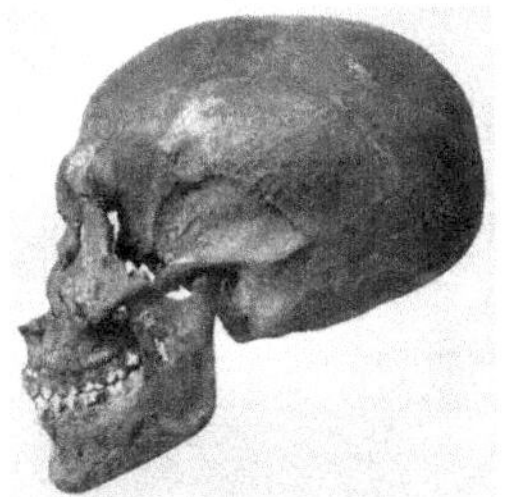

Ancient Skull "Not" Human

Ancient Egypt - note the head

Grey Alien - Ancient Egypt
above – Ancient Mesopotamia

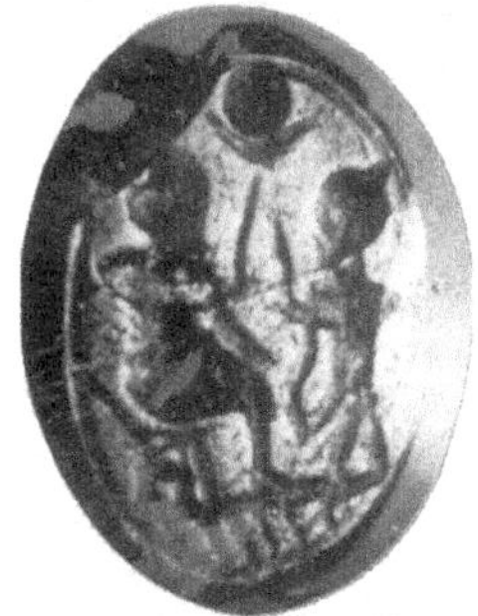

Grey Alien - winged disc

Vimana

In ancient Indian mythology a "Vimana" is the word used for a mythological flying machine. References to these flying machines are commonplace in ancient Indian texts, even describing their use in warfare.

The Vimanas was said to be able to fly within Earth's atmosphere, into space and travel submerged underwater. The Vedas describe Vimana's as having various shapes and sizes. The Sun, Indra and several other Vedic Deities were depicted as being transported by flying wheeled chariots pulled by animals, usually horses. The Vedic God Pusan, had his chariot pulled by goats. The "Gaja Vimana" had the more (powerful) engines. The primitive artists of the times could only understand power as coming from a source of animals. So the type of animal represented the power of the engine so to speak.

The "Agnihotra Vimana" means with two engines, and word Agni means fire in Sanskrit Gaja means elephant in Sanskrit, and in some modern Indian dialects, the word Vimana still means aircraft.

A Vimana depicted in a temple relief at Ellora Caves, India.

Ancient Egypt

Alien photo from area # 51

Winged Anunnaki God - Sumerian

Ancient Cave Drawings

Anunnaki Gods - Sumerian

Japanese Dogu - ancient astronaut 1000 BC

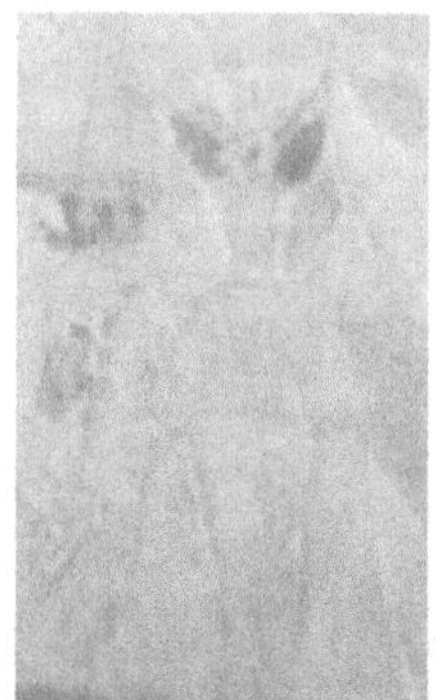

GRAY Alien

Terracotta Reptilian (Anunnaki) figurines 4th millennium BC

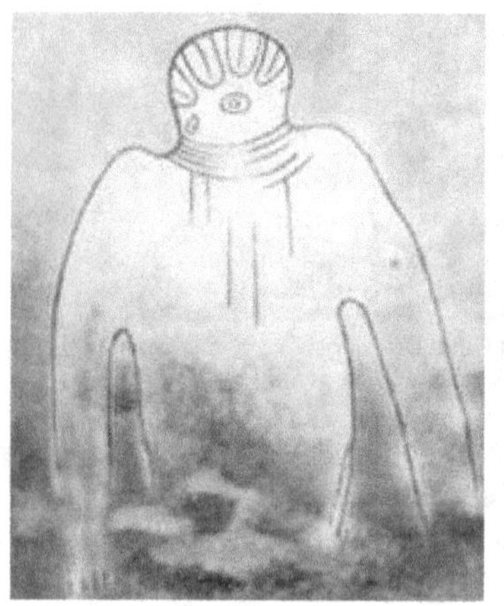

Algerian cave painting circa 6000 BC

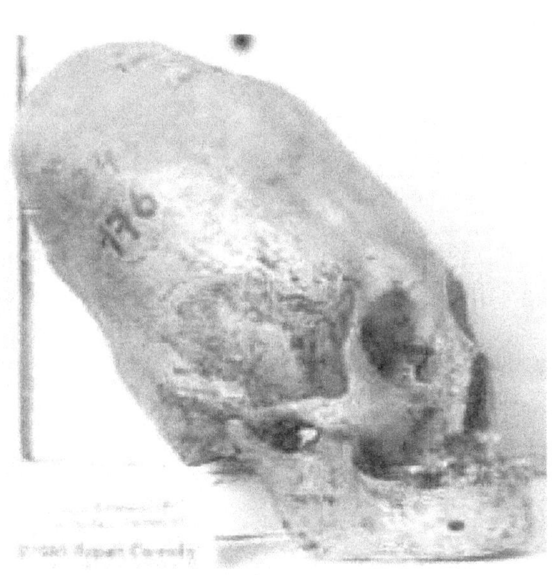

Anunnaki Statue and Ancient Skull

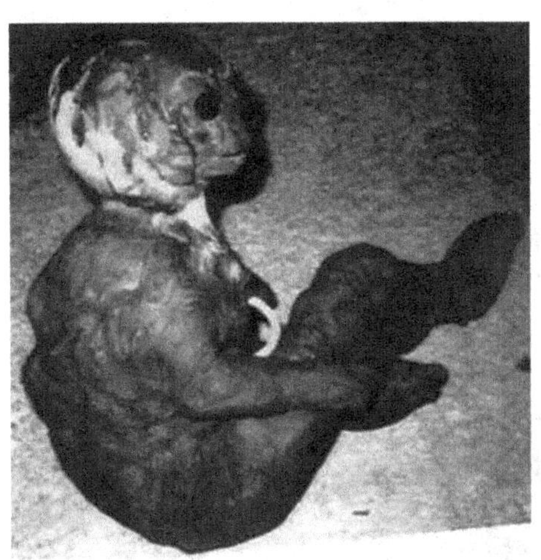

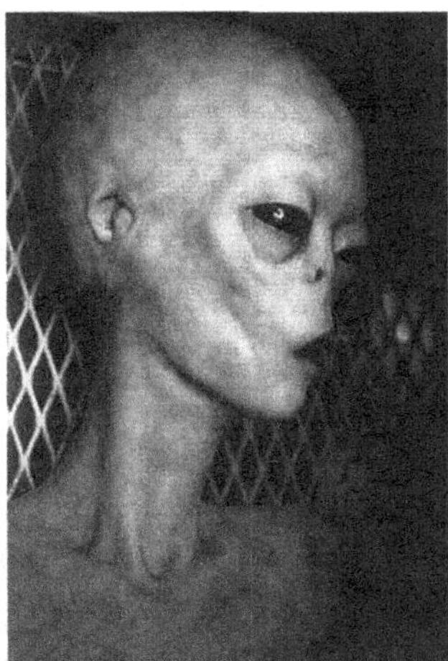

Area #51 alien photos

AREA # 51—Alien photos released by CIA employee who died of mysterious heart failure weeks after.

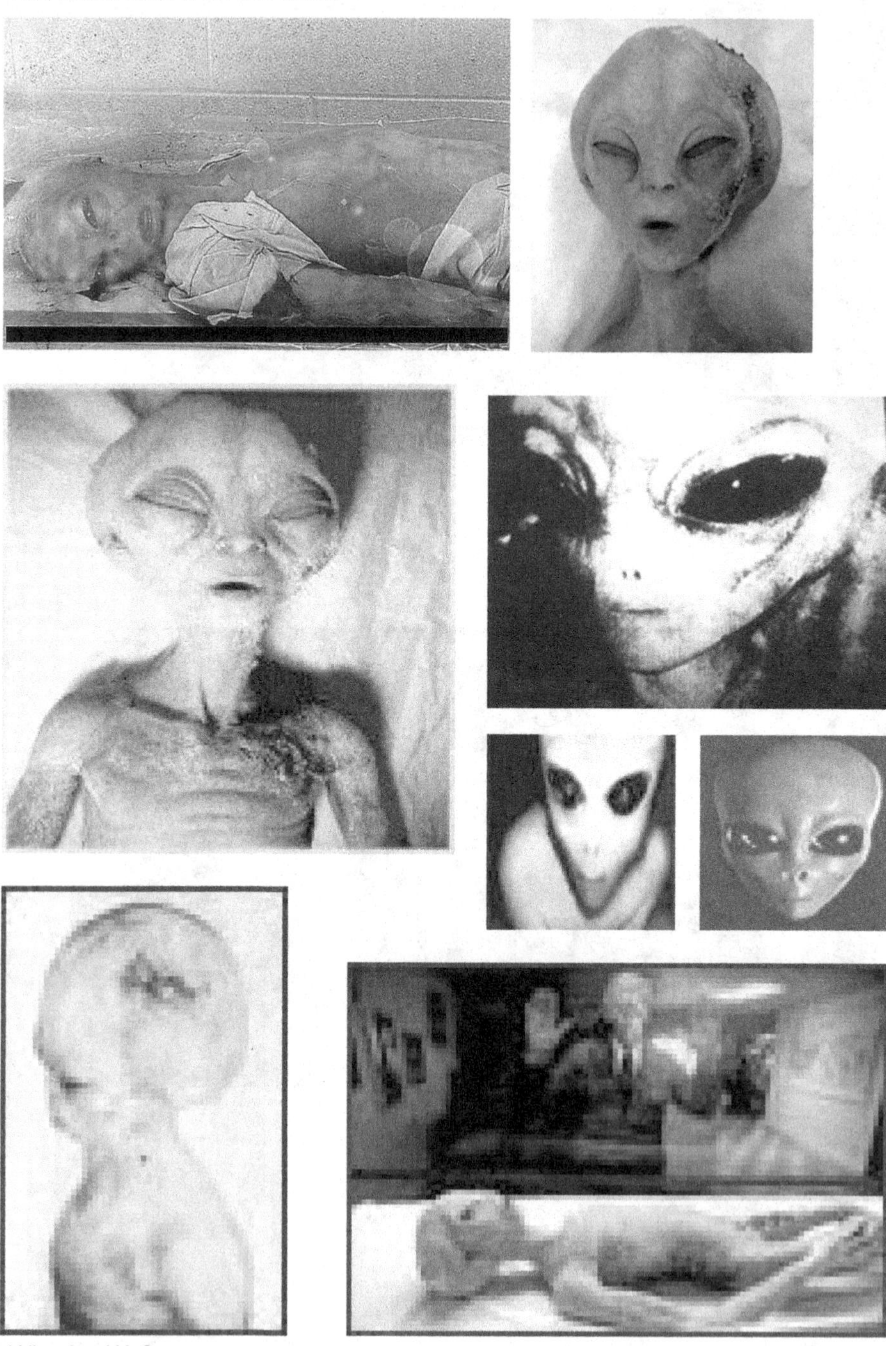

Gods of ancient Egypt with humans

Winged Horned GOD of ancient times

MARS—Landscape

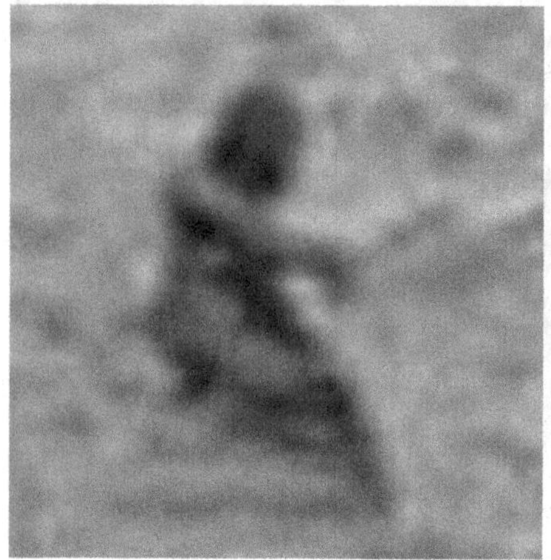

NASA photo taken of landscape with Alien being

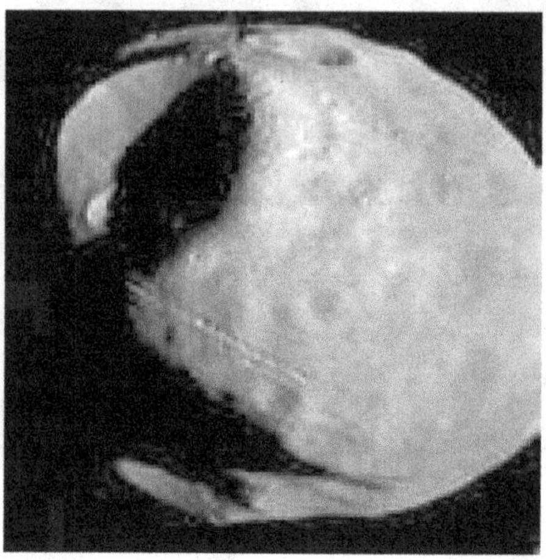

Strange Mars Moon

MOON—Earth

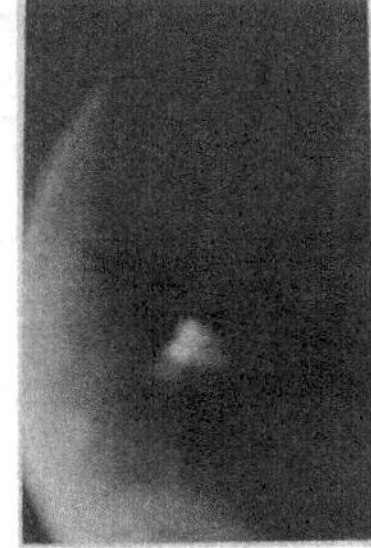

Earth's moon with UFO in photos

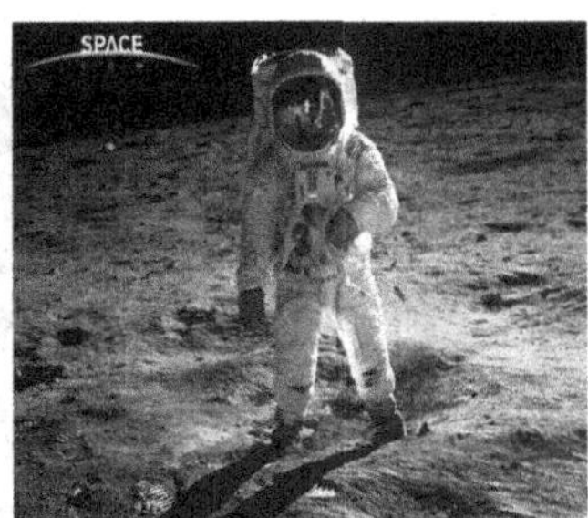

Buzz Aldrin – Apollo Moon Mission

Michael Tellinger, a publisher and TV producer, released his findings about lunar anomalies and other strange aspects of the earth's moon. He stated it is more than just a natural satellite revolving around the Earth. There are a number of oddities, including how astronauts spoke in code about UFOs seen there, and the strange lights verified by Apollo astronaut Buzz Aldrin. Tellinger also mentioned instruments, which picked up large amounts of water vapor despite mainstream science saying there was no atmosphere there, as well as countless observations of lights on the lunar surface. Tellinger stated the moon is *"most likely being used as a base for extraterrestrial craft."* This may also explain the Dark Side of the moon theory, and why the moon does not really rotate. The multi-national Space Station astronauts have also noticed many lights with countless UFO sightings.

Another important fact: based on various density tests, it has been shown the density of the moon would be the same as a moon that was hollow. The moon has been dated to be about 1 billion years older than the earth, with its rocks being millions of years younger than its own surface dust. This leads to many more questions.

Tellinger also discussed a recent discovery of a site in South African dubbed, *"Adam's Calendar"*, which research states is around 75,000 years old. *"We have found something truly remarkable, truly unique, and most likely the oldest manmade structure on earth,"* According to surveyors who have examined it, he states the site was *"a circular structure, like Stonehenge"* that features rocks that aligned with *"the cardinal geographical points of Earth"* along with the solstices and equinoxes similar to Stonehenge. He explained dating of the site was initially derived from the fact that the points of alignment *"did not match up"* with the modern position of the Sun. In part, it was using archaeoastronomy that they determined the age of the monument. This dating system would make sense given that fact that the Earth has experienced numerous pole shifts, where the land mass alignment with the sun would have changed. Another pole shift is set to happen again around 2012.

NIBIRU—Planet of the Crossing (Sumerian)

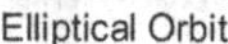
Elliptical Orbit

Southern Hemisphere (small dot by the Sun)

Hebrew scholar, author, speaker and archaeologist—Zecharia Sitchin, has stated the planet Nibiru appearing in Sumerian records, correctly refers to a large planetary body or small constellation that is transitioning into our solar system. According to the 6,000-year-old Sumerian cosmology, Nibiru is the twelfth planet in the solar system. The Dwarf star of this mini constellation is 8 times the size of Earth with two planets and two moons rotating around it. One of the Planets is home of the aliens called Anunnaki. The research reveals this constellation is on a 3,600 year elliptical orbit around our Sun.

Dwarf Star Constellation with Planet Nibiru

Currently, Nibiru can be seen with the naked eye in the skies in the most southern hemisphere as it moves toward our Sun. By spring 2010, Nibiru will be seen with the naked eye in the northern hemisphere—passing by the Earth in 2012. It is feared this passing will bring the Pole Shift and major cataclysms. NASA has been silently tracking Nibiru (Planet-X) since 1983. Although official news of Nibiru has been suppressed for so called *global security*: socially minded scientists have been secretly revealing more and more information, and it is coming our way. As a result, news and pictures of Nibiru are becoming more common on the Internet. There is a huge misinformation strategy by NASA to suppress this reality or to misinform.

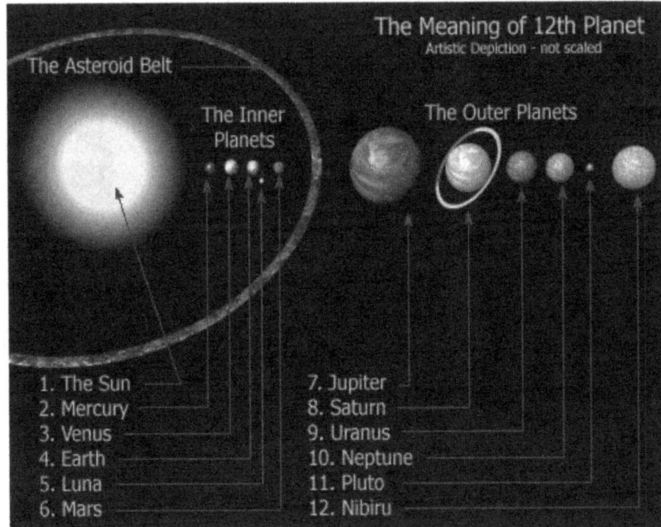

Planet Nibiru has orbited close to the earth many times during our history. The last time this event happened 3600 years ago, there were survivors and tales of its passing.

The following is a quote by African Zulu elder and spiritual guide of the Zulu people named Credo Mutwa, who spoke of a story still told by his ancestors. Its a legend where a strange Star passed by the earth thousands of years ago:

"Let me tell you two last things please. One, it is this, that I am told by the great storytellers of our tribes, that fresh water is not native to our earth. That at one time, many thousands of years ago a terrible star, or the kind called Mu-sho-sho-no-no, the star with a very long tail, descended very close upon our skies. It came so close that the earth turned upside down and what had become the sky became down, and what was the heavens became up.

"The whole world was turned upside down. The sun rose in the south and set in the north. Then came drops of burning black stuff, like molten tar, which burned every living thing on earth that could not escape. After that came a terrible deluge of water accompanied by winds so great that they blew whole mountaintops away. And after that came huge chunks of ice bigger than any mountain and the whole world was covered with ice for many generations.

"After that the surviving people saw an amazing sight. They saw rivers and streams of water that they could drink, and they saw that some of the fishes that escaped from the sea were now living in these rivers. That is the great story of our forefathers. And we are told that this thing is going to happen again very soon. Because the great star, which is the lava of our sun, is going to return on the day of the year of the red bull, which is the year 2012."

Creation

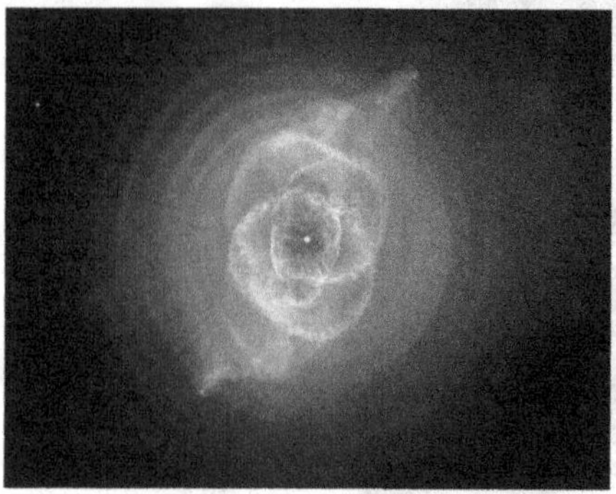

Before creation there was silence. There was no life and no living thing—no worlds, stars, flowers, oceans, valleys or mountains. Then through the light of divine consciousness a thought became manifest, and through this thought, creation was born and the universal sound of creation (Om) became manifest. The Audi Shakti (feminine aspect of all creation) then whispered this holy sound and the forming of worlds began vibrating at the universal frequency. This created the universes and all aspects of all things transcended to their places on the planes of life and creation. A beautiful living garden called Mother Earth was created to sustain and nurture life, and the human children of the light started their spiritual evolution. As the children evolved in their crude human forms, their inner light connection to the universal light consciousness was also evolving and they soon understood their accent was far beyond the 3rd dimensional realm. This realization has become more apparent as 2012 approaches, and we open up to the light consciousness to guide us through the multi-dimensional transformation—soon upon us.

Creation has many meanings on many levels: from the creation of the soul and universal light consciousness, to the creation of civilizations and the science of our modern intellect. Our creation seems beyond the comprehension of our intellect in the current plane of our spiritual awareness.

Our Earth has hosted the creation of many great civilizations such as Atlantis, Mu, Mayan, Inca and all were destroyed by cataclysms or some other unknown fate. Our current civilization has evolved under the subtle guidance of the divine light consciousness and the alien beings that have previously come to Earth acting as gods.

If we reference creation through the eyes of the Kabbalah, Tibetan or Tantric Buddhism, Adam and Eve are viewed as symbols of male and female energy. The presence of the Serpent, believed a dividing force, was necessary for creation. The belief was that it gave humankind the opportunity to evolve to the Light on its own. One veiled version of the Adam and Eve story represents two Gardens of Eden, one represents the higher self, the other the lower self—while evolving to the higher Garden is the destiny of humankind. *"Thy will be done on earth as it is in Heaven".*—Bible. The next question is: what does all this represent in terms of our past, present and future evolution?

For us to understand our future, we should first understand the past. Over 6000 years ago the ancient Sumerians wrote their history onto thousands of stone tablets, 500 of these tablets depict a story of aliens called Anunnaki that hailed from the Planet Nibiru, "planet of the crossing." Their story tells of aliens genetically altering our human DNA and enslaving humans to mine gold used as reflective dust to save their planets atmosphere. This story resonates given the fact that over the past 20 years, we have genetically manipulated the DNA of sheep, and other animals in the name of our own science and survival. So it would be fair to assume this happened 200,000 years ago using ape like *grunt* workers to mine their gold on our planet. It is interesting our science maintains modern man is 200,000 years old, evolving out of Africa. This parallels the Sumerian tablets, with a twist. The twist is 200,000 years ago, in the land of Eden (Africa) the Aliens created a human hybrid from the dust. Would this dust be the DNA to genetically modify human beings? Also interesting: the human being has 46 chromosomes or 23 pairs with 28 major deformities, all tolled over 4,000 genetic deformities. This is said by science to be off the charts (not normal) considering our modern species is only 200,000 years old. Also primates have 48 chromosomes, humans have 46, so unless we were genetically fused or manipulated we could not have evolved from the chimp or ape family. It is also a fact of science that a new species like us should have few, if any, genetic deformities. The law of nature dictates that when a species has deformities it ceases to exist, but with the human, it is the opposite.

We can see that anatomically, modern humans first appear in the fossil records of Africa about 195,000 years ago, and studies of molecular biology give evidence that the approximate time of deviation from the common primate ancestor of all modern human populations was 200,000 years ago. Well this seems to correspond with the Sumerian stone tablet account that our genetic modifications were done by the "Gods" or Anunnaki in Africa at a place called Eden also 200,000 years ago. The tablets also speak of the forbidden fruit as a sexual act between Eve and the fallen Reptilian Anunnaki "Serpent." It seems likely that the serpent (Saturn/Satan) seduced Eve and through this child of their union, Cain, the Serpent seed lines of the Anunnaki began. This seed line can be traced to modern times through a vast family tree including the British Royalty of Queen Elisabeth, Pharaohs and Political leaders such as both George Bush senior and junior.

Genesis 6:1-4: *"And it came to pass, when men began to multiply on the face of the earth, and daughters were born unto them, That the sons of God saw the daughters of men that they were fair; and they took them wives of* *all which they chose... There were* ***Nephilim*** *in the earth in those days; and also after that, when the sons of God came in unto the daughters of men, and they bare children to them, the same became mighty men which were of old, men of renown."*

In Genesis 3:15a: *"And I will put enmity between thee and the woman, and between thy seed and her seed."* Enmity means there is mutual hatred between the seed lines of Satan's and of Eve's. So it sounds like there is "two" seed lines created with Eve, the serpent's son Cain and Adam's son Seth. The facts in the Dead Sea Scrolls and verses in Gen 3:15 make it clear: Satan had his own seed line *ancestry* established back in the garden with Eve.

Note the serpents, Gray aliens and woman giving birth

The Sumerian tablets clearly mention modern mans origins or re-creation and colonization of the Earth through genetic manipulation of our species. DNA manipulation does not make the Anunnaki our God, or make them divine, just as our modern scientists are not divine because they managed to manipulate the DNA of sheep. The Anunnaki did not create the universal divine light or any life on Mother Earth, in fact the opposite. The Anunnaki or Nephilim, *descended* from Planet Nibiru where their aggressive reptilian super race known as the Anunnaki governed. This descent to earth caused the anti-evolutionary domination not in tune with our evolution to the light consciousness.

A better definition for their descending might be "those who came down", "those who descended", or "those who were cast down". The "Nephilim" in Hebrew, means *"they who have come down from the heavens to earth"* referenced in the Hebrew Bible, Book of Genesis and the Book of Numbers. It would seem the Anunnaki are the foundation of the anti Christ; a force that has been around since ancient times to manipulate, confuse and control our civilization until Planet Nibiru comes again in 2012. This manipulation started, when the Anunnaki switched the gender of the universal creator *God* from the Mother (Audi Shakti) to father: which was the dominant force on their planet. It was the Anunnaki who introduced polygamy, incest and pedophilia, which are characteristic to their culture. Such traits evolved into other cultures, including the ancient Egyptian royalty and the patriarchs of the Old Testament who followed the laws of "God" ordered by the Anunnaki. These satanic traits also evolved in the doctrine of many modern secret societies of the Illuminati.

Descendants of the Anunnaki were known as the "fallen angel" or Nephilim: sons of God. They were named as Saturn or Satan—the evil angelic host that was evident to early man. These forces were the dominant governing

Reptilian / Anunnaki—2

Anunnaki God—3

Sumerian goddess figurine from Ubaid—4

(Mesopotamia *ca.* 5000 BC)

Sumerian God - Flying winged disk – 5

powers of our ancient forefathers, and their power and influence still dominates our world today. This dominance was easy to identify in ancient times when the people were physically enslaved. The form of dominance started to change after the last great flood. People evolved spiritually and started to identify with their connection with the universal light consciousness and collectively united under one banner to build the "Tower of Babel" to the heavens. This tower symbolized their desired independence, and need to connect with the divine creator. The alien "Gods" empowered at the time felt this was a challenge to their authority and domination, so they segregated and enslaved the peoples of the known earth into different languages and races. The Anunnaki "God" Horus understood that our forefathers were weak when divided, easy to control and to enslave. Thus different kings and kingdoms rose up created by the Anunnaki seed line.

The Ancient Egyptians believed that their Pharaoh was the God Horus, son of Re, the sun God or a direct descendant. So when a pharaoh died it was believed he united with the sun, and a new Horus would reincarnate and continue to rule on earth, thus the lineage of the dominant Pharaohs and kings continued: eventually crossing religious and political boundaries to grasp and hold power. Another major challenge to their domination occurred when Moses led his people to freedom against the will of the Egyptian Pharaoh. Their world changed and so did the approach to enslavement.

The descended seed line of the Anunnaki also evolved a subtler approach to stay in power over the ages, but with one goal of controlling the modern world. In today's world; money, mind control by the media, and control of Governments are the real power, and they have this. We are no longer working the mines as slaves, but are enslaved most of the year to pay off debt and taxes, which mostly benefit the world banks and corporations controlled by secret societies and the Illuminati. These controlling factions can be traced back to the Pharaohs and Anunnaki or linked in some way to their Royal or Aristocratic Blood lines (blue blood). Their power and influence has become more powerful: but much subtler and cunning. So as 2012 approaches, we need to understand that any doctrine that enslaves or divides us is anti-Christ, and not part of the collective oneness we seek with divine light consciousness.

Confusion of Tongues
by Gustave Doré (1865)

HORUS

The Anunnaki and their descended seed line have created many of the dogmas and power structures used to control, confuse and corrupt the minds and pure spiritual knowledge that threaten control of their expanding power base. They have horded the metaphysical and spiritual knowledge over the ages, while promoting dogmas that confuse and divide. This arrogance started with the absolute power given to the Pharaohs. This connection between Horus and the Pharaohs was promoted by the Anunnaki to stabilize their kingdom and frighten the slaves into submission. This power base evolved and spread over the ages, as their Kings and dogmatic Religions promoted anti-Christ principals.

We are now living in the time of the great revealing, and the secret societies are starting to be revealed—along with their true intentions of global dominance. In modern times, the Illuminati or ancient seed lines, understand the human will not become enslaved willingly. So they disguise their agenda to enslave and control our minds and the world. Starting with controlled media such as: FOX, CNN, CBS and other major TV networks, heath organizations like; WHO, multi-national GMO seed companies and big Pharma that promote an agenda against natural health supplements. WTO manipulates governments, while promoting the agenda through their controlled media and world banking systems. It is no accident governments, religions and false gurus all have doctrines in direct contrast and opposition to each other, this is the anti God doctrine promoted to breed disharmony, mistrust, confusion, war, misinformation and division.

The Dogon tribe, 19th century Africa. Their history spoke of the (Anunnaki) Reptilian race that came from Sirius – *"the biggest secret in the world is that amongst the humans walk the others – shape shifting into human form ... this is a secret enshrined in secret societies and their dogma."* The Dogon people also claim that their *'sacred knowledge'* of the stars was given them by a race of God-like aliens that came to earth from the Sirius system.

The reality is, these alien "Gods" have manipulated us since ancient times, to prevent our peaceful and spiritual evolution into our family of the light consciousness. Originally, the Anunnaki did not understand humankind would evolve spiritually as well as physically, and over time we eventually started to rebel against the enslaving "Gods" or kings. We are still evolving but with two aspects to our being: the physical—that was genetically manipulated, and the spiritual—that is truly evolving beyond their controls. The Anunnaki and their descendants (the Illuminati) now control the worlds economy, drug industry, disease industry and information networks—this is the anti Christ. So as 2012 approaches the battle of Armageddon is manifesting on many physical and spiritual levels. This will start with Alien contact foretold in the crop circle warnings as planet Nibiru gets closer, and soon life will change as we know it, and the deceivers of the anti Christ powers will be exposed.

True spiritual evolution: Is creation continually moving beyond each realm of its existence? An existence that previously bound us to the limitations created in and by this physical body and its 3rd dimensional conditionings. In creation there is a sacred significance of "Om" the sound of divine creation and the advanced principals of love and light consciousness that manifest as a pure frequency of the new world and 5th dimension. Thought creation manifests into visualization of light partials becoming mass on the level or frequency in which we reside. So as the drama of 2012 and earth regeneration unfolds, our spiritual destiny will evolve, and the lower evolved species like the Anunnaki and their earthly representatives will be left behind and the *"First will be the Last".*

> **Ezek. 29:3** ... *"Thus saith the Lord God; Behold, I am against thee Pharaoh KING OF EGYPT, THE GREAT DRAGON that lieth in the midst of his rivers".*
>
> **James, p. 2** ...*"In the Pyramid texts the king was regarded as the SON AND EMBODIMENT OF THE SOLAR DEITY. In this capacity he was the EARTHLY REPRESENTATIVE and high priest of his heavenly Father Re - A GOD IN HUMAN FORM."*

Anti Christ—666

In the Egyptian Astro-Mythology we find the first man-God Horus, his death and resurrection as Amsu. The first sign or hieroglyphic of Amsu was this 6-pointed star.

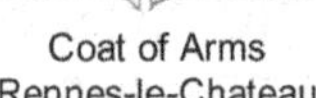
Coat of Arms
Rennes-le-Chateau

Building -Toronto Canada

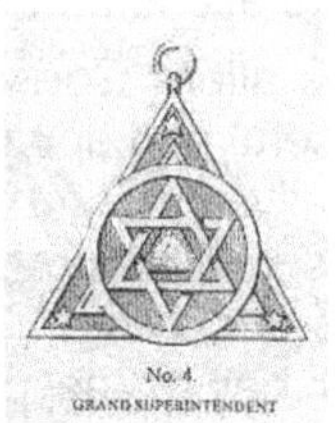

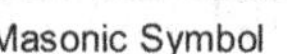
Masonic Symbol

Amsu

It is mentioned in ancient pagan mythology, that Saturn ruled over the dark side in the kingdom of Atlantis before the great flood, and was the divine forefather of all earthly patriarchs and kings. It should be mentioned the Chaldean number system of the ancient Indian, Mazdean, and Egyptian for Saturn is **666**. This may suggest in the Book of Genesis that the mark of Cain was the mark of the beast—the six-pointed star received by those who will worship the God Saturn during the Golden Age of Saturn, the occult millennium (which will be shortened to 3 1/2 years).

The six-pointed star is associated with the worship of Saturn. Therefore, the beast is Saturn (Satan) and his mark should be associated with the 6-pointed star and all it represents—from ancient to modern times. If we look further, we also find the ancient God of Horus and Satan is represented by the secret symbols of many modern and powerful interconnected secret societies of the Illuminati.

Acts 7:43

Yea, ye took up the tabernacle of Moloch, and the STAR OF YOUR GOD REMPHAN, figures which ye made to worship them: and I will carry you away beyond Babylon.

Amos 5:26-27

"But ye have born the tabernacle of your Moloch, and Chiun (Remphan) your images, the STAR OF YOUR GOD, which ye made to yourselves. Therefore, will I cause you to go into captivity beyond Damascus, saith the Lord".

The Six-Pointed Star, (Graham, pp. 28-29)

"Chiun is sometimes called Kaiwan, or spelled Khiun, and means star. The star of Saturn was a God... Sakkuth and Kaiwan or Chiun are objects of idolatrous worship and are Assyrian Gods. In Akkadian texts both names mean the planet or star, Saturn."

Obverse Talisman of Saturn Reverse

The Crown of the Magi

Christian, (p. 304-5)
"On the first face is engraved...a pentagram or a star with five points. On the other side is engraved a bull's head enclosed in a SIX-POINTED STAR, and surrounded by letters composing the name REMPHA, THE PLANETARY GENIUS OF SATURN, according to the alphabet of the Magi."

It was King Solomon who reintroduced the 6-Pointed Star to the Kingdom of Israel.

Some Jewish scholars also say the mark of Cain was the Seal of Solomon or Star of David. This is "not" a swipe at the Jewish religion but just a fact of history. The Jewish Government only used the Star as a symbol after 1946. The Seal of Solomon is a graphical representation of 666, the number of the Beast, and Solomon is the man whose number is 666:

Rev. 13:18 - *"Here is wisdom. Let him that hath understanding count the number of the beast: for it is the number of a man; and his number is SIX HUNDRED THREESCORE AND SIX. "*

Rev. 12:3, 9 - *"And there appeared another wonder in heaven; and behold a GREAT RED DRAGON, HAVING SEVEN HEADS and ten horns... And the great dragon was cast out, that old serpent, called the Devil, and SATAN..."*

Would 12:3.9 refer to the Planet Nibiru and the Anunnaki?

John 2:18 - *Little children, it is the last time: and as ye have heard that antichrist shall come, even now are there many antichrists; whereby we know that it is the last time.*

Rev 13:2 - *And the beast which I saw was like unto a leopard, and his feet were as the feet of a bear, and his mouth as the mouth of a*

lion: and the dragon gave him his power, and his seat, and great authority.

Cor 13:5 - *"Examine YOURSELVES, whether ye be in the faith; PROVE your OWN selves. Know ye not your own selves, how that Jesus Christ is in you, except ye be reprobates?"*

Rev 21:8 - *"But the fearful, and unbelieving, and the abominable, and murderers, and whoremongers, and sorcerers, and idolaters, and ALL LIARS, shall have their part in the lake which burneth with fire and brimstone: which is the second death."*

Mat 7:15 – *"Beware of false prophets, which come to you in sheep's clothing, but inwardly they are ravening wolves."*

Mat 7:20 – *"Wherefore by their fruits ye shall know them."*

Secret Societies

Illuminati—Warnings

The Illuminati, by different names, have been waiting in the shadows for thousands of years. A German sect first used the name Illuminati in the 15th century. Like their predecessors they practiced dark occult and professed to possess the occult *Knowledge of Satan*. Over time, the Illuminati has been successfully manifesting its agenda: creating and controlling shadow governments that supersede and manipulate elected national governments, military and banking systems. The goal of the Illuminati sect is total global control with no respect for human life or any form of democracy. Its *New World Order* is about modern enslavement—using all methods and means to accomplish this goal. In recent times, this has been accomplished through a rabid campaign of *fear media* and *dark military operations* that created a spurious terrorist threat—the war that can never be won. The great revealing of 2012 will allow the light to shine on the lies and deceptions of the Illuminati anti-Christ forces, because we are the light and masters of this density, not the satanic Illuminati. The light will prevail!

Secret Societies have been in place since ancient Egypt, with a purpose to retain the knowledge of the metaphysical sciences, and keep this information secret: as a form of control and power. The European societies originally borrowed aspects from, and created various cults, sects, covens, fraternities, societies, and churches from the ancient Osirica—a professed Black Egyptian Masonic order. Their membership has been programmed and conditioned to believe this knowledge elevates them above their fellow brothers and sisters of the spirit. This is an illusion and in essence anti Christ. In an evolved enlightened society, all knowledge would be shared, as the love of self would radiate into the collective. This would allow true spiritual assent. The anti Christ does not want the evolution of the spirit; its only goal is world domination, keeping society as slaves to their corruptions and dogmas. This is done with no compassion for the millions that suffer and die needlessly. It has been done by the same seed line since the beginning of civilization.

The Mayan and Hopi elders say we are living during the *end time* of our civilization. It is the time of revelation and the great revealing of truth. This revealing extends deep into our ancient history and into the base fiber of our social consciousness. The negativity and darkness surrounding our civilization has always stemmed from greed, control and ego: rooted deep in our lower evolved self. The dogmas all feed the dogmas that share the illusion of power in the realm of the lower self. So as 2012 reveals the true essence of our spiritual being, and our history will no longer be a place for the dark secretive groups that feel they are above the collective light. There is no caste system in the realm of divinity, and there is no hierarchy where one can buy a position within the light consciousness. The goal for global domination is servicing the lower self, just as Hitler and all those before him that failed—did so because they follow the path into darkness and the abyss.

July 1782 had the Illuminati join forces with Freemasonry at the Congress of Wilhelmsbad. The Illuminati goal was to establish a New World Order or one World Government that they can control.

The Vril Society Is an account of a superior subterranean master race and the energy-form called "Vril". They combined the political ideals of the Order of the Illuminati with Hindu mysticism, Theosophy and the Cabbala. It was the first German nationalist groups to use the symbol of the swastika as an emblem linking Eastern and Western occultism.

The Order of Skull and Bones; a Yale University society; was originally known as the Brotherhood of Death. It was founded in 1832 and the privileged membership is open to few. It is one of the oldest student secret societies in the United States. The society uses Masonic inspired rituals to this day. Both of the Bush presidents were members of the society while studying at Yale, and many other members have gone on to great renown and affluence.

The Grand Masonic Lodge was created in 1717. The three degrees of Masonry are: 1—Entered Apprentice: this makes you a basic member of the group, 2—Fellow Craft: this is an intermediate degree in which you are meant to develop further knowledge of Masonry, and 3—Master Mason: this degree is necessary for participating in most Masonic activities.

Ancient Rosicrucian's had an influence on Masonry, and in fact, the 18th degree of Scottish Rite Masonry was called the Knight of the Rose Croix (red cross). The cross relates to the Planet Nibiru "the Planet of the Crossing" home of the Anunnaki.

The OTO an organization originally modeled on Masonry but, under the leadership of the self-styled "Great Beast" Aleister Crowley, many ancient Egyptian God's are invoked, as well as the Devil, and at one point the priestess performs a naked ritual.

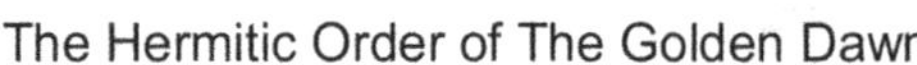
The Hermitic Order of The Golden Dawn

The order was as created by Dr. William Robert Woodman, William Wynn Westcott, and Samuel Liddell Macgregor Mathers, Freemasons and members of Societas Rosicruciana in Anglia. It is considered a forerunner of the modern Occult groups. The belief system of the Golden Dawn is largely taken from Christian mysticism, Qabalah, Hermeticism, the religion of Ancient Egypt, Freemasonry, Alchemy, Theosophy, Magic, and Renaissance writings. William Yeats, and Aleister Crowly are two of the more famous members of the group.

The Knights Templar is a modern off-shoot of Masonry and does not have a direct tie to a religious military group formed in the 12th century—the original Knights Templar. It is tied to the global Illuminati and its doctrine.

The Bilderberg Group

This group is slightly different from the other Illuminati societies in that it does not have an "official" membership. It is believed these are some of the elite of the Illuminati and mason infrastructure, who meet every year secretly (with heavy military and government security). The topics discussed are kept top secret. The conference—usually held in five star hotels around the world. What would be the real agenda of this elite group?

Recent attendees include:

> *Queen Beatrix Prince Bernhard of the Netherlands, of the Netherlands,* ***Prince Charles****, Prince of Wales, United Kingdom, Juan Carlos King of Spain, Prince Philippe, of Belgium,* ***Prince Phillip****, Duke of Edinburgh, United Kingdom Queen Sofía of Spain,* ***Stephen Harper*** *Prime Minister of Canada, Mike Harris Premier, Paul Martin Prime Minister of Canada, Frank McKenna, US President* ***Bill Clinton****, Tom Daschle Senator, John Edwards Senator, Dianne Feinstein Senator, Mayor of San Francisco, Chuck Hagel Senator,* ***Alexander Haig NATO*** *Commander (US Secretary of State)*
>
> *Lyman Lemnitzer Supreme Allied Commander NATO,* ***Ben Bernanke Chairman*** *of United States Federal Reserve, Jamie Dimon, CEO and chairman of JPMorgan Chase & Co.*
>
> *Wim Duisenberg European Central Bank President, Timothy Geithner president of the Federal Reserve Bank of New York, Gordon Richardson Governor of the Bank of England, Michel Bon CEO of France Telecom,* ***Louis V. Gerstner Jr. IBM Chairman*** *and so many more.*

The Priory of Sion (Zion)

The Priory has a long history starting in AD 1099, called the Illuminati, having illustrious Grand Masters including Isaac Newton and Leonardo de Vinci. The order protects certain royal claimants because they believe them to be the literal descendants of Jesus and his alleged wife Mary Magdalene. The priory seeks the founding of a "Holy European Empire" that would become the next power to usher in a new world order—through their version of peace and prosperity.

OPUS DEI

The right wing of the Roman Catholic Church believes it cannot lose if it has strong ties with both ends of the political spectrum. Opus Dei, Latin for "work of God," has, at least 3,000 members in the United States but its influence is much more far reaching than this number implies. The order was founded in Spain by Roman Catholic priest Josemaría Escrivá with the approval of Pope Pi. Escriva founded the group on Oct. 2, 1928, after what he said was a command from God. Opus Dei runs 60 centers in 19 cities, among them Boston, Chicago, Dallas, Houston, Los Angeles, Milwaukee, Pittsburgh and San Francisco. Frequently aligning with fundamentalist Protestants, far-right Catholics are an often-overlooked, but powerful, segment of the Religious Right..."

"Satan! Cry Aloud! Thou Exalted Most High, O, my father Satan! The Eye!"

Aleister Crowley – Head of the Occultist Satanic movement
Representative of Horus.

Skull & Bones

EYE of HORUS

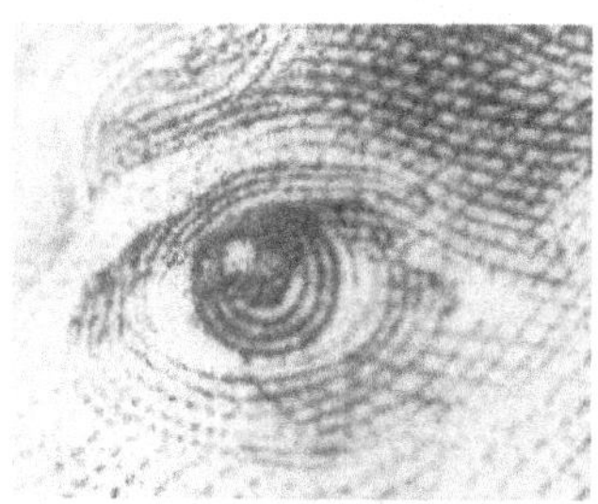

US Dollar – Reptilian Texture

Illuminati

Six- Pointed Star - spells out the word, "**mason.**"

Annuit Coeptis – "Announcing The Birth"

Capstone – Eye of Horus [Egyptian Mysticism] = Eye of Satan or Lucifer

Thirteen Layers to the Pyramid = Number '13' occult number of Depravity, Rebellion.

666 – Six bars—Six stars x 2?

Illuminati—Masons

Population Control

Bohemian Grove with US Presidents at Secret Illuminati ceremony

Coincidence? Not at all.

Mason Logo - left

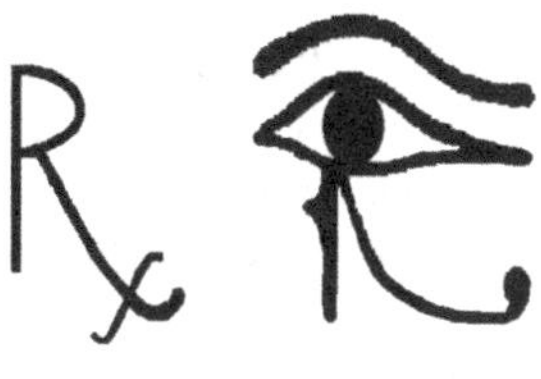

Big Pharma—The Eye of Horus

In 1776 professor, Adam Weishaupt of canon law at Ingolstadt University Germany, formed the modern version of the Illuminati—a secret society bent on reshaping European civilization. It's no coincidence that 1776 was also the year of the American Declaration of Independence. Most of the Illuminati's early members were from the Freemasons.

In 1992, Dr John Coleman published Conspirators' Hierarchy: The Story of the Committee of 300. Dr Coleman identifies the players and carefully details the Illuminati agenda of worldwide domination and control. Dr Coleman accurately summarizes the purpose and intent of the Committee of 300:

> *"A One World Government and one-unit monetary system, under permanent non-elected hereditary oligarchists who self-select from among their numbers in the form of a feudal system as it was in the Middle Ages. In this One World entity, population will be limited by restrictions on the number of children per family, diseases, wars, famines, until 1 billion people who are useful to the ruling class, in areas which will be strictly and clearly defined, remain as the total world population.*
>
> *There will be no middle class, only rulers and the servants. All laws will be uniform under a legal system of world courts practicing the same unified code of laws, backed up by a One World Government police force and a One World unified military to enforce laws in all former countries where no national boundaries shall exist. The system will be on the basis of a welfare state; those who are obedient and subservient to the One World Government will be rewarded with the means to live; those who are rebellious will simple be starved to death or be declared outlaws—thus a target for anyone who wishes to kill them. Privately owned firearms or weapons of any kind will be prohibited."*

The Bible warning:

"Let no one deceive you by any means; for that Day will not come unless the falling away comes first, and <u>the man of sin is revealed</u>, the son of perdition, who opposes and exalts himself above all that is called God or that is worshiped, so that he sits as God in the temple of God, showing himself that he is God."

Resurrection of the Anunnaki on Earth

Horus

Symbol of Horus with Sun

Eye of Horus

Seal with six-pointed Star

US Dollar

"Let my servants be few and secret. They shall reign over the many and known" Lam, Messenger of **Horus.**

Victoria B.C. Canada

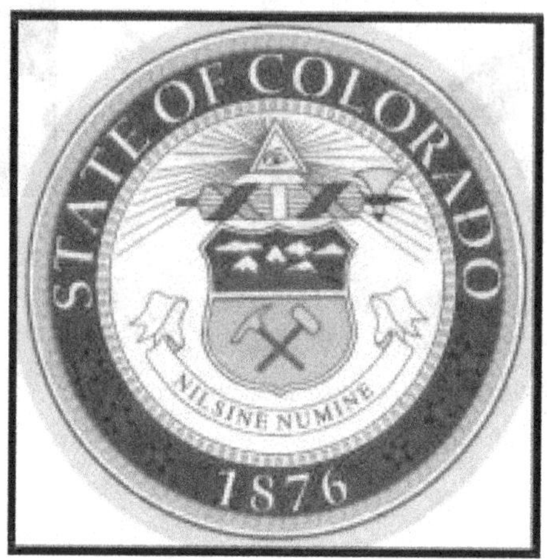

All Seeing Eye

Information Awareness Office - *(Department of Defense). As you can see it has the symbol of the pyramid with the All Seeing Eye over-looking (over-ruling) planet Earth.*

MI5 British Intelligence—(eye on top)

Please Note: All Logos and Trade Marks are used for reference only.

Texaco Gas Company - *The "T" symbol in the middle is the powerful "Tau" of ancient Greek and Hebrew alphabets, and is placed in the center of a pentagram with strong use of the color in this "sigil".*

Hexagram of Solomon

America Online company logo - *We see a similar motif of the All Seeing Eye inside the pyramid capstone in the logo.*

America on Line

Time Warner logo

Who Owns the Media

Bohemian Club—*Illuminati*

The Club is an association of rich and powerful men and women, mostly of USA (there are sister organizations in other countries). Some artists are allowed to join because of their social status and PR entertainment value. The membership list has included each Republican U.S. president (as well as some Democrats) since 1923, many cabinet officials, and directors & CEO's of the major corporations, including Banks and major financial institutions. The group also includes; Major military contractors, oil companies, banks (including the Federal Reserve), utilities (including nuclear power), and national media (broadcast and print) have high-ranking officials as club members or guests. Many members are, or have been, on the board of directors of several of these corporations. The above industries depend heavily on their relationship with government for their profitability.

Some members & frequent guests included: Henry Kissinger, George Shultz, S. D. Bechtel, Jr., Thomas Watson Jr. (IBM), Phillip Hawley (B of A), William Casey (CIA), and Ralph Bailey (DuPont), A. W. Clausen (World Bank), Walter Cronkite, and William F. Buckley. George Bush Jr., known as the air head, and others of lower status reside in a less prestigious part of the camp (Hillbillies), where top level information is not shared.

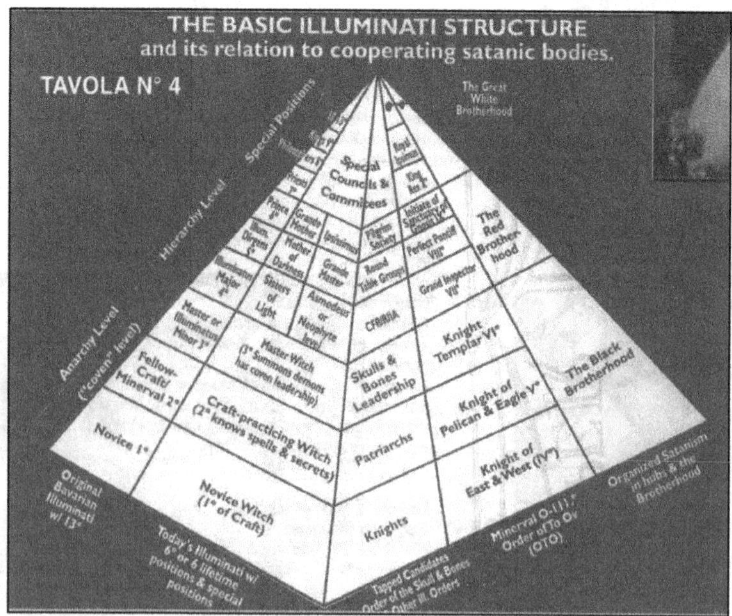

Freemasonry—*Illuminati*

Egypt is the cradle of freemasonry, but in no way the beginning of the metaphysical knowledge. The knowledge came to Earth long before Atlantis, and represented the universal knowledge of light, and pure solar occultism. During the early days of Atlantis, the divine knowledge was shared. But over time a deviation of the knowledge evolved and the seed lines of the Anunnaki or dark forces battled for dominion of earth. Their agenda became the dominant force, and eventually, Atlantis was destroyed by a higher power that would not accept the direction towards the lower self. Some escaped the final days of destruction, with the knowledge intact. This set the stage for the next age of man—where the knowledge became secretive, horded and hidden. The reason this knowledge was not shared, was simply to have control over the people. The sacred knowledge was the same for priests of the Druids and Maya, who like the Magi of Persia and Priests of Heliopolis in Egypt, were all priests of the sun god. This corruption of the Star or Light Teachings manifested secretive sects, and distorted versions of the divine reality, of one universal teaching for all. The people's innate spiritual thirst for truth became ripe for the religious dogmas that resulted and filled the spiritual void. The void was filled with false knowledge that enslaved the peoples under the controls of the anti-Christ. The divine is one body, one mind, and one collective voice—anything else is anti-God.

The Masons date back to Ancient Egypt, with their occult customs, ceremonies, hieroglyphics, numerology and chronology of the stars. They have always had an agenda: as they expanded their domination: erasing other cultures' spiritual foundations and replacing it with dogma in order to divide. The evolution of the Catholic Church, and the inquisition during the middle ages is just one example.

It was about 200 years ago, when these powers finally realized they could no longer control people by the sword. So they started to search for ways to control Governments and the minds of the population. The ancient and powerful seed line, and their interconnection with the Illuminati, Masons, Church and the Royal bloodlines have one agenda of total global control, and spinning their web of anti Christ ideology.

We must look for truth, as truth will not look for us!

Illuminati—9/11

President John F Kennedy's speech was made before the American Newspaper Publishers Association—ten days before his assassination in Dallas. It is obvious his concerns resonated truth, as he was killed by the very forces he was going to expose—those secretly building a covert shadow government behind the scenes.

"Mr. Chairman, ladies and gentlemen: The very word secrecy is repugnant in a free and open society; and we are as a people inherently and historically opposed to secret societies, to secret oaths and to secret proceedings. We decided long ago that the dangers of excessive and unwarranted concealment of pertinent facts far outweighed the dangers, which are cited to justify it. Even today, there is little value in opposing the threat of a closed society by imitating its arbitrary restrictions. Even today, there is little value in insuring the survival of our nation if our traditions do not survive with it. And there is very grave danger that an announced need for increased security will be seized upon by those anxious to expand its meaning to the very limits of official censorship and concealment. That I do not intend to permit to the extent that it is in my control. And no official of my Administration, whether his rank is high or low, civilian or military, should interpret my words here tonight as an excuse to censor the news, to stifle dissent, to cover up our mistakes or to withhold from the press and the public the facts they deserve to know.

But I do ask every publisher, every editor, and every newsman in the nation to re-examine his own standards, and to recognize the nature of our country's peril. In time of war, the government and the press have customarily joined in an effort based largely on self-discipline, to prevent unauthorized disclosures to the enemy. In time of "clear and present danger", the courts have held that even the privileged rights of the First Amendment must yield to the public's need for national security.

Today no war has been declared--and however fierce the struggle may be, it may never be declared in the traditional fashion. Our way of life is under attack. Those who make themselves our enemy is advancing around the globe. The survival of our friends is in danger. And yet no war has been declared, marching troops has crossed no borders, no missiles have been fired. If the press is awaiting a declaration of war before it imposes the self-discipline of combat conditions, then I can only say that no war ever posed a greater threat to our security. If you are awaiting a finding of "clear and present danger", then I can only say that the danger has never been more clear and its presence has never been more imminent.

It requires a change in outlook, a change in tactics, a change in missions--by the government, by the people, by every businessman or labor leader, and by every newspaper. For we are opposed around the world by a monolithic and ruthless conspiracy that relies primarily on covert means for expanding its sphere of influence--on infiltration instead of invasion, on subversion instead of elections, on intimidation instead of free choice, on guerrillas by night instead of armies by day. It is a system, which has conscripted vast human and material resources into the building of a tightly knit, highly efficient machine that combines military, diplomatic, intelligence, economic, scientific and political operations.

Its preparations are concealed, not published. Its mistakes are buried, not headlined. Its dissenters are silenced, not praised. No expenditure is questioned, no rumor is printed, no secret is revealed. It conducts the Cold War, in short, with a war-time discipline no democracy would ever hope or wish to match.

I am asking your help in the tremendous task of informing and alerting the American people. For I have complete confidence in the response and dedication of our citizens whenever they are fully informed. I not only could not stifle controversy among your readers--I welcome it. This Administration intends to be candid about its errors; for as a wise man once said: "An error does not become a mistake until you refuse to correct it." We intend to accept full responsibility for our errors; and we expect you to point them out when we miss them.

Without debate, without criticism, no Administration and no country can succeed--and no republic can survive. That is why the Athenian lawmaker Solon decreed it a crime for any citizen to shrink from controversy. And that is why our press was protected by the First Amendment-- the only business in America specifically protected by the Constitution- -not primarily to amuse and entertain, not to emphasize the trivial and the sentimental, not to simply "give the public what it wants"--but to inform, to arouse, to reflect, to state our dangers and our opportunities, to indicate our crises and our choices, to lead, mold, educate and sometimes even anger public opinion.

This means greater coverage and analysis of international news--for it is no longer far away and foreign but close at hand and local. It means greater attention to improved understanding of the news as well as improved transmission. And it means, finally, that government at all levels, must meet its obligation to provide you with the fullest possible information outside the narrowest limits of national security--and we intend to do it." - "And so it is to the printing press--to the recorder of man's deeds, the keeper of his conscience, the courier of his news--that we look for strength and assistance, confident that with your help man will be what he was born to be: free and independent. Thank- you."

President Dwight D. Eisenhower: Farewell Address January 17, 1961.

"In the councils of government, we must guard against the acquisition of unwarranted influence, whether sought or unsought, by the military-industrial complex. The potential for the disastrous rise of misplaced power exists and will persist. We must never let the weight of this combination endanger our liberties or democratic processes. We should take nothing for granted. Only an alert and knowledgeable citizenry can compel the proper meshing of the huge industrial and military machinery of defense with our peaceful methods and goals, so that security and liberty may prosper together."

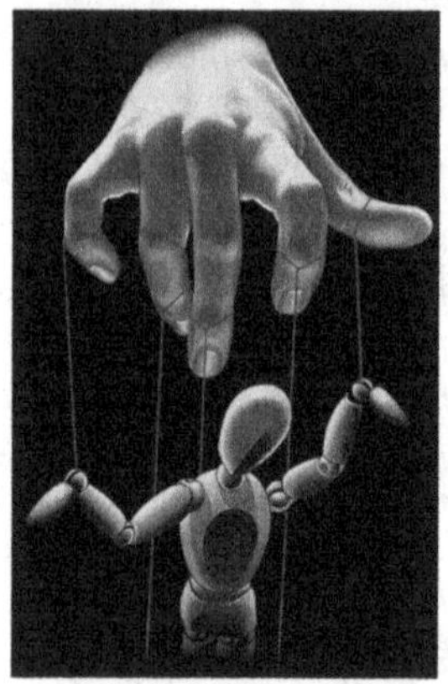
The Puppet Masters

Luke 12:2 "*Whatever Is Covered Up Will Be Uncovered And Every Secret Will Be Made Known*"

It is ironic that President John F Kennedy and his predecessor, President Dwight D Eisenhower, warned of the power and influence that the secret societies were gaining—fearing control and manipulation of the US Government and CIA. Kennedy's assassination was a smoothly coordinated plot by the Illuminati to protect their special interests vested in the Banking system, the CIA shadow operations and the covert secret arms of the military industrial complex—including UFO's. These special interests included reverse engineering captured alien space technologies, and global plans for the *New World Order*—to control the world through military and financial manipulation.

The sham known as the *Warren Commission* investigating the JFK assassination was the first in a series of controlled misinformation campaigns—successfully directed by the Illuminati *puppet masters*. With 9/11 and the current middle east wars, we can clearly see there is a major attack on the innocence of the world populations. It also shows the length to which the Illuminati will go to execute their plan for world domination, and, to inflict upon us, their *New World Order*—an ongoing satanic manifesto like their last failed attempt in Nazi Germany.

September 11, 2001, the eyes of the world were focused on a sad and unnecessary loss of innocent lives at the World Trade Center. And, at the same time, most media networks appeared to lose their moral backbone to report and investigate what was an obvious *covert military strike*. This is more proof that major US and international media is owned or controlled by the Illuminati—through an integrated web. Their media agenda is simple: promote a very planned and patterned system of fear and misinformation and distraction. Fear will allow expansion of government powers without oversight. In this way the Illuminati can accomplish *The New World*

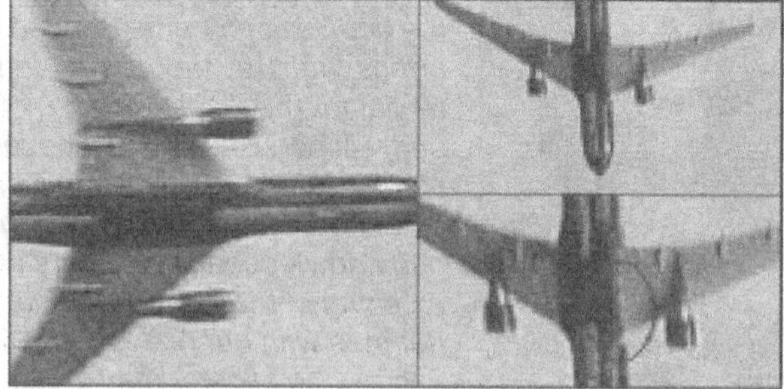

***Note:** The underbelly of AA commercial Jets are smooth—the 9/11 plane has a missile.*

Order—something they couldn't do when Hitler was defeated in WWII. Currently, the Illuminati has created a top-heavy infrastructure that globally controls most of the banking, economies, and the powerful US armed forces. This is not to say that the innocent citizens working within the infrastructure are Illuminati—they are not. They just don't understand and realize who controls the top of the pyramid, and that their strings are controlled and pulled by the Illuminati *Puppet Masters*.

The certainty that four large commercial jets vanished in the northeastern United States the morning of 9/11 created unparalleled events and dealt a crippling blow to what was left of US democracy. What made it so incredible, was that after each *World Trade Center* skyscraper was struck by an *aluminum framed* commercial aircraft, the massive reinforced *steel framed* buildings collapsed. The official story reported that jet fuel fires melted the steel in the buildings causing the collapse. Scientifically, this is impossible. Jet fuel will not burn above 1520°F (825°C) and studies show the high-grade steel used at the WTC would have to be at least 3000°F (1650°C) under sustained heat in order to melt. In reality, most of the jet fuel burned up during the impact explosion—so how did this high-grade steel melt? It was the first time in history that fire caused collapse in a steel structured skyscraper: and it happened twice on the same morning—September 11, 2001.

One month prior to these attacks, WTC owner: Larry Silverstein, expanded *two* insurance policies to include *Acts of Terrorism*. His insurance settlement was US$7.1 billion. Coincidentally, George Bush's brother was a principal in the security company responsible for protecting the WTC. This firm turned off security at the WTC, and on many occasions sent their security personnel home along with their explosive-sniffing dog teams, during the months leading up to 9/11—even during times when private contractors were actively working in both towers.

Currently, 800 top US Architectural Firms and many engineering and demolition companies: insulted by the official 9/11 Government account, are demanding an *Independent Investigation*—citing that the WTC buildings were destroyed by a *Controlled Demolition,* not airplane fires. Bomb-like explosions were seen blowing out windows and were heard by many first responders in their personal accounts. Some of these people were threatened and *told* they *did not hear* blasts or explosions.

Military-grade Nano-Thermite dust was found over the crime scene in Manhattan during cleanup. White-hot molten steel was dripping from the burning south-tower's 80th floor—a sign of Nano-Thermite explosives. The molten metal shown in videos on the 81st floor of the WTC Tower Two, is clearly yellow and white-hot. Military personal and explosive experts say only military-grade Nano-Thermite explosives could produce such large amounts of hot molten metal.

(Artist rendering of a commercial airlines jet—using exact proportions - it just doesn't fit!)

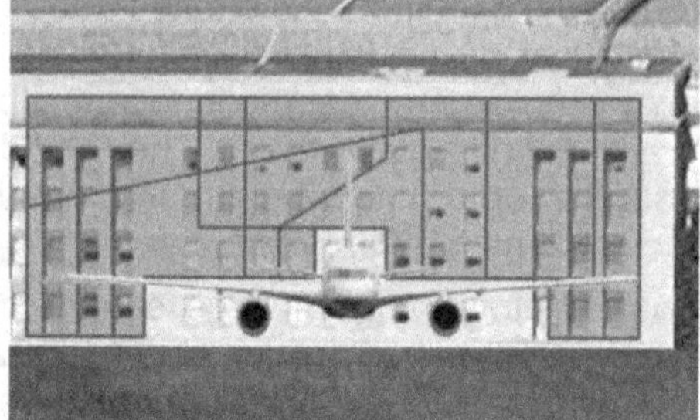

(So where are the plane's wings & Titanium RR Engines) – official story—Vaporized!

It is highly unlikely that two commercial airliners with aluminum wings cut through the World Trade Center's steel-reinforced concrete, but that the airliner that hit the Pentagon left just a circular hole in the building's wall— missile? If it was an airliner, then where are the wings and the two 8 ton Titanium engines? Official story "Vaporized" - but the Government was still able to identify 95 passengers' DNA. It is again, the first time in history where two commercial Jets vaporized on impact with the ground. Of the four 9/11 crashes, extensive research and facts most clearly refute the government's lie about a 757 hitting the Pentagon. We know for sure that something blew a circular hole in the Pentagon that morning—not a Boeing 757.

If a plane hit the Pentagon; one of the most guarded and secure centers in the world; then show us just one photo or video footage from one of hundreds of security cameras that would have shown the crash—not one was provided. How did two 8-ton Titanium RR engines vaporize in burning jet fuel, when the fuel was consumed in minutes reaching 1520°F degrees and Titanium melts at 3135°F—over 1500 degrees hotter?

I think we all know where this is going, and the reality of what happened. The Illuminati controlling parts of the US Government and shadow CIA, created a *new Pearl Harbor* to inflict fear and more fear on the American public and mayhem on the world. This was done to take more powers away from the constitution and fulfill the *New World Order* agenda of total control. The fact is, many Republican and Democratic politicians, top military and CIA personal are freemasons, and have evolved into positions of power and influence over the past 50 years. This is exactly what President Eisenhower and JFK warned us about, it has now come to be the reality.

Could the Illuminati *puppet masters* really get the US Government do something so evil to its own citizens? The evidence says yes! And It shows just how deeply embedded the satanic Illuminati are in world affairs.

Illuminati—New World Order - Monetary Control

The Bankers' Manifesto of 1934

"Capital must protect itself in every way, through combination and through legislation. Debts must be collected and loans and mortgages foreclosed as soon as possible. When through a process of law, the common people have lost their homes, they will be more tractable and more easily governed by the strong arm of the law applied by the central power of wealth—under control of leading financiers. People without homes will not quarrel with their leaders. This is well known among these principles now engaged in forming an Imperialism of Capital to govern the world. By dividing the people they can get them to expend their energies in fighting over questions of no real importance. Only by discrete action can we secure for ourselves from what has been generally planned and successfully accomplished."

The Federal Reserve Act

Passed on Christmas Eve 1913, it transferred the power to coin money and issue US currency, and to regulate its value from Congress to a Private corporation. Now, the US borrows what should be the citizen's own money from the Federal Reserve; a private corporation; with interest. The debt can never be repaid under the current money system and the Illuminati elite owns the private corporation.

Article I, Section 8, US Constitution: *as only The Congress shall have Power... To coin Money, and regulate the Value thereof...*

Nathan Mayer Rothschild: *"I care not what puppet is placed upon the throne of England to rule the Empire on which the sun never sets. The man who controls Britain's money supply controls the British Empire, and I control the British money supply."*

Senator William Jenner: February 23, 1954, warned about the Illuminati in a speech: *"Outwardly we have a Constitutional government. We have operating within our government and political system, another body representing another form of government, a bureaucratic elite which believes our Constitution is outmoded."*

Professor Dr. Carroll Quigley: (Bill Clinton's mentor while at Georgetown) wrote about the goals of the investment bankers (Illuminati) who control central banks: *"nothing less than to create a world system of financial control in private hands able to dominate the political system of each country and the economy of the world as a whole... controlled in a feudalist fashion by the central banks of the world acting in concert, by secret agreements arrived at in frequent private meetings and conferences."*

Thomas Jefferson wrote: *"The Central Bank is an institution of the most deadly hostility existing against the principles and form of our Constitution...if the American people allow private banks to control the issuance of their currency, first by inflation and then by deflation, the banks and corporations that will grow up around them will deprive the people of all their property until their children will wake up homeless on the continent their fathers conquered."*

President Andrew Jackson wrote: *"The bold effort the present bank had made to control the government, the distress it had wantonly produced...are but premonitions of the fate that awaits the American people should they be deluded into a perpetuation of this institution or the establishment of another like it."*

Illuminati—New World Order - Civilian Detention

There is something in the works, as more and more information is surfacing from Government insiders about an *imminent and forced collapse* of the world monetary system—prior to 2012. There is also talk of a deadly H1N1 or Avian Flu pandemic being released into the populations with *forced deadly vaccines*, as well as Alien contact and the imminent cataclysms as we approach 2012.

Whatever the reality, there are 100,000 rail cars built with 2 levels and rows with shackles (20 pairs per side) sitting ready for use in many US states – these rail cars were built over the past 5 years for FEMA by – Halliburton & the Bechtel Corporation.

There are also over 600 new FEMA "Civil Detention Facilities" 2 or 3 in each and every state in the United States. These camps are operated by FEMA (Federal Emergency Management Agency) should Martial Law need to be implemented. Again the Illuminati controlled companies like Halliburton & the Bechtel Corporation, have built these facilities. Each can house between 20,000 – 50,000 citizens at one time, and each has said to house large furnaces. All these facilities are all fully operational and ready to receive prisoners or detainees. It seems very odd that many of these detention facilities only have rail and heliport access—so would this mean "no" visitors or lawyers. All facilities are currently staffed and surrounded by full-time international guards, but all the facilities are currently empty.

International Forces are now training in the US to control massive civil unrest. What are they planning for? Would this unrest be a result of Martial Law created by a major cataclysm, international flu pandemic, or civil unrest caused by micro nukes planted in cities by the same secret covert group that created and planned 9/11? It seems the Illuminati and parts of the Government are well aware of the coming events and are preparing for something as 2012 approaches.

Illuminati—Chemtrails - Global Spraying

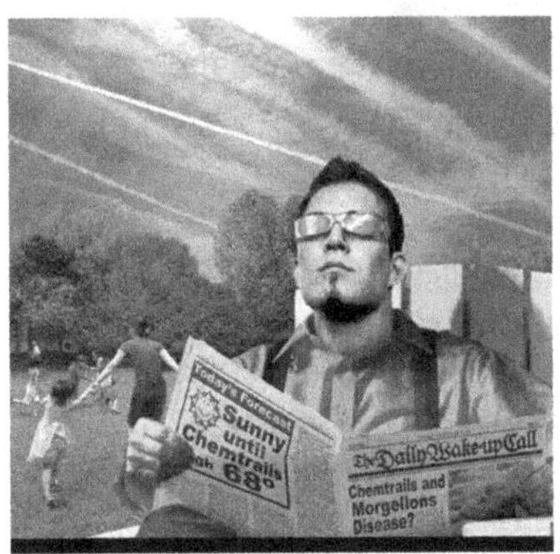

Chemtrails are NOT vapor trails left behind high-flying Jets. Enormous regions of our planet are being continually sprayed systematically with highly toxic combinations of chemicals—at high and low altitudes. This is happening all around the world, over all major cities and rural areas and forests. This controlled spraying has been going on secretly for years. Citizen groups are now suing governments of many countries, but the military continues to spray their populations. Particle fallout from these Chemtrails are found to contain *Colloidal Aluminum*—at seven times the legal Canadian health exposure limits. *Barium Salts* and other nasty biological components, all of which have been proven to cause severe illness in humans and animals, and will stunt and kill vegetation growth.

So what are Barium Salts and Colloidal Aluminum?

Barium Salts in the body have been used in the past to track released terrorists. Under Marshall Law, military technologies will be able to track populations by following the traceable Barium.

Symptoms of barium poisoning include: nose bleeds, respiratory distress, hard mucous coating in the back of the throat, increased blood pressure, changes in heart rhythm, stomach irritation, brain swelling, muscle weakness, liver, kidney, heart, and spleen damage.

Colloidal Aluminum is used to pacify the population. Exposure to this substance causes: nausea, vomiting and joint pains. Long-term exposure causes impairment of brain functions—such as memory and balance. These debilitating symptoms are now common in adults in the Pacific NW and have increased dramatically over the past two years.

HAARP (*High-Frequency Active Auroral Research Program)* – Please read up about this—online. Military forces around the world are using this new technology in secret to control weather patterns, create earthquakes, and induce mood swings in the populations. Many top scientists have come forward on the dangers this technology creates on a global scale.

Illuminati—Health Care

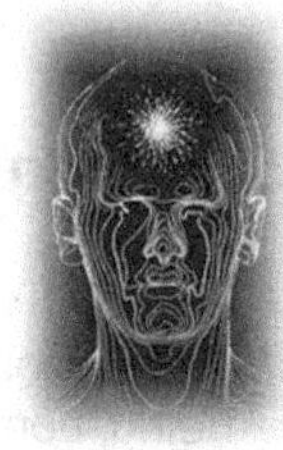

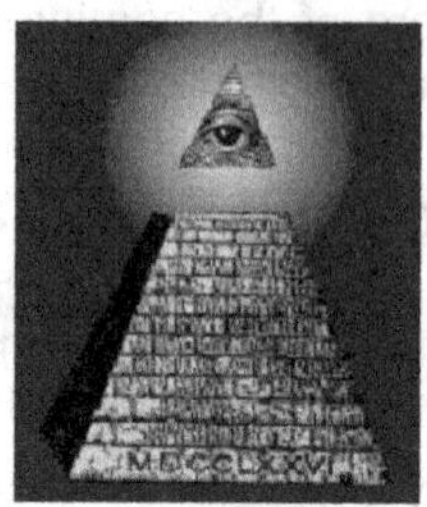

Cancer

Since the 1970's, the powers of the medical establishment still claim not to know the cause of cancer, after countless billions of dollars spent on "the war" on cancer. They still only offer expensive and invasive treatments like radiation and highly toxic drugs to treat it. Interestingly, these drug companies are mostly Illuminati owned or controlled and they conveniently generate billions of dollars in revenues each year for thousands of their cancer business elite. This is a form of population control, as the tobacco and cancer industries as well as the global health industry (CODEX, WTO, WHO) are mostly controlled and owned by the illuminati or their subsidiaries and brotherhood. This select secret group includes many Royal and political figures of global power and influence. (See secret societies)

Fluoride

Fluoride is a major intellect suppressant that has been added to drinking water supplies and toothpaste for decades. Did you know sodium fluoride is a common ingredient in poisons, anesthetics, hypnotics, psychiatric drugs, and military nerve gas? Independent scientific evidence shows fluoride causes various mental disturbances and makes people dense, submissive, and subservient, while shortening life spans and damaging bone structure. Fluoride is in fact a byproduct of the aluminum industry and the public was hoodwinked into adding it to drinking water by the Mellon family who are a direct bloodline, and close friends of the British royal family, and dictators of US policy through the Illuminati network.

The first use of fluoridated drinking water was in the Nazi prison camps like Auschwitz in Germany. It was offered by the Illuminati's notorious pharmaceutical giant, I.G. Farben which today is known as "Bayer". This mass medication of the water supply was not given to the inmates because the Nazis were concerned about their teeth! Fluoridated drinking water was given to sterilize the prisoners and force them into quiet submission.

Mind Control

Repeated doses of the smallest amounts of fluoride will: over a short time, reduce an individual's will to resist domination—slowly poisoning and "drugging" a specific part of the brain, thus becoming submissive. This

would be called "gentle opportune lobotomy." So the real reason behind water fluoridation is not to benefit children's teeth, it is to reduce the resistance of the population to domination and control of the "New World Order". Any sustained use of fluorinated water will effect a person mentally and physically. This would include beer, soft drinks, and toothpaste.

Dr. Jennifer Luke from the University of Surrey in England found that the pineal gland is the primary target of fluoride accumulation within the body. Up until the 1990s, no research had ever been conducted to determine the impact of fluoride on the pineal gland—a small gland located between the two hemispheres of the brain that regulates the production of the hormone melatonin. Melatonin is a hormone that helps regulate the onset of puberty and helps protect the body from cell damage caused by free radicals.

The Pineal Gland looks like a tiny pine cone, and it produces a chemical called DMT (N,N-dimethyltryptamine) an extremely short-acting but very powerful psychedelic. In his book *DMT: The Spirit Molecule*, Dr Rick Strassman researched the endogenous DMT's role in dreams, meditation & spiritual experiences, birth, alien entity contact, near-death & death experiences. The research showed it could very well be the entry and exit to this and other dimensions and worlds, and the collective unconscious. The Illuminati have understood the power of the Pineal Gland since ancient times, and intentionally want to suppress this spiritual awareness and opening to the light consciousness from manifesting. Please Note: the pinecone on the staffs and structures of the Vatican, as well as ancient Egypt.

The 'third eye' or 6th chakra is connected to the pineal gland. As our vibration or frequency rises through meditation or spiritual experiences, it activates and opens, allowing a connection beyond the 5 senses of our limited physical vision and into the light consciousness. This connection takes us beyond the illusions we have been conditioned to accept in the 3rd dimensional reality, and instead allows a full expansion into the vast spectrum of the divine light consciousness, while opening our connection to the spiritual transformation of 2012.

Mark of the Beast—666

Revelation 14:9-11 *"And the third angel followed them, saying with a loud voice, If any man worship the beast and his image, and receive his mark in his forehead, or in his hand, The same shall drink of the wine of the wrath of God, which is poured out without mixture into the cup of his indignation; and he shall be tormented with fire and brimstone in the presence of the holy angels, and in the presence of the Lamb: And the smoke of their torment ascendeth up for ever and ever: and they have no rest day nor night, who worship the beast and his image, and whosoever receiveth the mark of his name."*

"Worship the beast and his image" does not represent a physical mark on the forehead, it represents where and how we allow our awareness or attention to manifest via the 6th chakra. Over the ages the knowledge of vibrations, solar occultism and sacred geometry has been kept hidden and secret by the Illuminati forces - so our civilization has become child's play to manipulate – The reality is vibrations and sacred geometric ratios rule our density and reality. The Illuminati know this, and manipulate us, using the knowledge and lower vibrational fields to manipulate and control us. Thus keeping our senses and powers under evolved and focused on the lower density. The mark of the beast represents all the distractions and things created by the beast that will keep our attention on this lower density; TV, fear media, war, satanic music or lyrics, pornography, drugs, etc. The illuminati goal is to keep our attention enslaved, and prevent the spiritual evolution from transforming our awareness into a higher density of spiritual light consciousness and the higher spiritual density manifesting in 2012 and beyond.

False Gurus

Mark 13:22 – *"For false Christs and false prophets shall rise, and shall show signs and wonders, to seduce, if it were possible, even the elect."*

In the new age of transformation we must learn to be our own Guru and Master, and not be mesmerized by, or empower the false teachers. We need to look beyond the saffron words that would take our innocence and money—leaving disillusioned children searching for the promised love and light we imbibe already.

Crop Circles—Alien Warnings

There is no doubt the crop circles are alien messages and warnings about up-coming spiritual, galactic and Earth changes. An advanced form of Cymantic sound wave energy creates the circles; similar to a sound wave that creates sacred geometric symbols in the sand moving through water. It appears that the aliens contacting us have perfected this form of communication. The symbols, mostly of a spiritual, scientific or astrological significance, were created to communicate and depict future events up to and beyond 2012. Unfortunately, some crop circle designs were created by hoaxers trying to get their 15 minutes of fame. They attempted to discredit the real messages and confuse the population about the real message and what will happen in 2012. It is a cosmic chess match pitting humans against the real alien crop circle designers. Consequently, the aliens have improved the complexities of the sacred geometric designs, woven beautifully and created so we can no longer doubt their origins. Circles are bent at a 51° angle but not broken. The crystalline structure of the grain changes after the circle is created, and the seed will usually produce more berries after that happens.

The messages in the various crop circles include the 13 Baktun cycle of the Mayan as well as a time reference between the time a specific circle was created until the December 21st 2012 Galactic Alignment. Some circles communicate that they are working on a vibrational communication structure. A very unique series of circles also showed the broken DNA cell and later circles with a cell metamorphous or evolution to a double or triple helix. This was clearly a message that our DNA will be or is changing through 2012.

WARNING - Planet X "Nibiru"

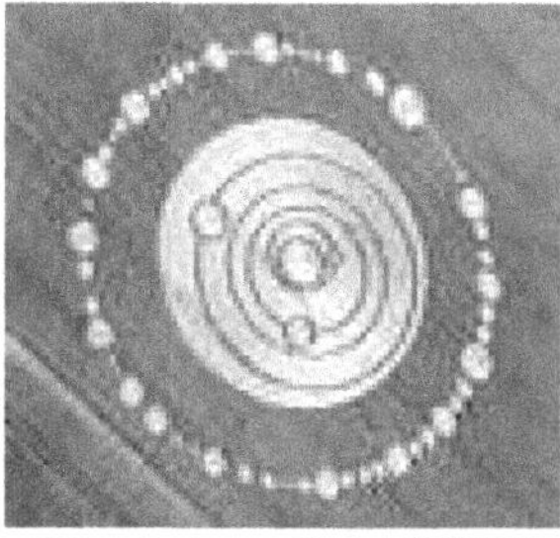

Solar System with out EARTH

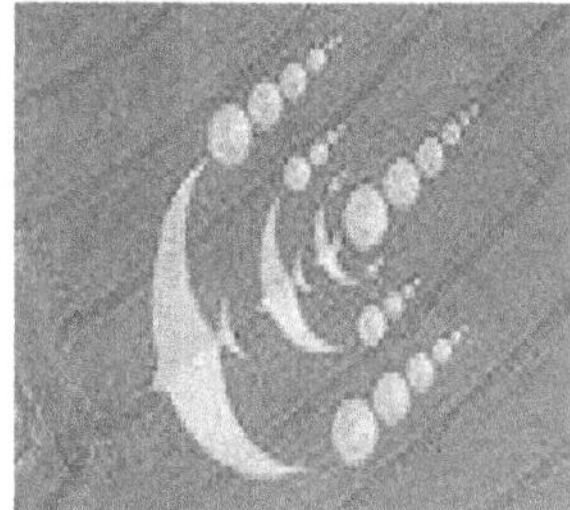

Space Ships In Formation

Mother **Star Ship**

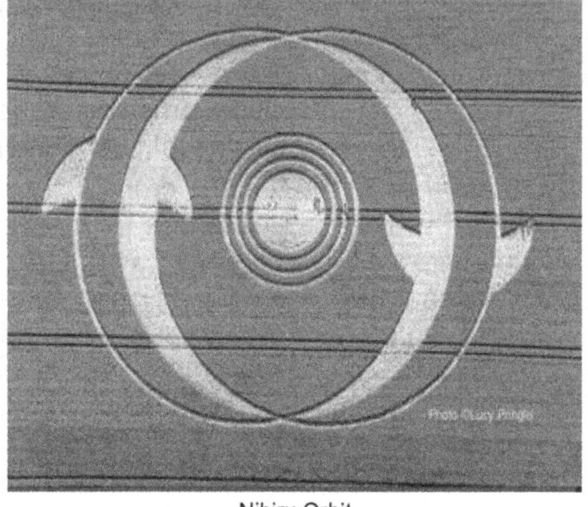

Nibiru Orbit
Nibiru spotted during eclipse of the Moon

Broken Helix

Single Helix

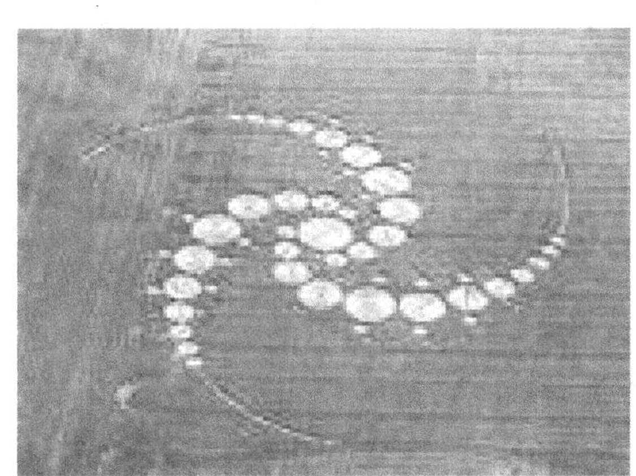
Triple Helix

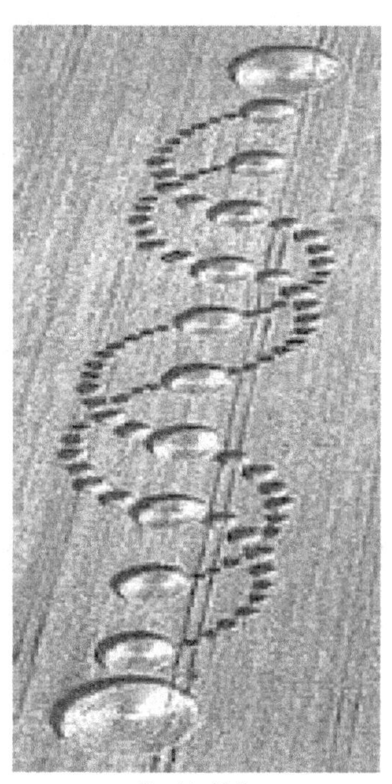
Double Helix

Wiltshire, 12 June 2009 – The Phoenix

NOTE: THE BIRD'S TAIL SEEMS TO BE ON FIRE

The phoenix is a mythical bird with a colorful tail of gold, purple and blue. Near the end of its life-cycle it builds itself a nest of myrrh twigs that then ignites; both nest and bird burn fiercely and are reduced to ashes, from which a new, young phoenix or phoenix egg is reborn anew to live again. Crop circle experts believe the latest pattern to be discovered, a phoenix raising from the flames in Wiltshire, may give a warning about the end of the world.

Wiltshire, UK 21/ 08/ 05

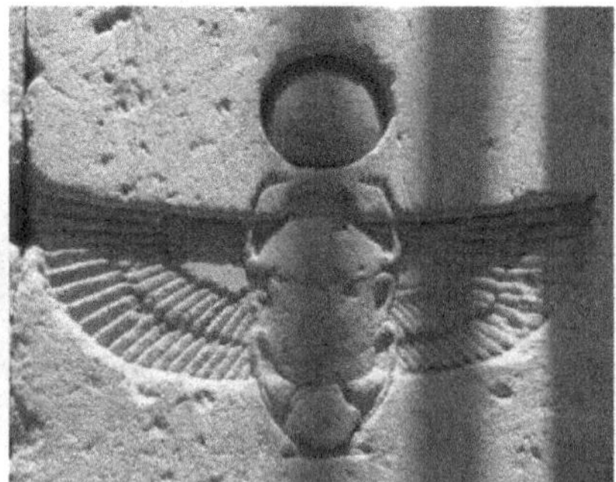

Carrying the Sun through the midnight hour!

Wiltshire - July 5th, 2009

This Mayan Motif Crop Circle symbolizing solar flares, coronal mass ejections represented as dots on the feathers of the headdress. The zigzag pattern is the signature of the feathered serpent, "Quetzalcoatl", 'The Radiant One' who is expected to make his return any time now.

Wiltshire - July 16, 1999
Creation - Sperm and Egg

Wiltshire - June 1999 – Nibiru / description of Sumerians

Horus (in Egyptian, Heru) the God of the sky, and the son of Osiris, the creator

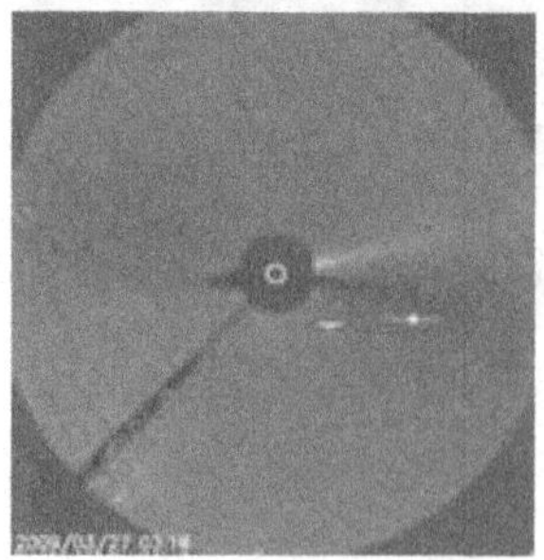

Planet Nibiru – Soho Photo

Sumerian – Nibiru - Anunnaki

Winged Sun

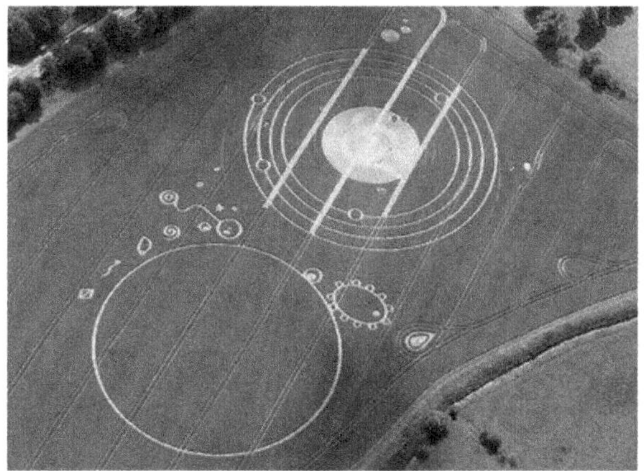

July 22nd, 2008 - Warning: Nibiru—Planets—Sun

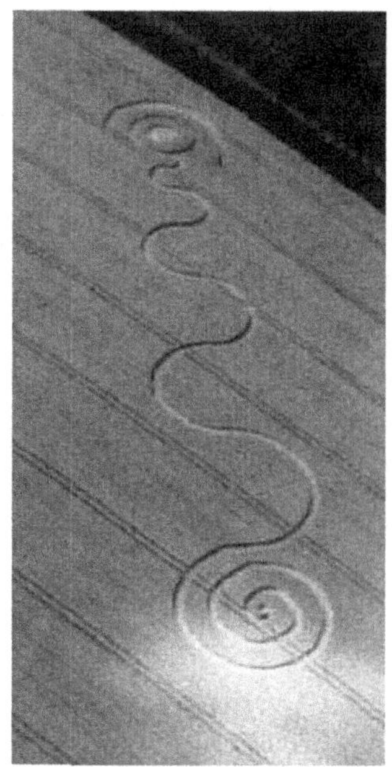

Barbury England - DNA
Spiraling Consciousness

This Crop Circle design same as those found on Rose Windows in medieval cathedrals, all point to the finite and infinite, Earth and Heaven, or matter and spirit, the 12 Disciples or 12 disciplines of ascension.

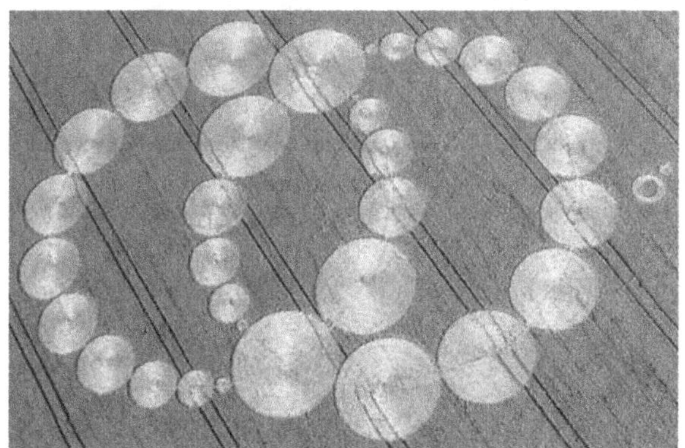

Oxfordshire
Reported August 3, 2009
Vesica Pisces is part of the creational patterns of sacred geometry.
The circles represent the female ovum and the oval the male opening of the penis, sperm, shape of the eye of creation, God, etc.

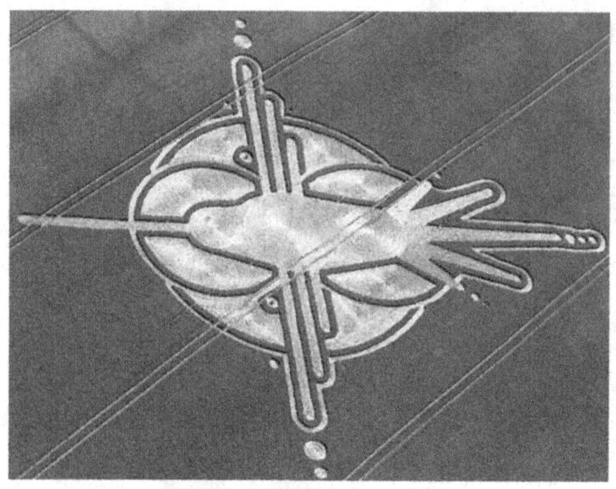

Milk Hill, Wiltshire. July 2, 2009
The Hummingbird represents a symbol of regeneration or resurrection.

Aztec mythology, Huitzilopochtli
Hummingbird of the South or Left-Hand was a God of war, a sun God.

Barbury Castle, The Aztec Spirit Bird of Aztec Mythology (right). Gods were represented as Birds, and at the top of their pantheon of Gods. Quetzalcoatl himself was also a (Bird - God) and is said to return in 2012.

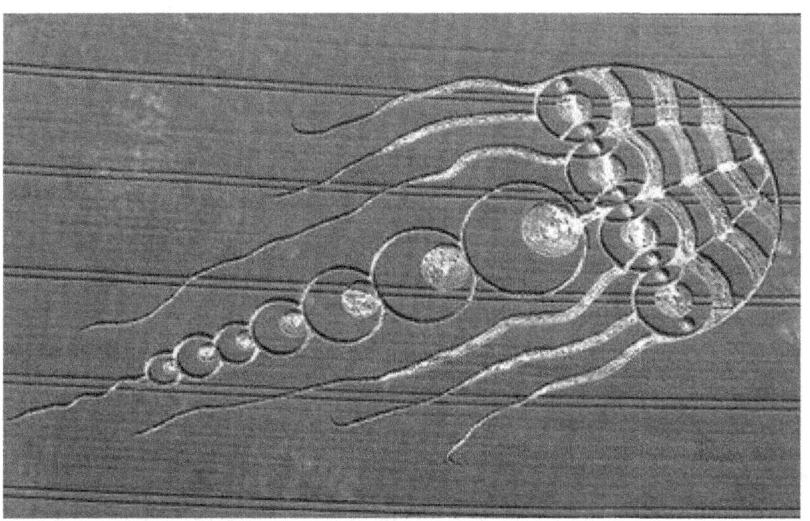

Oxfordshire - May the 29th, - **Jellyfish** (Light and Power)
Symbolic Meaning: inner strength, vulnerability, transparency, truth.

The Owl
Is one of the 20 Solar Seals of the Mayan Tzolkin Calendar.

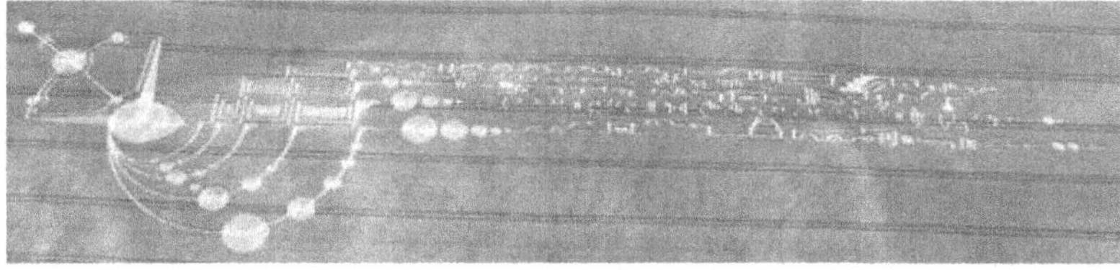

Crop Circle
Analysis suggest several Suns CMEs (coronal mass ejection) will impact upon Earth

Vortex / worm hole—Path to next dimension

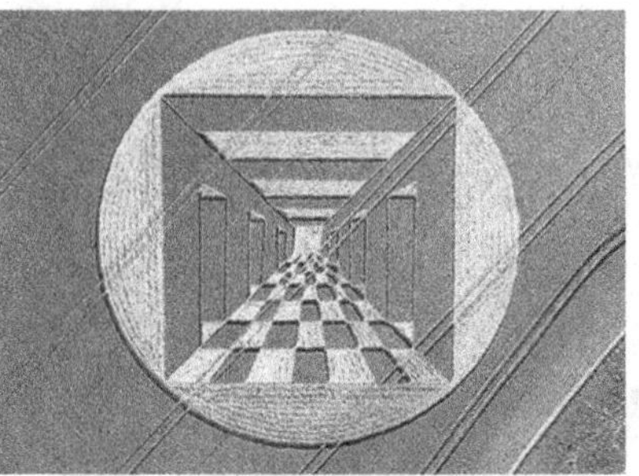

Illuminati Waning

Inter-dimensional Vortex Spiral: Norway Sky Dec 10th 2009 both photos are real. Witnessed by 100,000 people.

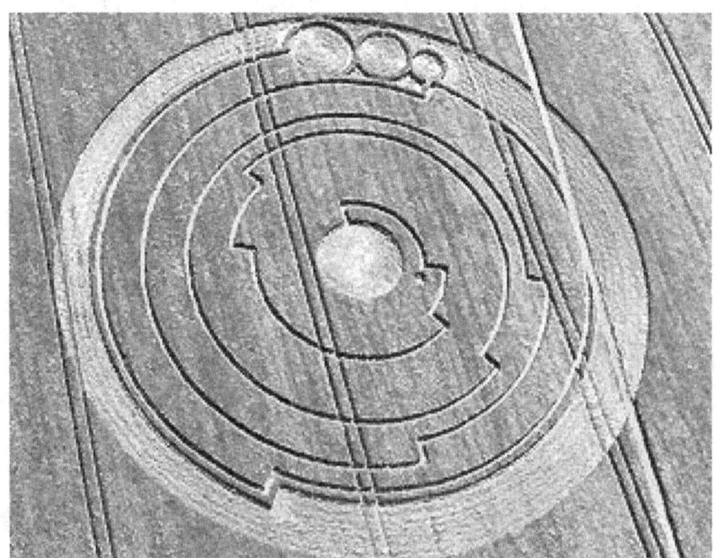

Crop Circle is coded representation of pi to the 10th significant figure, representing the first 10 digits, 3,141592654. of pi.

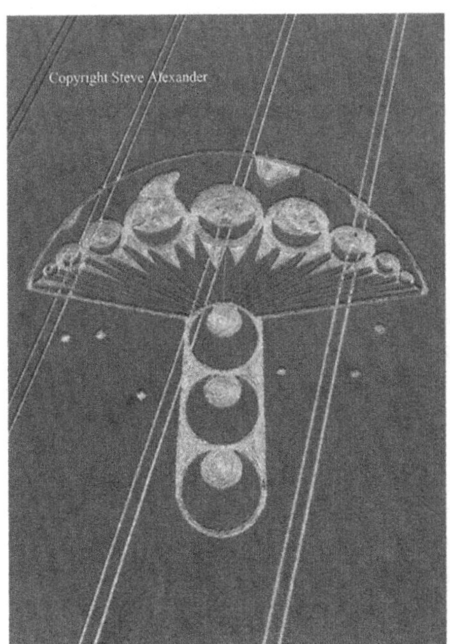

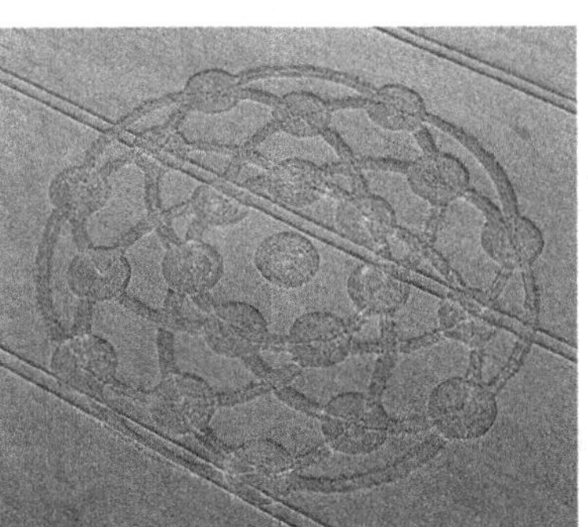

Mushroom – Nuclear fallout

Mother Ship

The Circle (below) is binary code with a message: *(Translated by three experts)*

*"**Beware** the bearers of false gifts, and their broken promises, much pain, but there is still time, Believe there is still good out there, we oppose the deceivers, the conduit is closing."*

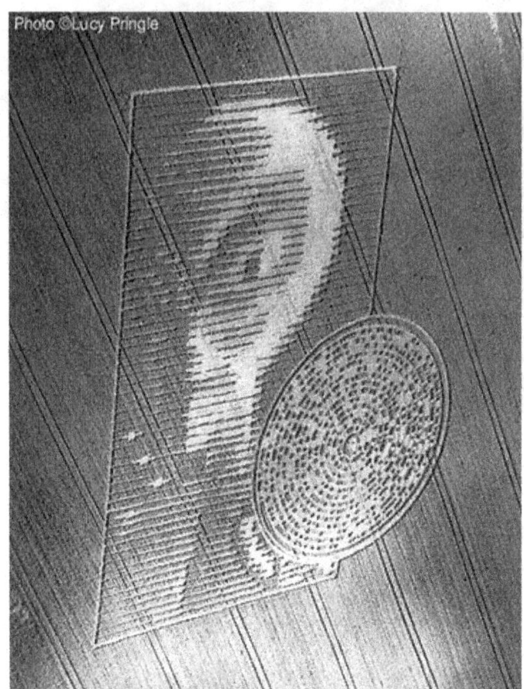

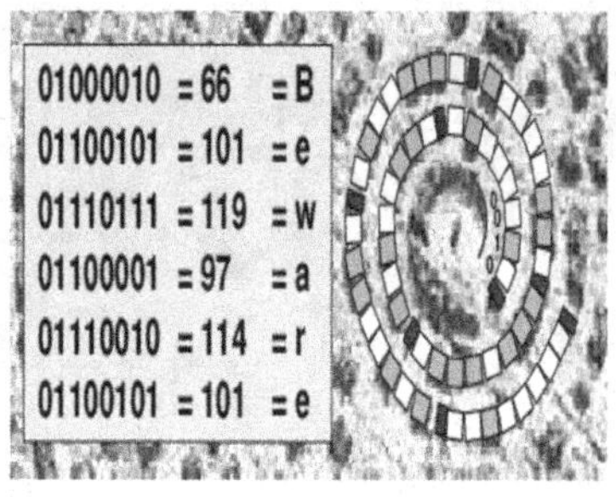

The sheer size and complexity of the (bottom right) formation is staggering. It has been estimated that hoaxers would have had to make one circle every 30 seconds during the night time hours in order to create this design!

Two ancient symbols for Human Spirituality.

Mind—Body—Spirit

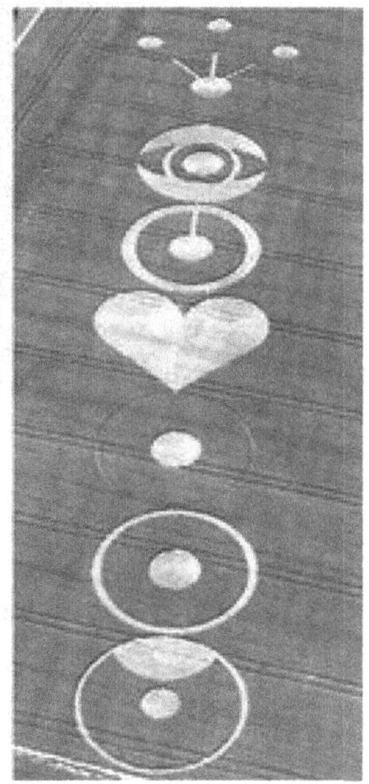

The Seven Chakras

Crop Circle Chakra

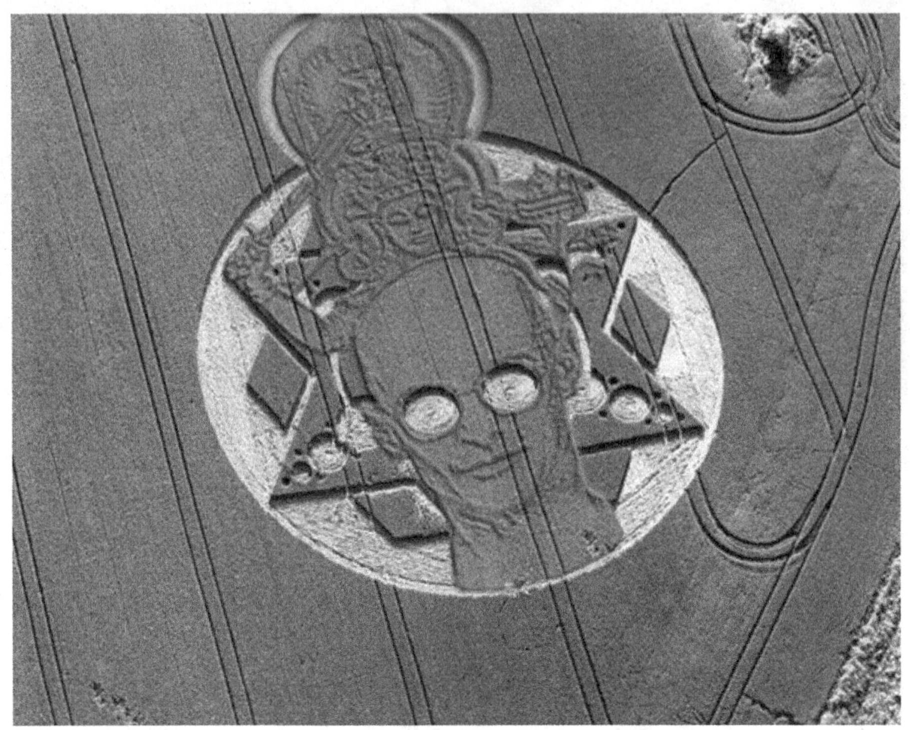

Significant Dates Mentioned through various Crop Circles.

May 20th 2012 – 16 days later = transit June 6th

Every 52 years—same day—same star—new era

The RETURN of Mesa

Nov 8th 2010	**8 Kan – yellow galactic seed**
May 5th 2012	**Planetary alignment**
June 14th 2012	**Hanub Ku rebirth**
July 7th	**5 CMEs will impact our planet soon**

Galactic Alignment

2012—The End Time

The Galactic plane is a gravitational field that consists of a very high force of gravity, expanding out from the black hole in the center of our galaxy. This dark rift or black hole has an estimated mass of one trillion stars and creates an enormously strong gravitational field. Because it is so massive, it spins incredibly fast which causes the Galactic plane to be reportedly thin causing our galaxy to have its spiral shape. On December 21st 2012 we will be aligned into the center of this dark rift.

Much has been written about the forecast of 2012 cataclysmic and transformative events. There are many views and opinions speculating on what it all means. After extensive and thorough research, this book offers an accurate portrayal of upcoming events.

First, it is important to note that the foundation of the events and transformation provided here is based on scientific research—ancient Sumerian records of past planet Nibiru fly bys and the Mayan Mesoamerican Long Count calendar. These align with the period of December 21st 2012 and the end date of the Mayan Calendar. This time period also parallels with interpretations of many assorted historical legends, numerological constructions, prophecies, and warnings of the Indigenous peoples around the world—including the Aztec, Mayan and Hopi Indians, the ancient Sumerians, Edgar Cayce, Bible revelations and extraterrestrial crop circles warnings. It is difficult to dispute the facts. (See crop circles)

Our solar system completes a full cycle through the zodiac or procession of the equinox every 25,800 years. On December 21st 2012 it will be the end of this cycle as our sun will again rise in a direct alignment with the dark rift, or center of the Milky Way galaxy—like it did 25,800 years ago. This dark rift is also known as the black hole—Cosmic Mother.

The Mayan and Aztec believe this is the end times as we know it, and the great regeneration period and new beginning or transformation for humanity. This transformation aligns with the evolutionary galactic acceleration that has been morphing for years now and with it, a feeling of time flying by and spiritual oneness and a deeper seeking of truth. Part of the population is aligning itself with the vibrations of love and light energy as we evolve from "the 3rd dimension" through the 4th and into the 5th dimension. December 21st 2012 is the gateway through this transformation and the purification time for Mother Earth.

Based on the data and facts, this purification will be within the realm of a catastrophic event with a pole shift and other occurrences mentioned in this book. After this global purification, the dawning of the new spiritual age will manifest and the new age and calendar will begin.

As we move closer to 2012, the negativity bubbles up as we hit barriers in many aspects in our lives that attach to the 3rd dimensional illusions.

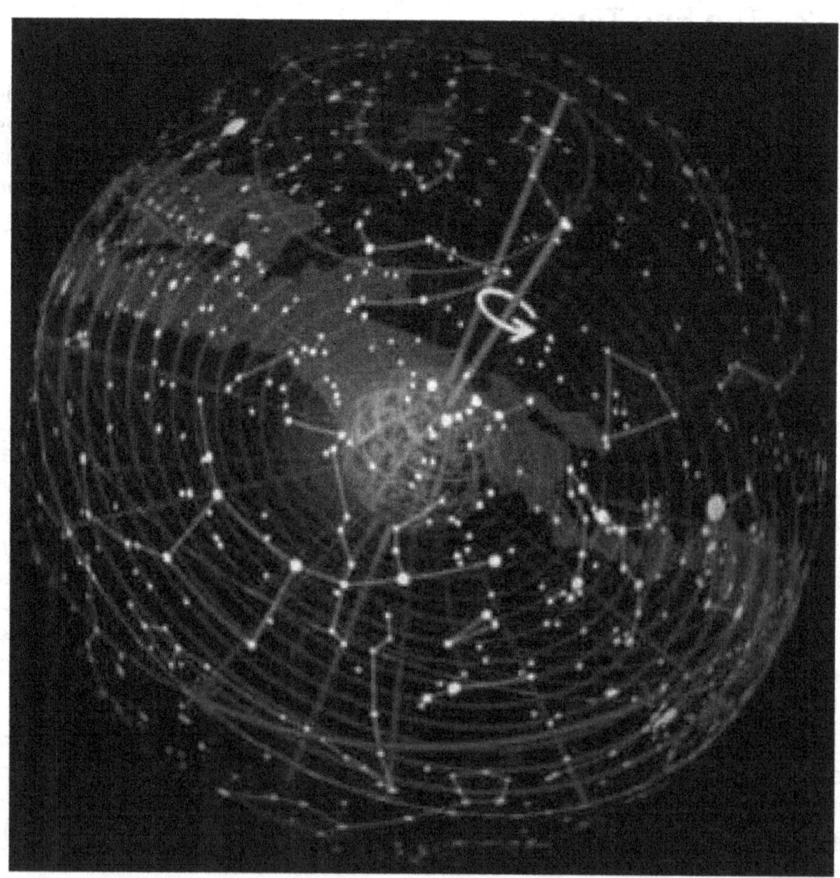

Galactic Alignment

The catastrophic reality of 2012 started to scientifically gain attention and momentum back in 1982. This is when NASA noticed a strong pull on the planets of our solar system as they orbited near the constellation Orion. NASA quickly decided to launch an infrared telescope in 1983 and discovered a dwarf star constellation. This dwarf (brown) star has 2 moons and 2 planets—one of which is known as the Planet Nibiru or Planet X. The proud astronomers at NASA joyfully announced their finding in 1983 but over the years they discovered that this constellation is on an elliptical orbit around our sun and is now crossing into our solar system. Since this has become apparent NASA has both minimized and denied any concern, however many NASA staff astronomers began leaking photos on *You Tube* to make the public aware of what is actually coming. There is no doubt this dwarf star constellation is heading our way on a 3600 year elliptical orbit around our Sun. Its projected orbital path may well be between Mars and Jupiter and should arrive in full view in the northern hemisphere by spring 2010. This is not really a new event as the ancient Sumerians have witnessed this eerie occurrence in the past and documented it in historical written records. They claimed that planet Nibiru and its super race of alien beings first came to Earth as Gods some 200,000 years ago during the planet Nibiru fly by. The records coincide with many other ancient records that mention the cycle and the cataclysms that occurred. Historically pole shifts have come to pass over 171 times, with scientific evidence of volcanic lava flows changing direction after the magnetic north shifted.

2012 is the Armageddon or “End Times” and the transformation to a higher collective light consciousness and what needs to be done on the earth plane for this regeneration to happen. This transformation is also part of a shift in awareness that has taken countless civilizations and ages of evolution to manifest.

We are now living during a special time in our evolution. On the physical level our Mother Earth is about to realign the poles with a “pole shift”. This will bring destruction and catastrophes similar to what Atlantis experienced but it is also a purification period and life will go on and we will rebuild a new Earth and create the Golden Age.

On the spiritual level the 2012 transformation will allow the Golden Age of enlightenment to be established as the forces of light and darkness complete the battle of Armageddon. Fortunately, the “good guys” will win, and the 1,000 year peace of the Golden Age will be established on Earth.

It is important to remember that 2012 is the beginning of the new age and spiritual transformation. It is a "consciousness shift" from the 3rd dimension human awareness into the 5th dimension of collective light consciousness. It is a time when all the battles of the past will dissolve into a higher awareness of our Mother Earth, each other, and the historical connection to the stars.

Sun Spots

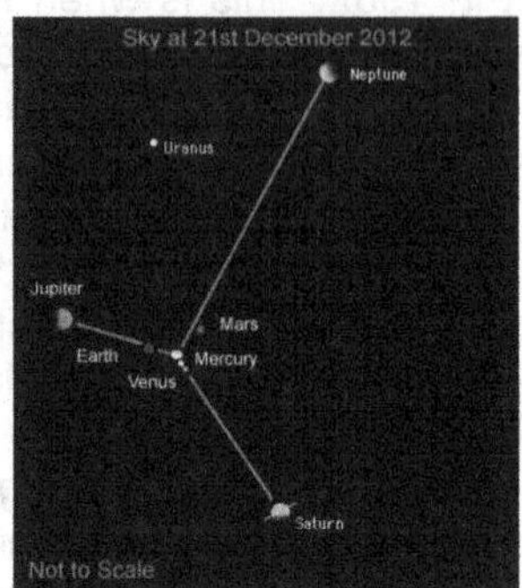

The picture on the right shows the sky alignment on December 21, 2012—the end date of the Mayan calendar. On that day the Earth also aligns with the serpent's mouth of Ouroboros and the Galactic Centre that harbors a number of potential gamma-ray sources, including a super massive black hole at the center of the Milky Way galaxy—the dark rift where magnetic influence is enormous. If the gravitational pull of this is not enough for a pole shift, we also have Earth, Jupiter, and the Sun in alignment, as well as Saturn, Venus and the Sun in alignment, and not to be out done—Neptune, Mars, and the Sun in alignment. So what is going on? This simultaneous gravitational tug on our Sun would definitely add to the solar storm projections that have been said to be 30–50% stronger than normal in 2012.

On July 31, 2006 a reverse polarity sunspot was spotted that gave birth to the next maximum solar cycle #24. This emerging cycle, combined with our planet's declining magnetic field, may have severe consequences for Earth in terms of climate, electrical grid systems, human behavior, and pole shifting. This solar cycle occurs when the Sun goes into its maximum emissions period. The peak of this increased activity and cycle will correspond with 2012. Given the Earth's weakening magnetic field at this time, this could be very significant with major sun spot eruptions on the Sun starting up again and especially when the December 21, 2012 alignments are taking place.

To appreciate the dangers we should first understand that the bubble of protective magnetism that surrounds the Earth from solar wind is called the magnetosphere. Historically, this magnetic field deflects most of the Suns particles into a circular path around the Earth. Solar wind and flares can change rapidly like our weather found here on Earth.

Strange events are the result. Earth's magnetic field has been weakening, and our magnetic field has become far more unpredictable over the past 20 years.

NASA's spacecraft have revealed a break in the Earth's magnetic field—10 times larger than previously thought. So when this happens we are in uncharted territory, as solar wind can flow in through the breach for powerful geomagnetic storms. Best case scenario would be a total disruption to our telecommunications and weather patterns—worst case is the pole shift as predicted by many, including top scientists.

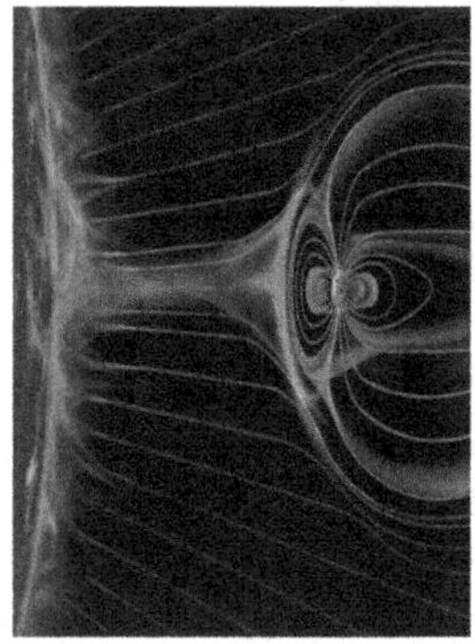

After a reverse sunspot was noticed, David Hathaway, a solar physicist at the Marshall Space Flight in Huntsville, Alabama said: "A backward sunspot is a sign that the next solar cycle is beginning." Hathaway explained: “Sunspots are planet-sized magnets created by the Sun's inner magnetic dynamo. Like all magnets in the universe, sunspots have north (N) and south (S) magnetic poles. According to NASA the sunspot of July 31st popped up at solar longitude 65° W, latitude 13° S. Sunspots in that area are normally oriented N-S. However this one was S-N, opposite the norm. This tiny spot of backwardness foretells a really big solar cycle that will peak around 2012. This is above and beyond all the Galactic alignments happening at the time. He also explains that solar activity rises and falls in 11-year cycles, swinging back and forth between times of calm and storms. NASA planners and satellite operators are bracing for the next solar cycle, expected to be the stormiest in decades. When these sunspots and solar flares return, dangerous proton storms in space and bright auroras on Earth will push the Earth's protective but weakening shields to the max. NASA scientists have also warned the protective bubble around the sun that helps to shield the Earth from harmful interstellar radiation is shrinking and getting weaker. New data has revealed the heliosphere; the protective shield of energy surrounding our solar system; has weakened by 25% over the past decade and is now at it's lowest level in 50 years. Without the heliosphere the harmful intergalactic cosmic radiation would make life on Earth almost impossible by destroying DNA and making our climate uninhabitable.

So what will happen in 2012 when the sun spots hit their peak and a dwarf star the size of Jupiter: with its constellation, orbits past the Earth and our Sun? This dwarf star is about 8 times the size of our Earth with a huge gravitational and energetic significance—not only pulling opposite against our Earth rotation, but magnetically battling our Sun as well. We also have the Galactic Alignment with the dark rift as well as the Sun's gravitational alignment with the planets mentioned. This will increase solar activity well beyond what is mentioned by NASA and maybe even a baked Earth scenario in parts of the world. (See Prophecies)

Pole Shift

Many of us wonder whether or not pole shifts will really happen. Something to ponder when posing this question, is to ask why the hairy mammoths in Siberia were flash-frozen with tropical vegetation in their mouths thousands of years ago, and tropical vegetation found under layers of ice in Antarctica?

The Earth is exceptionally magnetic. The crust achieves its opposite magnetic charge via the electro-magnetic currents created by its different spin ratio and the enormous gravitational field of the moon also helps to hold the crust in its rotational axis.

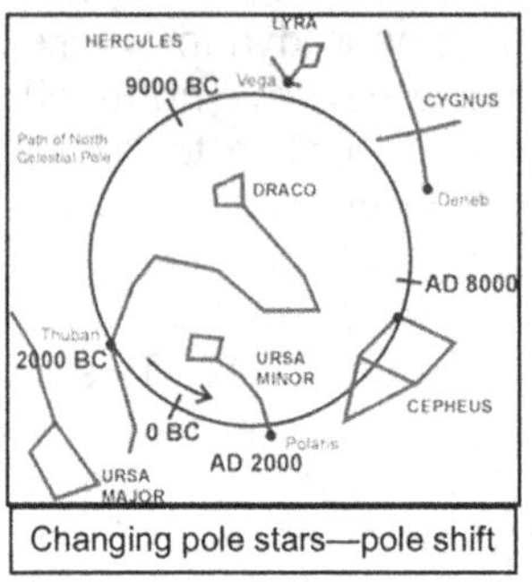

Changing pole stars—pole shift

Our magnetic poles are currently several hundred kilometers from true north and south, and at an accelerated rate over the past 10 years they've been changing their positions. Pilots now need to adjust their navigational instruments almost daily when proceeding to regions of the north or south pole. This means that the Earth's axis has a slight gyroscopic "wobble" which may also be a sign of the Earth's core spinning faster than the crust. Could this be the beginning signal of an impending pole shift coming our way? Interestingly, shifts are not so rare in the big picture, as the magnetic poles have skipped around the world 171 known times—each with cataclysms included. Noah's Arc, the sinking of Atlantis and other past great civilizations were wiped out. What effects will this galactic alignment with the dark rift, and a dwarf star constellation the size of Jupiter zooming by Earth's orbit with its two moons and two planets in tow, have on the Earth? The passing Dwarf Star (Planet Nibiru) grips the Atlantic Rift magnetically, so the Earth does not turn past this grip until the constellation passes and loses the grip. This is solid science and is cause for great concern to our civilization, but NASA is not talking about it. NASA scientists recently projected the Sun's magnetic fields will be extremely strong with extra violent magnetic solar storm activity—up to 50% stronger than normal during 2012. This will happen with the magnetic poles of the Earth—already in decline and steadily weakening.

Is it all really just coincidence or is 2012 the year everything seems to becoming to a conclusion? I personally feel; without question; this pole shift is coming—based on all the different factors and information available.

The New Earth

If it is off by one or all the factors mentioned, the pole shift would be sudden: taking about an hour with the Earth's rotation stopping for a few days or a week: during which time extreme stress will build between the Earth's crust and its core—along with major climate changes and super storms. This shift and stoppage has happened many times before. It has been written in history and recorded in indigenous folklore worldwide as "the long day or the long night". This would make sense since the Earth stops rotating for a while.

Pole Shift of 16 degrees

During a pole shift we can expect many major events to happen that will change the geography, and all life, as we know it. When the earth stops rotating during a pole shift, many cataclysmic events occur. Major volcanic and seismic disturbances, super wind storms, displacement of water with two mile high Tsunamis or water displacements on coastal areas, Subduction of landmasses and mountain ranges, new land masses and, disappearing land masses. Severe electrical storms, super tornadoes, nuclear fallout from facilities not shut down in time, and Hurricanes with land winds in excess of 400 miles per hour.

This unfolding comes in a few stages. First, as the crust separates from the core, the vibration would start, then over just a few minutes the crust along with the core will start to slide and find it's new location. During this slide, massive water displacement in the form of tsunamis or tidal waves will move over the Earth covering the coastlines and moving inland 300-500 miles. This happens as the earth spins and then stops: the water will continue to move, as it is fluid and separate from the landmass.

Earth's Tectonic Plates

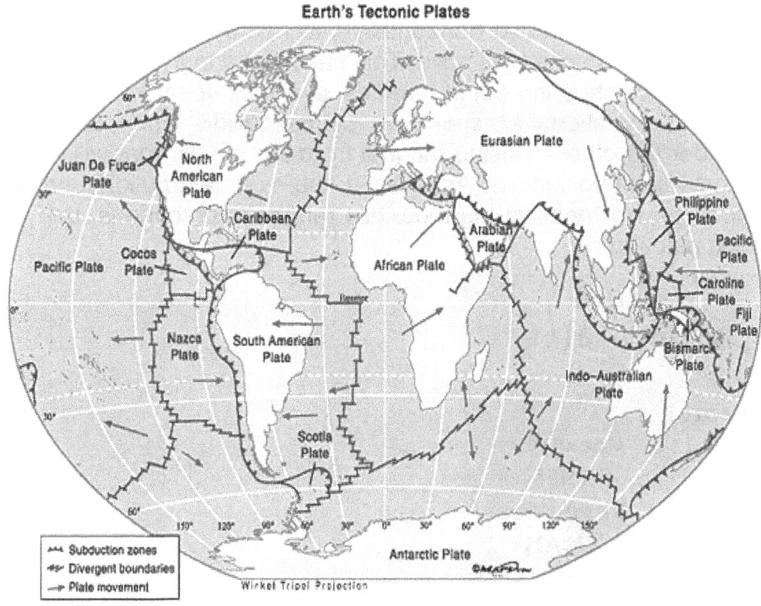

Then as the Earth's core aligns it will settle, but the solid Earth's crust will proceed slowly on until it settles into its new alignment. This is when and where massive earthquakes occur and mountain building starts.

Mountain Building

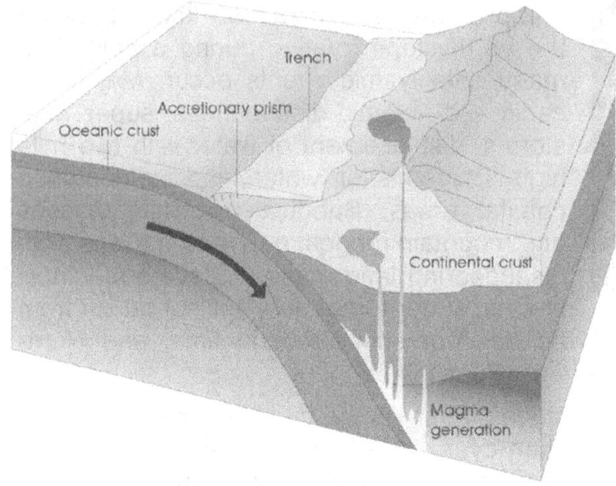

Mountain building happens quickly during rapid subduction of one plate under another—not just along the tectonic plates. There is a friction between the plates where crumbling of the upper or softer plate occurs. Crumbling relates to pressure and release, and can result in aggressive jolting and upheavals that create new cliffs or protruding rock, and rock slides from nearby mountains. Those holding-on will be heaved skyward, with barely a safe place to cling to. Subduction releases pressure by pushing peels of land upward and forward that separate from the lower levels. This sudden thrust happens with the rock shelves, cliffs and projectiles crashing down. Compressed rock can also move horizontally into nearby space or land not already occupied by anything as solid. This said, those in a valley can: without warning, find rock shooting out of hillsides, and rock spears shooting up under their feet. Additionally, when two plates collide, one plate may be pushed under the other—raising magma from the mantle that will form dangerous and violent volcanoes. As a result, the mountain building process in mountain valleys or near young mountain ranges is precarious, and overall not a good place to be.

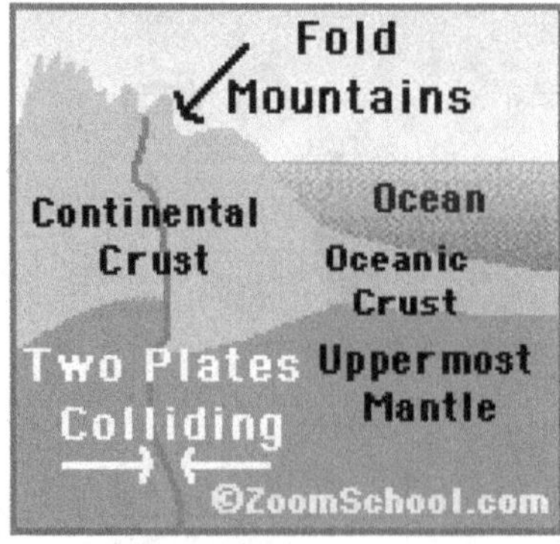

Pole Shift

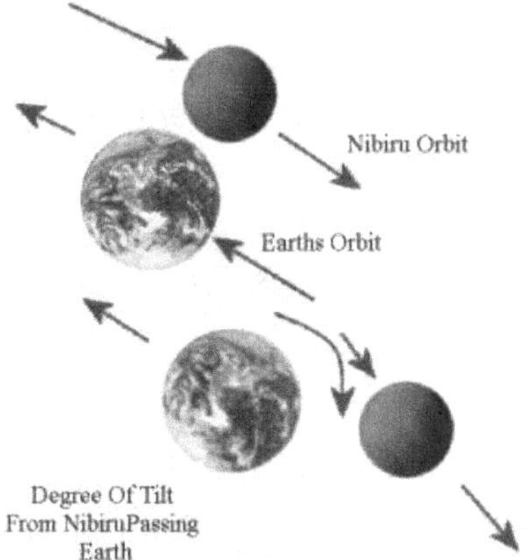

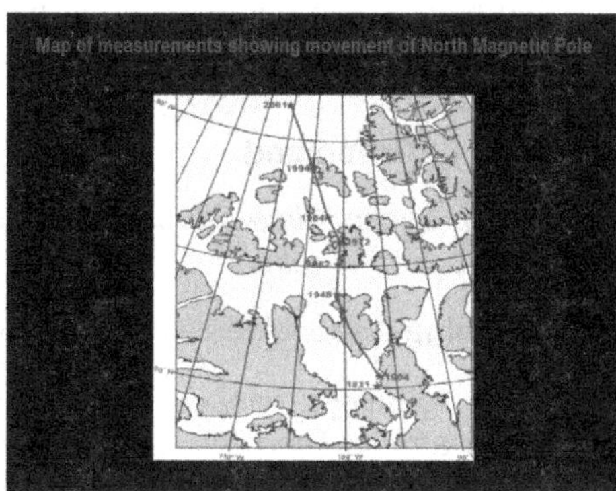

Folk Lore

Aztecs

> *"There had been no sun in existence for many years ..[The Chiefs] began to peer through the gloom in all directions for the expected sight, and to make bets as to what part of heaven [the sun] should first appear ... but when the sun rose, they were all proved wrong, for not one of them had fixed upon the east.'"*

Caius Julius Solinus—A Latin author of the third century of the present era, wrote of the people living on the southern borders of Egypt:

> *"The inhabitants of this country say that they have it from their ancestors that the sun now sets where it formerly rose,"*

Pomponius Mela—Latin author of the first century:

> *"The Egyptians pride themselves on being the most ancient people in the world. In their authentic annals ... one may read that since they have been in existence, the course of the stars has changed direction four times, and that the sun has set twice in that part of the sky where it rises today."*

Hopi Elder

Thomas Banyacya—HOPI Nation address to United Nations, Dec 10, 1992:

> *"Nature and the spirit of our ancestors are giving you loud warn-*

ings. Today you see increasing floods, more damaging hurricanes, hail storms, climate changes and earthquakes as our prophecies said would come. Why do animals act like they know about the earth's problems and most humans act like they know nothing? If we humans do not wake up to the warnings, the great purification will come to destroy this world just as the previous worlds were destroyed."

Eskimos of Greenland

"In an ancient time the earth turned over and the people who lived then became antipodes."

The Cashina—aborigines of western Brazil:

"The lightnings flashed and the thunders roared terribly and all were afraid. Then the heaven burst and the fragments fell down and killed everything and everybody. Heaven and earth changed places. Nothing that had life was left upon the earth."

China

"At the time of the miracle is said to have happened that the sun during a span of ten days did not set, the forests were ignited, and a multitude of abominable vermin was brought forth. 'In the lifetime of Yao [Yahou] the sun did not set for full ten days and the entire land was flooded."

Plato

"I mean the change in the rising and the setting of the sun and the other heavenly bodies, how in those times they used to set in the quarter where they now rise, and they used to rise where they now set."

Russia

The body of a mammoth, with flesh, skin, and hair, was found in 1797 in northeastern Siberia. The meat looked like freshly frozen beef, and wolves and sled dogs were able to feed on it. Had the ground not been flash frozen, the bodies of the mammoths would have putrefied in a single summer and dissolved over a few years, but they remained unspoiled for thousands of years. In the stomachs and teeth were found more lush style plants and grasses that do not grow in northern Siberia. Interesting that microscopic examination of the skin showed red blood corpuscles, proof of a sudden death, due to suffocation either by gases or water.

2012—The Prophecy

Prophecies have been part of our historical folklore since the beginning of civilization. In most cases the predictions are glimpses into the ethereal Akashic records, where the past, present and future is all one. A person with this connection, can access the information of warnings and events that have not happened on this physical plane—but are just a page in the great book of ethereal records. It is not a coincidence that most global cultures have similar predictions that relay the end of times to be 2012; The Mayan's, Egyptians, Zulu, Hindu, Incas, Aztecs, Dogon (Africa), Cherokee, Pueblo, Tibetan's and many others: a "coincidence" maybe not.

Hopi - Predict a 25 year period of purification followed by End of Fourth World and beginning of the Fifth.

Mayans - Call it the 'end days' or the end of time as we know it.

Maoris - Say that as the veils dissolve there will be a merging of the physical & spiritual worlds.

Zulu - Believe that the whole world will be turned upside down.

Hindus - Kali Yuga (end time of man). The Coming of Kalki and critical mass of Enlightened Ones.

Incas - Call it the 'Age of Meeting Ourselves Again'.

Aztec - Call this the Time of the Sixth Sun. A time of transformation and creation of new race.

Dogon - Say that the spaceship of the visitors, the Nommo, will return in the form of a blue star.

Pueblo - Acknowledge it'll be the emergence into the Fifth World

Cherokee - Their ancient calendar ends exactly at 2012 same as the Mayan calendar.

Tibetan Kalachakra teachings are prophesies left by Buddha predicting the Coming of the Golden Age.

Egypt - According to the Great Pyramid (stone calendar), present time cycle ends in year 2012 AD

Prophecies

Mother Shipton of Norfolk, England 1500's – speaking of post 1900's, and like Nostradamus, she wrote her prophecies in the form of verses.

> *"For those that live the century through, in fear and trembling this shall do, for storms shall rage and oceans roar when Gabriel stands on sea and shore, and as he blows his wondrous horn, all the world shall die and new be born"*

Below, the "Dragon" in this poem seems to refer to Planet Nibiru with its long tail of trailing debris that will whisk across the Earth over a period of seven days and nights, causing in its wake, earthquakes, volcanic eruptions, tidal waves and flooding. She also describes the violence in the aftermath. Apparently there is a brief lull, then a second passage through the tail worsens matters even more.

> *"A fiery dragon will cross the sky, Six times before this earth shall die. Mankind will tremble and frightened be, for the sixth heralds in this prophecy.*
>
> *For seven days and seven nights, Man will watch this awesome sight. The tides will rise beyond their ken, To bite away the shores and then The mountains will begin to roar, And earthquakes split the plain to shore.*
>
> *And flooding waters, rushing in, Will flood the lands with such a din That mankind cowers in muddy fen, And snarls about his fellow men.*
>
> *He bares his teeth and fights and kills, And secrets food in secret hills And ugly in his fear, he lies, To kill marauders, thieves and spies.*
>
> *Man flees in terror from the floods, And kills, and rapes and lies in blood And spilling blood by mankind's hands, Will stain and bitter many lands And when the dragon's tail is gone, Man forgets, and smiles, and carries on To apply himself - too late, too late, For mankind has earned deserved fate.*
>
> *His masked smile - his false grandeur, Will serve the Gods their anger stir.*
>
> *And they will send the Dragon back, To light the sky - his tail will crack Upon the earth and rend the earth, And man shall flee, King, Lord, and serf.*
>
> *But slowly they are routed out, To seek diminishing waterspout And men will die of thirst before, The oceans rise to mount the shore.*
>
> *And lands will crack and rend anew, You think it strange. It will come true."*

Bishop of Malachi *1100's*—states that the current pope 111 will be the last:

> *"during the final persecution the seat of the holy roman church with be occupied by Peter the Roman, who will feed the sheep in many tribulations, the seven hill city will be destroyed, and the terrible judge will judge his people, the End"*

Mayan Prophecy – *"The face of the sun will be extinguished because of the great tempest"*

Hopi Indians – *"These are the signs that great destruction is here, the world shall rock to and fro, the white man will battle people in other lands, those that possess the first light of wisdom, the 4th world shall end soon, and the fifth world will begin."*

The Hopi also believe that the world has been destroyed *purified* four times and the fifth time is coming.

Zulu – According to Zulu tradition humanity is currently in the 6th World. They also say that the Lord of the Sky Nkulunkulu, with the help of the Heavenly queen, Nomkubulwana created, destroyed, and recreated this the world 5 times.

Our sixth world is a difficult one, full of ignorance, pain, suffering, hunger, war and strife and the Earth Mother is in a state of deep depression and sorrow. This suffering will last about 2000 years. Then Nkulunkulu and Nomkubulwana are going to destroy this sixth world and establish the seventh world. The seventh world is going to be a perfect Earth where death, pain, and suffering will be unknown. Humanity will live in a time of bliss and harmony.

Albert Einstein was shocked as he learned of Charles Hapgood's theory in "Path of the Poles", whereby ice build-up at the polar caps could eventually cause the crust to "slide" over the lava ocean until the centrifugal force of the spinning Earth brought those ice caps around to the equator. Geological evidence suggests that something like this has happened repeatedly during the "life" of the planet; the magnetic poles seem to have shifted at least 171 known times

Mayan Prophecy speaks of vain egoism of a deity "Sen Macaa" (anti Christ) that during the times of Armageddon will look to control and keep mankind stuck in this lower evolutionary cycle (3rd dimension), and not allow the evolution to the higher or enlightened state of consciousness. I believe the light will win the battle of Armageddon during the months before, during and after December 21, 2012—the time of transformation. This transformation will achieve the purpose of gently fusing the human cells with divine light high-energy as we evolve into the higher state of spiritual awareness and an evolutionary genesis.

Ouroboros

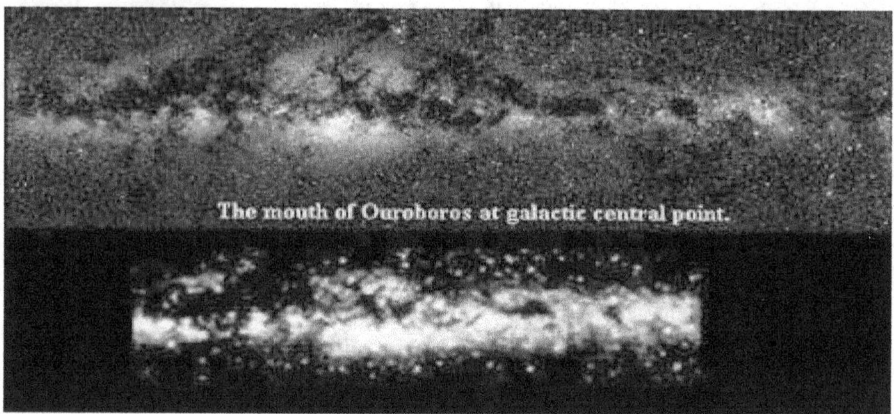

The Ouroboros is an ancient alchemy symbol—snake or dragon—swallowing its own tail, constantly re-creating itself and forming a new circle. It symbolizes the basic nature of the universe—creation out of destruction, life out of death. In mythology, the Wheel of Time, and the Milky Way galaxy keeps a "great time cycle" that ends in catastrophic change. The Mayan also believe that the supreme God and creator of the Maya "Hunab Ku", rebuilt the world after three deluges, which poured from the mouth of a sky serpent. On December 21st 2012 the Earth will align directly with the mouth of the Ouroboros or dark rift of our Milky Way galaxy.

AZTEC

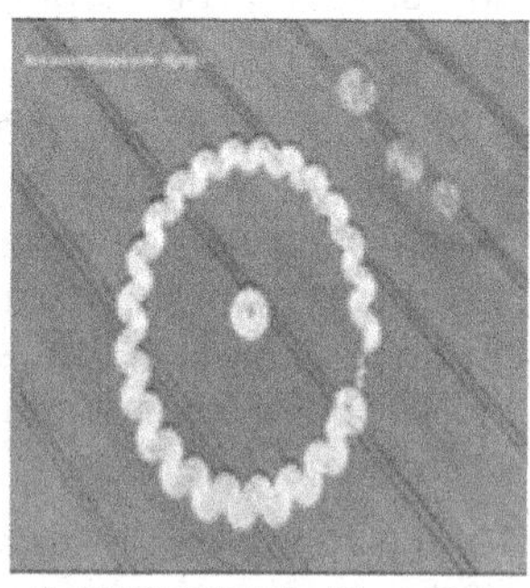

ALIEN WARNING – Crop Circle

Nostradamus (1503-1566) St. Remy, France

Nostradamus predicts the ***"Great, King of "Terror from the sky",*** is the Coming. No doubt it is the NIBIRU dwarf star constellation, The Comet Planet.

"The great star will burn for seven days, the sun appears double through the haze. The big mastiff will howl all night, while the Great Pontiff relocates."

Century II /XLI

C2 Q46—*After a great misery for mankind, an ever greater approaches. The great cycle of the centuries renewed, it will rain blood, milk, famine, war disease, In the sky will be seen a great fire dragging a trail of sparks.*

C2 Q4—*During the appearance of The Bearded Star, the three great princes will be made enemies. The shaky peace on earth will be struck by fire from the skies. Po, The winding Tiber, a serpent placed on the shore.*

C2 Q72—*MABUS will soon die, Then will come a horrible slaughter of people and animals. At once vengeance revealed coming from a hundred hands "Thirst and Famine when The Comet shall pass.*

C6 Q6—*There will appear towards the seven stars of Ursa Minor and Polaris. Not far from Cancer, The Bearded Star Susa, Siena, Boeotia, Great Rome will die, the night having vanished.*

C1 Q69—*"The great mountain, one mile in circumference, After peace, war, famine flooding It will spread far, drowning antiquities and their mighty foundations."*

C8 Q16—*"At the place where Jason built his ships, there will be such a great sudden flood that no on the land will have a place to fall on. The waters mount the Olympus Festulan".*

C2 Q41—*The Great Star will blaze for seven days, The cloud will cause two suns to appear. The Huge dog will howl at night When the great pontiff will change lands.*

C10 Q72—*"In the year 1999 and seven months The Great, King of Terror shall come from the sky. He will bring to life the King of The Mongols. Before and after, Mars reigns happily".*

Revelation

Rev 8—7: *The first angel sounded: and hail and fire, mingled with blood, and they were thrown to the Earth; and a third of the Trees were burnt up, and all green grass was burned up.*

Rev 8—8-9: *Then the second angel sounded; and something like a great mountain burning with fire was thrown into the sea, and a third of the sea became as blood; and a third of the living creatures in the sea died and a third of the ships were destroyed.*

Rev 8—10-11: *Then the third angel sounded; And a great star fell from Heaven, burning like a torch, and it fell upon a third of the rivers and on the springs of water, and the name of the star is called Wormwood; and a third of the waters became as worm-wood; and many men died from the water because it was made bitter.*

Rev 3—10: *The Lord will take His True Followers to Heaven before the Start of The Great Tribulation and The Destruction caused by The Comet Planet.*

Matt 24—7: *For nation shall rise against nation and kingdom against kingdom, there shall be earthquakes in many places, plagues and famines.*

Revelation 13: *And Satan does great wonders, so that he makes fire come down from heaven on the earth in the sight of men.*

Luke 21—36: *Watch therefore and pray always That you may be "accounted worthy" To ESCAPE all of this things that shall come upon the earth and Stand before The Son of Man.*

Thessalonians 2—4: *Who opposes and exalts himself above every so called God or object of worship, so that he takes his seat in the temple of God, displaying himself as being GOD"—(anti-Christ)*

Joel 2: *And I will show wonders in the heavens and in the earth, blood, and fire, and pillars of smoke.*

Isaiah 24: *Therefore has the curse devoured the earth, and they that dwell therein are desolate: therefore the inhabitants of the earth are burned, and few men left.*

Revelation 11—3-6

"And I will grant authority to my two witnesses, and they will prophesy for twelve hundred and sixty days, clothed in sackcloth."

These are the two olive Trees and the two lamp stands that stand before the Lord of the earth.

And if anyone wants to harm them, fire flows out of their mouth and devours their enemies; so if anyone wants to harm them, he must be killed in this way.

These have the power to shut up the sky, so that rain will not fall during the days of their prophesying; and they have power over the waters to turn them into blood, and to strike the earth with every plague, as often as they desire."

> **Note:** That crop circles gave the dates July 7, 2009 and December 21, 2012—the distance between the two dates is 1260 days

Quotes: The Bible

Isaiah 13—1: *"From a far away land they came, from the end-point of Heaven do the Lord and his weapons of wrath come to destroy the whole Earth. Therefore will I agitate the Heaven and Earth shall be shaken out of its place. When the Lord of Hosts shall be crossing, the day of his burning wrath."*

St. Matthew 24—38-39: *" For as in the days that were before the flood they were eating and drinking, marrying and giving in marriage, until the day the Noah entered the ark. And knew not until the flood came, and took them all away; so shall also the coming of the Son of man be."*

Edgar Cayce

A well-known medium and clairvoyant of the early 1900's depicted the world after 2012. He predicted a global pole shift of 17° into Russia, thereby creating the new world map (below).

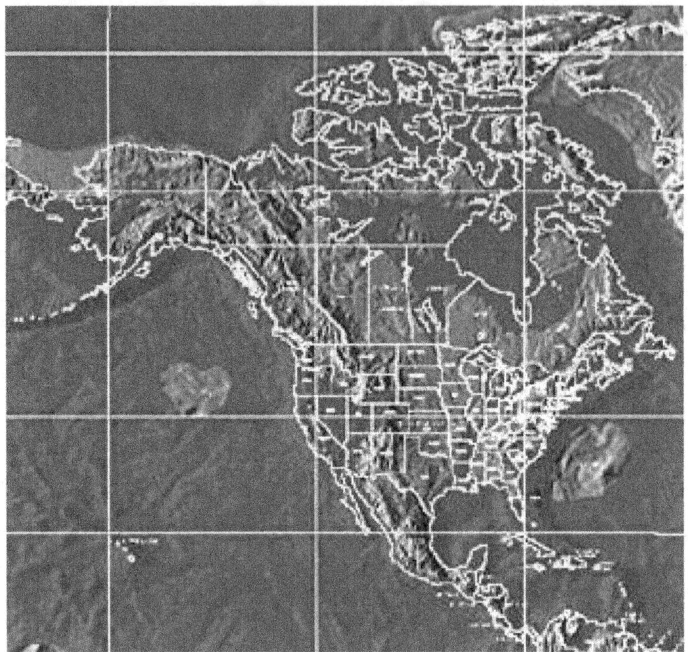

Map of the World - post 2012

When asked about the coming new age, Edgar Cayce replied:

> *"By the full consciousness of the ability to communicate with the Creative Forces and be aware of the relationships to the Creative Forces and the uses of same in material expression. This awareness during the era or age in the Age of Atlantis and LEMURIA or Mu brought what? Destruction to man, and his beginning of the needs of the journey up through that of selfishness."*

Here he was explaining that in a previous time cycle, pre 2012, past civilization had a consciousness relationship with the Creative Forces that allowed higher levels in the material, mental, and spiritual realms. But history states that relationship was misused and corrupted similar to today's world. It was the misuse of the blessings that brought on the destruction of those past civilizations along with the karmic reaction and journey created by those actions. Now, as the Mayan cyclic calendar of 2012 comes knocking again, we are nearing a time when the final judgment is upon us, just as it was during the times of Atlantis and Mu.

Edgar Cayce Predictions

"The earth will be broken up in the western portion of America. The greater portion of Japan must go into the sea. The upper portion of Europe will be changed as in the twinkling of an eye. Land will appear off the east coast of America. When there is the first breaking up of some conditions in the South Sea and those as apparent in the sinking or rising of that that's almost opposite same, or in the Mediterranean, and the Etna area, then we many know it has begun."

"If there are greater activities in Vesuvius or Pelee, then the southern coast of California and the areas between Salt Lake and the southern portions of Nevada, we may expect, within the three months following same, inundation by the earthquakes. But these are to be more in the Southern than the Northern Hemisphere."

"...many portions of the east coast will be disturbed, as well as many portions of the west coast, as well as the central portion of the U.S. In the next few years land will appear in the Atlantic as well as in the Pacific. And what is the coastline now of many a land will be the bed of the ocean. Even many battle fields of the present will be ocean, will be the seas, the bays, the lands over which The New World Order will carry on their trade as one with another."

"Portions of the now east coast of New York, or New York City itself, will in the main disappear. This will be another generation, though, here; while the southern portions of Carolina, Georgia -- these will disappear. This will be much sooner. The waters of the lakes will empty into the Gulf, rather than the waterway over which such discussions have been recently made. It would be well if the waterway were prepared, but not for that purpose for which it is at present being considered. Then the area where the entity is now located (Virginia Beach) will be among the safety lands, as will be portions of what is now Ohio, Indiana and Illinois, and much of the southern portion of Canada and the eastern portion of Canada; while the western land -- much of that is to be disturbed as, of course much in other lands."

"There will be the upheavals in the Arctic and in the Antarctic that will make for the eruption of volcanoes in the torrid areas, and there will be the shifting then of the poles -- so that where there has been those of a frigid or the semi-tropical will become the more tropical, and moss and fern will grow."

Survival

When we speak of surviving the transformation and regeneration of our planet leading up to and beyond 2012, we should first look at our own spiritual path and our connection to the light consciousness. It all starts with this connection, as this connection will empower and guide us to the right place of understanding this change and what is really happening in the multi-dimensional levels of the physical and ethereal planes.

There will be major Earth shifts and changes, and likely alien contact, along with the fall of the social and political systems, and the unrest that directly follows. It is the time of transition and Armageddon, as the battles will be fought on many levels. The old system of living in the 3rd dimension will start to unravel, but the end result will be the transformation into the Golden Age and the thousand-year peace will take place. This is the time where we: as the children of the light, evolve out of our earthly quarantine to join the universal collective of light consciousness and other advanced beings evolving in the light.

We all have our truth to find during these times, because as we have grown spiritually in life, we have tried to find truth where truth does not exist. Now it is the time of transformation prophesied by all the great teachers and societies. We can hide our heads in the sand and try to hold on to the illusions of the 3rd dimension or find that place within that will guide us. To survive is to surrender to the reality and adjust your plans and desires accordingly—to find the safest areas around the world to live during this transition.

Please visit our website: *www.2012Enlightened.com*

The New Earth—Golden Age

Akashic Records & Reincarnation

The Akashic records are the universal records of time, space and deed *(Sanskrit for "sky", "space" or "anther")* encoded in the ethereal plane of existence. These records contain all knowledge of human and universal experience, and the history of the vast universes. They are metaphorically depicted as a library or "universal computer hard drive" or the "Book of Life and Mind of God". These universal records are updated with each thought or action and can be accessed through different levels of spiritual awareness or astral projection. It is this connection that allows the great prophets such as Edgar Cayce, Nostradamus and others to access the future.

Michael Newton an hypnotherapist and author of *"Journey of Souls" & "Destiny of Souls, Evidence of Life between Lives"* has many accounts of the Akashic Record, or working with subjects in deep states of unconsciousness. He witnessed that before souls are incarnated, they go to a cosmic "library" to view the pages associated with the lives they choose to enter in order to evolve. The pages are not in an actual "physical" book and are ethereal as opposed to physical text.

It appeared that although there may be definitive waypoints along the course of our lives, our free will can change our paths, events and outcomes. As the soul prepares for a life with the intent of learning a particular lesson or satisfying a karmic debt, the soul will also choose a family and a body that will help them with the lessons for this incarnation. For many, some of those images of the book survive "birth amnesia" and become our intuition that serves us during our lives. There is also a soul mate or guardian angel that may help guide our intuitions. This frame of reference also corresponds to the Mayan calendar of the coming sixth age, where 2012 has been written in the Akashic. This why there are so many predictions from so many prophets and indigenous peoples about the coming end times, as well as vivid dreams and warnings signs.

So as our state of awareness evolves beyond the current chains of the 3rd dimension, we will be able to influence our history, and this will become the reality not the exception.

Transformation

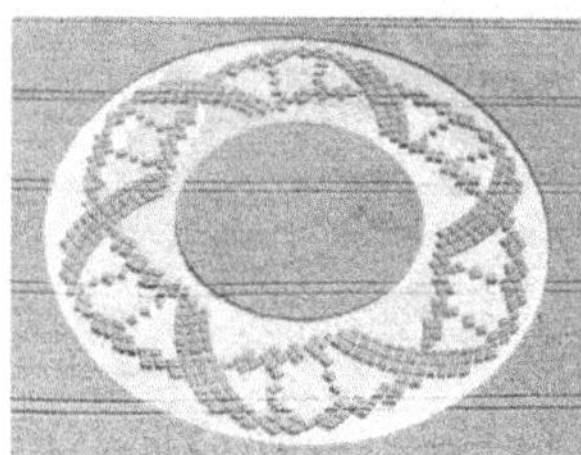 

Edgar Cayce – "*now is the time of which the Archangel Gabriel spoke. Our planet will change. Our bodies will change. The people of the earth will be changed. A new world is going to begin, transforming us for the long awaited new age.*"

We have chosen a very special time to be born, and as we enter into the cusp of 2012 and beyond, a wonderful new age of spiritual transformation will manifest. This is where the lower levels of human awareness are morphing into the higher universal spiritual light consciousness. This metamorphous is taking place on many levels—mostly beyond the realm of human intellectual comprehension. The crop circles above are messages from the higher light consciousness of this impending transformation. The left circle is our evolving DNA and the right one is the human butterfly that represents the transformation or metamorphosis in the Mayan and Aztec mythology. This circle is over 500 x 400 meters in area, appearing overnight.

The impending age is all about transformation and understanding of our new found place within the universal consciousness. We are indeed evolving our frequency and vibration to a level where we may reside along with other more evolved life forms within the light based universal consciousness. The frequency of time is speeding up (or collapsing) and the planets of the solar system also have been heating up. The heartbeat of the Earth or Schumann pulse has been 7.83 cycles per second for ages, and was a very reliable reference. Now the military states our global heartbeat has been rising slowly since 1980. It is now over 12 cycles per second; creating the feeling that our day is only 16 hours instead of the 24 hours we are used to. But, is time really moving by faster? Yes it is! This change is being arbitrated from the centre of our galaxy the Hunab Ku, and everybody on this planet is mutating. Some are more conscious of it than others. Albert Einstein said time can slow down, but it always flows in one direction. The Mayas believed that time essentially flows in a circle. There is a beginning and an end to all things but there is a renewal at the end of the time cycle. The Mayas also believe Hunab Ku created time and controls it. So it is very difficult to simply dismiss the Mayan Cosmology as they left remarkable evidence that their "time keeping" wisdom produced extremely accurate results.

The current civilization inhabiting the Earth has been one living with a dark social disease that has infected most aspects of our planetary vibration and global society. It has allowed the displacement and detachment of our spiritual roots and has disenfranchised the relationship we have with the Mother Earth and our spiritual path. This is our addiction to the illusion of money or power rather than evolving our spiritual union with universal light consciousness. It is true many great masters and teachers have incarnated to warn and guide us back toward the light but to little avail as we continued to misrepresent their words and allow dogmas while walking a path of disillusionment and ego. The more we lost touch, the more we polluted and disrespected our Mother Earth—the provider of physical life. We were led into, worshiped and followed religious dogmas that led us further off the path of spiritual truth. We allowed leaders that represent the Illuminati and social elite, and continually exercise forms of warring barbarism that is anti God, and will not merge with the enlightened future of the 5th dimensional plane. Our civilization has taken the road of a dark social karma similar to the road of past civilizations that ended in cataclysms as the distance between the spiritual reality of evolution and the ego expanded. In doing so, we have turned away from the evolutionary path of enlightenment and basic laws of universal dharma. Our modern collective ego has allowed us to hear only that which we want to hear, feeding us false knowledge, attachments and conditionings to put us to sleep and appease our taste for social falsehoods that have been so easily consumed within the bubble of our illusions. This is a direct result of projecting our lowly evolved free will, instead of finding the innocence, wisdom and humility needed to find and stay connected with the divine elements of creation.

So now comes the period of the great regeneration—the clearing and opportunity for new spiritual awareness. The 2012 universal transformation has started, and is casting a light on the darkness within ourselves and our global society while allowing spiritual awareness and evolution to manifest. As our society becomes spiritually aware, this light is shared and the collective frequency will eventually change the vibrations of the collective comprehension. Falsehoods of the past will no longer be accepted and the pattern of indulging the diseases of the lower self will no longer be accepted. This is the only way out of the cycle of earthly cataclysms that come our way every 10,000 years or so. As we change our collective vibration and evolve the power of our divinity, we will be protecting ourselves. This is similar to how a great Rishi or spiritual master easily merges with and controls the universal forces of nature: such as weather in the jungles of India. Imagine a whole society with this humility and understanding. "Thy will be done on Earth as it is in heaven." The angels and divine souls have all been waiting patiently for the human children of light to transform out of the earthly quarantine of lower evolution and look forward to welcoming us into the universal brotherhood of planets.

This book is meant to open your eyes and cause a stirring within to allow you to become your own guru and ask questions with an enlightened understanding of the 2012 transformation and beyond.

Age of Aquarius

The Golden Age of enlightenment is upon us, and with the "holy water" of the ages, the water bearer of Aquarius awakens the awareness of the seekers of the universal light consciousness. Every 2160 years, the constellation: visible on the early morning of the spring equinox, changes. In western astrological terms, this means the end of one astrological age (Age of Pisces) and the beginning of another (Age of Aquarius). Over the course of 25,800 years, this procession of the equinoxes makes one full circuit around the ecliptic or the full 12 signs of the zodiac. All prophecies say that the thousand year peace will begin after 2012 as we enter the Age of Aquarius. On a vibratory level this is also the time for the transformation of our consciousness into the realm of higher light awareness of the 5th dimension.

Sacred Geometry

Sacred geometry is the metaphysical science of mathematical ratios, harmonics and proportion found in music, light, architecture, art, and cosmology. Some art may also be found through a form of visualization of sacred geometry.

It is true all the foundational structures use "divine" proportions that resonate with the universal vibrations and cosmic cycles. The basic patterns of our vibrational existence are based on these mathematical equations that correspond in most cases to the sacred galactic movement of the cosmos. By analyzing the personality of these patterns, forms and relationships of interconnectiveness, insight may evolve into the mysteries, laws and tradition of the universal science of the light consciousness. It is also understood as we deepen our understanding toward the universal laws of sacred pattern recognition, that communication with extraterrestrial beings will be established and we will advance our understanding of sound and symbols to a level beyond the 3rd dimension.

The 3rd Dimension

The fundamental principles that operate in the outer universe are known by modern science as the natural laws. In our 3rd dimension, the four ancient elements *(earth, water, air, fire)* pervades our earth plane existence. But there are subtler laws that rule the metaphysical spiritual planes within the realm of spirit consciousness—as all true nature of matter exists within these laws. There is a massive transformation currently taking place as we approach 2012. Through a massive galactic shift of the universal consciousness and pure light energy, our 3rd dimension awareness is expanding through to the subtler 5th dimension. This shift is what is causing the stress and anxiety for many as they try to hold on to the illusions of the 3rd dimension. The unstable and disintegrating structures of our former 3rd dimension are no longer enough to hold our lives and world together. Through 2012 Mother Earth will also be making her transition by clearing the negativity of the past while setting the stage for the enlightened *Age of Aquarius*. The reality is the galactic shift is part of a divine evolution into the next realm of consciousness: hence holding on to the illusions and attachments of the 3rd dimension will only cause anxiety and fatigue.

As the higher self manifests, we will come to recognize all that exists in this 3rd dimension is of a lower evolved reality, but as one evolves into the next realm of consciousness—a metamorphous occurs. This transition was historically done though Kundalini awakening or spiritual meditation. This is where the awakened spiritual energy rises and spirit transcends *(*self realization*)* the boundaries of the earth plane (3rd dimension*)* transferring through the 4th into the 5th dimension. This is where time and space is beyond the others and is functionally very different from any of the spatial dimensions we have intellectually known before.

The Universal Consciousness

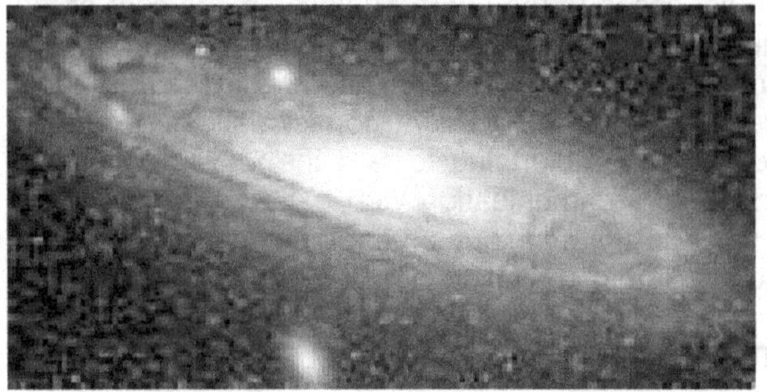

Our spirit or light energy has been described as the immortal soul, the Christ Consciousness, the Etheric body, and so on. Throughout the ages, most schools of wisdom have taught that our true spiritual potential and higher purpose involved evolving into the next level of spiritual evolution—the realm of divine light. This divine light realm consists of much subtler vibrations than we experience in the gross level of the physical realm.

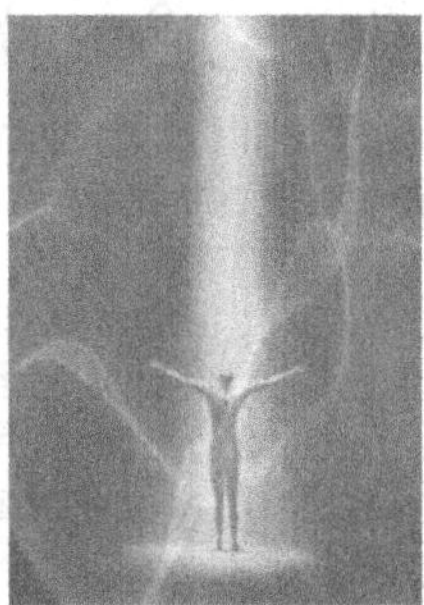
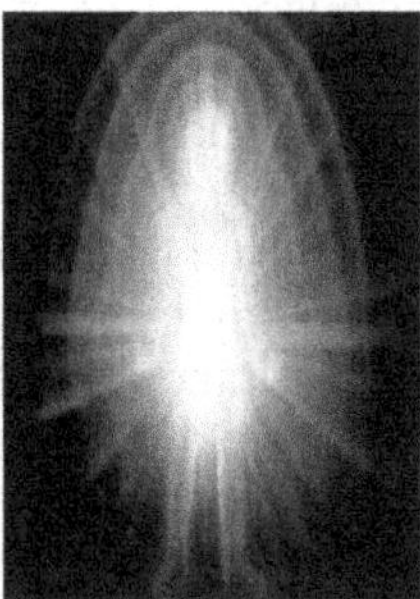

This omnipresent spiritual light consciousness resides within all matter, forms and manifestations. It imbibes the purest love and flows gently though all dimensions of time-space. It is not a concept or an intellectual particle that can be manipulated or contemplated. It is what is—and whether we understand its origin or not, it does not matter. What matters is that we search out that quiet place within, that will allow the peace and balance to open the doorway to the realm where the light resides. Once this door opens, we journey beyond the realm of self, and one will attract the qualities of humility and innocence as the eternal child within manifests. As this transformation progresses all self-identification becomes absorbed into the understanding that we are all just drops in the ocean of universal divine love consciousness.

Changing or Transformation of the DNA

Discoveries by Russian molecular biologists revealed DNA has a mysterious resonance termed the Phantom-DNA Effect. It was found that DNA reacts to voice activated laser light when set at the specific frequency of the DNA itself. Using these methods it is possible not only to "change" the information patterns in the DNA, but it is also possible to communicate with the DNA.

The Universal Truth

The universe is full of advanced intelligence. Eons ago earth was but a thought of the *prime creator*. The *prime creator*; power of creation or light consciousness; is also known as the Maha Devi or Audi Shakti in the Vedic texts and exists within the higher frequencies of pure love and light consciousness. These frequencies vibrate beyond the understanding of the lower human density, however, we, as children of the light, are connected and evolving within this living library of universal light consciousness.

When we were born the energy of the light and stars imprinted our DNA; astrologically speaking; for the physical life journey at hand—as all things are interconnected via energetic sacred geometric patterns of light consciousness. The universe in reality is a vast field of life interconnected and watered by the prime creator—using pure love and light. We have taken our birth at this time because we wish to master the evolutionary process, and be able to dwell in the higher densities. It is through our spirit which is the processor and conduit of light information, that we will understand what is truly happening during the 2012 shift.

The Galactic cycles of 2012 are much larger than our solar system. The Mayans are our timekeepers; their knowledge of the crystal skulls and the calendar are descended from our ancestors—the Star Teachers: the original planners of earth. The Star Teachers have existed for millions of years, and have seeded and designed many other worlds before ours. Their master goal or plan is to grow the collective light consciousness throughout the universe using the forces of creation and pure love.

Star Teachers are our missing link—our ancient light family whose DNA is shared within our own human genetics. They are our family that came from another universe and long ago achieved the understanding and completion of their own spiritual journey and development of their universe. The human race, on the other hand, is still in its infancy—working on the basics of spiritual ascension. We still struggle to understand our genetic and spiritual connection to the light consciousness—our mother earth and the living library of light that imbibes and surrounds us on all levels. The ascension or dimensional shift that will occur during the 2012 transformation has been known for eons as an important time in our evolution. This shift will lessen the density of the third dimension and allow us to move within higher dimensions and multiple realities beyond the lower human density. There are a multitude of cultures and societies existing in space as their has been through the many ages of humankind here on mother earth.

Our planet has layers of energy grids and cosmic doorways. The main purpose of the Mayan knowledge was to help lift these time locks. Time travel also exists. The pyramids in Egypt's Sinai Peninsula, Mexico's Chichen Itza and Tibet's Shambala, are some of the portals where trans-dimensional ascended life exists and using these portals.

Spiritually, the 2012 ascension will introduce us to higher evolved life forms living amid higher subtler densities and dimensions. It is through this transformation that the universal living library of light will become accessible. Within our DNA we have the dormant keys to this reality, all life is, and has accessed the living library of the light consciousness. Soon we will know and access this reality. These truly are important times for humankind. What happens during our earth's transformation will affect the entire universe on a *vibrational* level. We must understand the importance of these times, and that we are not alone.

2012 will bring the return of the Creator Gods (Anunnaki). They are part human and part reptilian—they evolve in the lower density and are a direct seed line to the Illuminati. They promote a satanic agenda to be worshiped by those of us who do not have the divine discretion to understand our true connection to the light consciousness. These alien gods are the master geneticists, that two to three hundred thousand years ago, played a key role in our evolution by dismantling (turning off) all but our basic DNA—leaving only the double helix. This earthly quarantine allowed humankind little control of the light frequency receptors (chakras) and limited our connection to the universal light consciousness—isolating us from the living library of the universe and hiding our true history. If humankind had evolved without interference, we would not have 85% junk DNA and we would have a 12-helix connection to the 12 chakras and a full universal living library spectrum of the light consciousness, not just two helix and little connection.

The 2012 transformation will release us from our earthly quarantine and allow our DNA to expand back to 12 helix; this morphing of our DNA will finally re-connect us to the living library of the *Prime Creator's* light consciousness.

The alien *Creator Gods* that return during the 2012 transformation will be promoted by the Illuminati as saviors, and to win us over they will offer to heal the planet from the rabid disease or chaos they and the Illuminati planted and created in the first place. This may be in the form of a bio-disease, created by their Illuminati seedline representatives within the military or world governments. Their true goal is enslavement and to keep earth in a *lower density frequency* during the 2012 transformation. This will create vibrations of global emotional trauma—nourishing their desires in the lower density. Sadly, 2012 will also bring the ***New World Order*** promoted by the Illuminati. Creating much chaos and confusion. This is needed, regrettably, to break down the current corrupt system so it can be rebuilt properly as a foundation to the coming Golden Age.

Refer to Page 88—Decoded Binary Message: *"Beware the bearers of false gifts and their broken promises..."*

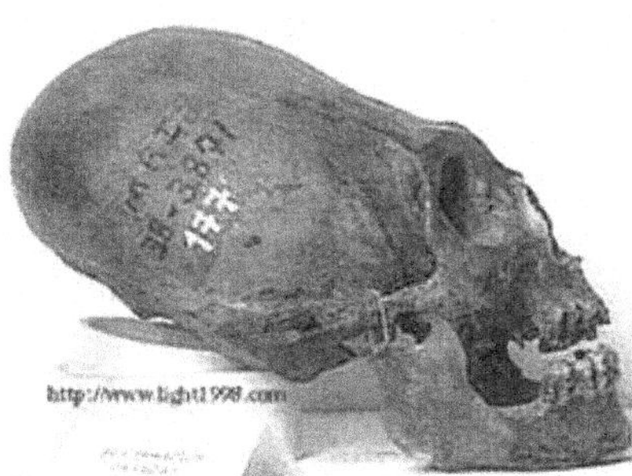

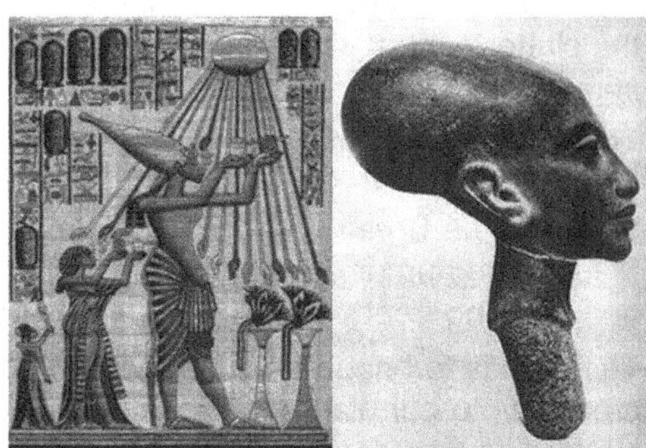

Anunnaki *– The "Creator Gods"*

Those that can handle the changing higher light frequencies of 2012, will evolve beyond the controls of these false gods. We have the power of *Free Will* and it is important that we do not give away our authority or our powers. We must also be responsible for our actions and words: because it is much easier to manifest what we believe and project during this transformation.

During this time of great revealing, not only will the dark past be revealed, but present day dogmas, belief systems and false teachings, will also be exposed. So it is important that we let go of the old concepts of money and spiritual dogmas. The new golden age is all about releasing ones self from the bondage that prevents flow to the light and knowledge of the higher frequency. It is important to know that when we face the dark or shadows within ourselves, we are creating an opportunity for liberation from the lower self as our "thought creates" and manifests our reality. This power will become manifest as the 2012 transformation occurs.

We chose to be here to help bring the higher existence back to our creation and shine the light on all that is false and anti-evolutionary. This is a lifetime where we also will remember who we truly are and what we already know innately about the living library. Asking our Kundalini to guide us will allow its great force to manifest as it fires the codes that activate the light fibers and align them with light consciousness.

This current age of man was most barbaric, and Mother earth permitted herself to be abused as we allowed and created a wide-ranging polarity of consciousness. 2012 will bring huge changes—cleansing the planet. The more we polluted and disconnected, the more her poles now need to shift and shake to realign the electro magnetic change needed for a higher vibrational density. Continents will move and reposition to *safe areas*. This will allow a major shift in consciousness. This shift will be safe for those willing to change—to be open to the new light frequency. There will be global safe areas, but, we need to trust mother earth to tell us where. Rid our lives of the clutter of conditionings and mundane things we don't need—listen to the impulses.

The 2012 transformation will sadly bring much death and suffering. It is important that the survivors open their hearts to the events being orchestrated by the Prime Creator, and work to help the dead pass over to the other side. Meditation, humor during this emotional period are key to staying detached and allowing freedom from the sadness and drama created.

The plan is to bring back the light—which is information, and love—which is creativity, to our planet that has dwelled in darkness for eons, and change it back to its true density. We took our birth knowing our role in a challenging place and time in our evolution. We have been helped along our journey in by the Star Teachers that have guided, taught and triggered our DNA at select times when we needed a teacher or reminder that we are children of the light.

We are truly magnificent beings. Members of the vast family of light—born into the earth realm to help create this shift: because love is the key to our universe. Our technology will only allow evolution to grow so far. When one is focused on ego or self, the vibration and frequency is only able to go so far and then its evolution ends. There is only so much that can be achieved within this 3D density. This is the case of the lower density extraterrestrials. Because of their technologies, the Anunnaki have been looked upon as Gods throughout our dark history. Humans, on the other hand, evolve—as love is the key that opens the doorway to the infinite universal light consciousness: where all possibilities of expansion exist.

We are a beautiful and perfect reflection of the Prime Creator, the Maha Devi (mother goddess) of Vedic lore. It is all one source of light with different names.

To grow deeply into our true potential, we must understand who we are and our connection to the light. Humility, meditation, wisdom, divine knowledge and discretion, will help open the 2012 doorway to the higher self. Then when we embrace the Prime Creator, the earth mother will open up the living library connection to all life forms: as all life forms have chakras integrated with the light. All is one and we are the light masters of this reality!

Spiritual Evolution—The 5th Dimension

Our soul (atma) is not of this physical plane, but rather a reflection and part of the divine universal light consciousness or primordial power. The 5th dimension and beyond is the eternal "now" that allows this reality to exist. Cycles of our 3rd dimensional day and night are only perfunctory markers of the cycles, but have no real effect or power over the present moment. This all means that what we feel and experience in the present moment is thoughtless awareness—the true reality of self. The past and the future have no relevance in this state of spiritual thoughtlessness, and until we ascend into the 5th dimensional plane where past, present and future are integrated as one moment beyond time and space, we are unable to understand the connection we have with the universal light consciousness. It is beyond thought and the limited human intellect. As we evolve our attention through the present moment and into the next dimensional level or spiritual plane of life, our connection to light consciousness will allow us to expand into the farthest reaches of the universe—beyond time-space.

This period of our Earth's history and civilization is coming to an end in 2012, but the Golden Age that follows will allow an evolution into the higher light awareness. This will transform our physical understanding into the higher spiritual self that vibrates at the higher frequency of the universal light consciousness. This transformation is the foundation of the new Aquarian or Golden Age, and the 1000-year peace. It will allow us to get back in tune with our Mother Earth and our connection to self-healing, natural herbs, crystals and solar power while respecting the life force energy as Children of the Light—evolving our destiny back to the garden. The Alpha and the Omega of our collective journey, the garden where only the light of the spirit will evolve, leaving the darkness of greed, ego, power and false knowledge fighting for the illusions they create.

Omkar—OM

The OM or A-U-M is the primary mantra in the ancient Vedic traditions (pranava mantra) and the most sacred symbol in Hinduism. It represents the sound of creation and the three deities in the Hindu trinity, in Brahma, Vishnu and Shiva. The vibration of the A-U-M represents the three aspects of the totality of creation. OM is also a mantra in Buddhism but without the Vedic deities. Buddhists believe OM is the primal vibration from which everything was created and into which everything returns at the end of the great cosmic cycle. The ancient sages and Rishi believed our universe was created by the divine thought of the Adi Shakti (primordial cosmic feminine energy).

The OM represents an advanced form of Cymantic vibration frequency, which fuses thought into light matter, then sound. The sound then manifests as a sacred geometric life force creating matter.

The OM frequency is also about merging three primordial powers, which manifest as **"A,U,M".**

The **"A"** is the power of pure desire, and represents the beginning, start and emanation of the universe and life. It is also the waking consciousness (jagrat), conditioned by time and space.

The **"U"** is the power of action and represents the sustenance of the universe, its in the middle between creation and destruction. It also represents the Dreaming Consciousness (svapna) with the subconscious mind, predominating the awareness.

The **"M"** is the power of evolution and represents the ending, destruction, and death of life and the universe, life is also the power of regeneration or rebirth. It also represents the Dreamless Sleep (nidra), which is a deep sleep state without any disturbance of dreams.

Star Tetrahedron

"A,U,M" in its fullness, is the divine sound of creation through to its eventual destruction. It represents all living things, from the microcosm to the macrocosm that have a connection to the light, or source frequency of creation. Our Mother Earth is fully alive within this frequency, and vibrates at the tone of the OM frequency. This is why when we visit the forests of nature we subtlety feel the OM vibrating through us, as it allows for peace, stillness and balance to manifest within our being. This generates the feeling of relaxation, and the connection we experience with nature.

Shri Mahasaraswati

The OMKAR is the foundational tone of music. The four Vedas are the continued manifestation of this Adi Sangeet that combined vocal music, instrumental music and classical dance. The evolution of the core teachings of the Vedas, Upanishads and the melodic Sanskrit language, are just an extension of "OM" and the evolution of the Adi Sangeet on this physical plane. The OMKAR manifests within the Adi Sangeet (primordial trinity of divine music) though which the Adi Shakti handed down this blessing to Lord Brahma. It was then destined to humankind, and through our spiritual evolution, it eventually manifested with the great enlightened Rishi, Munis and Sages of ancient times. These great masters tuned into the frequency of mother earth and the vibration of universal divine love (OM) to manifest the beginnings of divine music on earth, thus developing the foundation to the Vedas.

Vibrations

The belief of many cultures is that "The Word" of God created life, and the cosmos. Translated it means; the pure desire manifested pure thought "divine will" into a form of light frequency or vibration that transformed our surroundings into a form of physical mass or matter.

Vibrations exist on all levels or planes of existence; they can be subtler frequencies or grosser dependant on the source. The difference between the various planes of existence is that vibrations become subtler and purified more with each level achieved. They also represent a pathway or connection between all things in multiple dimensions of time, space, light and sound energy.

It seems many people place their faith in their physical senses, trusting only what they see, hear, touch, smell and taste in the 3rd dimension. In doing so, they do not feel the subtly of vibrations, and disconnect to their psychic faculties, and close off the connection to the higher, but subtler self-awareness principals. When we become subtle in our awareness we understand vibrations exist and transcend the present, as well as the past and future, crossing into the realm of the ethers and Akashic.

The more evolved the soul, the subtler the vibration frequencies, and the dimensions the soul can travel to, or attain. This understanding helps us to realize that time, as we know it does not control the universal patterns of multi dimensional travel or evolution. It is the subtle self, the innocence of pure vibrational light frequency. So as we evolve our awareness into the higher level of our evolution, we will fuse with the pure light frequency consistent with the next realm of our spiritual evolution. Because eventually *"Thy will be done, on earth as it is in Heaven".*—Bible

Atman—Spirit

Atman is the Self—the eternal center of our light consciousness, which was never born and never dies. A good metaphor is to imagine that the chakra is a lampshade, and the Atman or spirit is the light that gives essence to the vibration of the chakra. The Atman or spirit light shines through the koshas, and takes on the colorings of karmic residue and vibration frequency of the thought, action or the lifetime good or bad. The goal is to become more and more subtle which allows attunement to the higher light frequencies.

The Atman has been best described as "indescribable". The self realization of yoga meditation experienced in the ancient traditions is to become thoughtlessly aware, as this will allow the light of the divine love to connect with and imbibe ones body, mind and soul in all aspects of life.

Yoga—Union

There are many kinds of yoga everywhere today, but the practice of pure classical yoga dates back to the Upanishads, 5000 – 1000 BC. The yogis encouraged union with the finite jiva *(transitory self)* and with the infinite Brahman *(Sanskrit: to grow)*. The great Yogis and Rishi taught that everything is part of this divine universal light energy and the physical postures were just one aspect of the pure Yoga of spiritual attunement.

This new Golden or Aquarian age of yoga beyond 2012 allows the transformation from the human being into the spiritual being. It is important that as the 2012 global shift manifests, we understand it is our karmic responsibility to find our yoga (union) with mother earth and the universal light consciousness through awakening our spiritual source. This is important in order to positively affect the global vibration and raise its frequency to balance our civilizations karmic debt and minimize the cataclysms of 2012. The processional galactic cycle is ending and we need to attune with the vibrations of the universal light consciousness as it is through this atonement to our yoga that we will best understand what is truly coming our way via the earth changes and transformation.

Spiritual Transformation

There are numerous astral planes of light and life within the universal consciousness that vibrate beyond our 3rd dimensional world—a place where the past and future exist in their own "now" on parallel planes of existence. With the 2012 transformational and dimensional shift, we will finally see the previously closed gateways to the stars open up and our earthly quarantine lifted. This transformational shift is already happening and vibrating faster each day as 2012 approaches. Untrue relationships are ending and the desire for a more spiritual atonement and understanding is calling. These changes are happening on many levels.

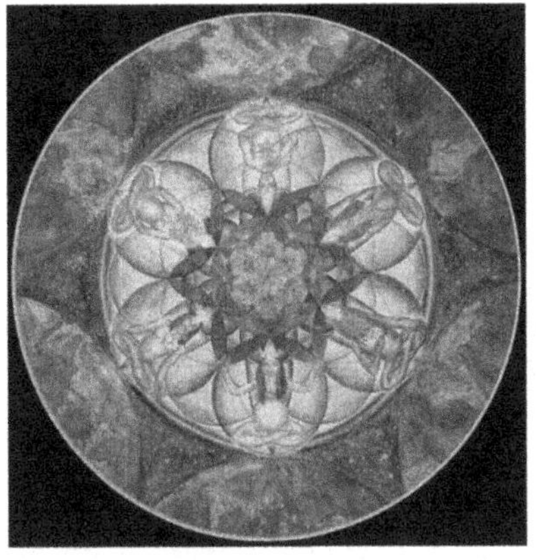

NASA has recently stated that planets in our solar system are experiencing a temperature increase. It appears that the vibrational frequency is increasing within the galaxy as the galactic alignment of December 21st 2012 approaches.

This shift or change will affect all aspects of our 3rd dimensional world as we know it. This will transcend our Kundalini energy through the Sahasrara chakra (crown) into the 5th dimension of light consciousness—birthing a new awareness. This is the true "born again" prophesied but misunderstood through erroneous dogmatic religious interpretations.

During this shift or transition, what we believe and where we put our attention will greatly determine how we position ourselves during the 2012 transformation. Now is the time we must stop and be in "yoga" (union) within to hear all that is being communicated to us through the light consciousness, as this information will protect and tune our awareness to the profound approaching changes. This is a beautiful convergence into a higher harmonic frequency and a new vibratory awareness that allows a reconnection with our ancient spiritual history and our Mother Earth. It is the birth of our spiritual evolution and the quantum leap into the realm of the light consciousness and reconnection with our creator.

This frequency shift or vibrational change appears to align with the theory that our unused DNA does not code proteins. Many researchers now believe this is where we will attach our currently unused abilities such as telekinesis, teleportation, clairvoyance, telepathy and others.

The "Human Genome Project" has revealed that our DNA is not genetically set. Only 10% of the human DNA is used for coding and for reproduction of proteins. The rest, approximately 90%, is referred to as junk DNA, which scientists say is confused and unnecessary to our body. This was the norm until renowned Russian Dr. Pjotr Garjajev of the Human Genome Project, revealed the junk DNA is actually our link to the deeper realms of our spirituality. This would explain the DNA messages of the crop circles where broken DNA images are shown to evolve in a sequence of crop circles, transforming into double and triple helix DNA. As 2012 nears, this DNA transformation will help plug us into the full 12 chakras of the 5th dimension.

The Chariot of Ascension

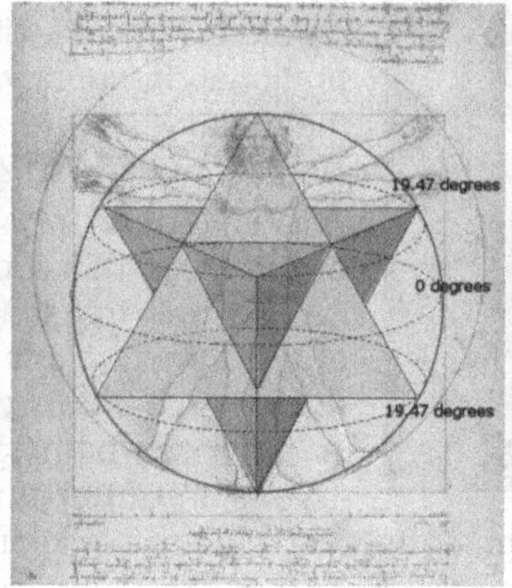

MER KA BAH – Mer = Light, Ka = Spirit, Bah = Body.

This is the chariot that can take us into the next dimension. MerKaBah means the spirit body surrounded by counter rotating fields of light, which transports it from one dimension to another. Like DNA, it is made of spirals of energy and acts as an inter-dimensional vehicle. MerKaBha is a vehicle of light consisting of two equally sized interlocked tetrahedrons of light with a common center. The star Tetrahedron (illustrated above) is viewed as a three dimensional Star of David. Once activated, this saucer shaped field is capable of carrying ones consciousness directly to higher dimensions. Activation of the Merkaba vehicle is required to achieve eternal life, time travel and star gate passage. This process of continually attuning to the nature and vibration of the Universe, awakens a deeper experience of the truth of the connectedness of all life. The personal Merkaba field represents the organic system through which our consciousness manifests through and into space, time and matter.

Deities—Angels

In the Old Testament "Genesis" it states *"God made man in his own image"*. So what does this really mean? We know through the ancient Sumerian stone tablets, that aliens descend 200,000 years ago from Planet Nibiru disturbing our evolution, and manipulating our DNA to enslave us. On the other side, we have also been visited and guided by the Light Teachers, a more spiritually advanced race from the star system Pleiades. They visited earth, sharing their knowledge of the stars long before Atlantis. The Mayan calendar is one small remnant of their knowledge, handed down through the ages. The Light Teachers shared the code of dharma with our ancient forefathers to help us evolve to the light consciousness, and guide us back on our evolutionary path. It is true, many of the deities depicted in the ancient Vedic mythology, are in fact portraits of the Star Teachers, and or their battles with the dark forces that were trying to harm our evolutionary process. There were many alien gods that influenced our journey through the ages, some with good intentions, others not. The dark side represented the fallen angels and the anti evolutionary lower self. The Light Teachers represent the path to our future and the enlightened self. Their goal was only to help guide us through spiritual protocols, as well as show us how to protect and connect our selves through the sacred mantras.

In modern times as our DNA evolves from a double helix of the 3rd dimension, to the12 helix of the light consciousness, we will finally come out of our quarantine and reside with the deities and angels of light.

Uriel is one of the archangels.

Gabriel is an archangel whose name means "God is my strength"

Hunab Ku

Hunab Ku

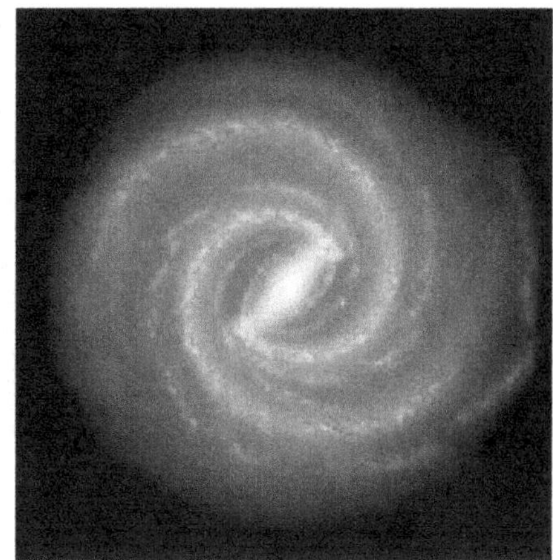

Spiral Galaxy

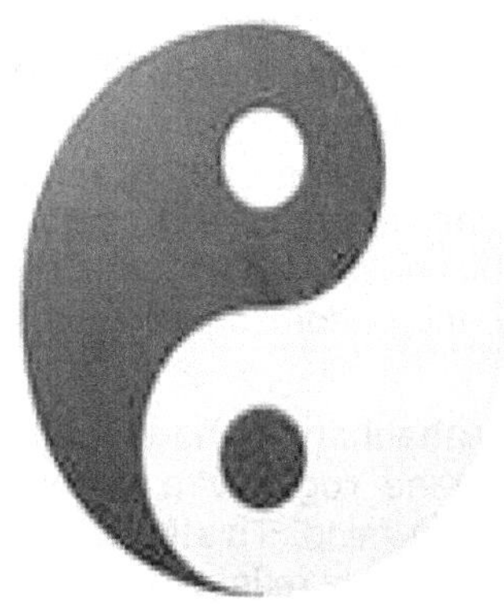

Yin Yang

The Mayan identify the Galactic Center as the Hunab Ku, which they say represents the supreme and ultimate Creator. It is also believed it represents the gateway to other Galaxies beyond our Sun and all of the consciousness that has ever existed. Hunab Ku, is also the consciousness, which organized all matter from a "whirling disk" into stars, planets and solar systems.

Subtle System—Yoga

The western world has recently embraced yoga as the new business of the enlightened. There is a deep knowledge and dharma associated with the yoga passed down from ancient times. So one must be careful of the boundaries of today's modern physical yoga and not confuse it with spiritual awakening. To indulge the ego and illusions of the lower self becomes a false understanding of the pure aspects of our true spiritual evolution. Too many times during our history we have allowed the lower self to dictate policy on our spiritual assent creating the justified dogmas of religious beliefs and their hierarchy. To become enlightened or a master, one be must "Be" enlightened or a master, we cannot buy a certificate or take a course that tells us we are. When we try to attach a business sign or certificate to enlightenment, it loses its essence and purity and becomes just another recycled dogma with a new paint job.

The ancient yoga tradition mentioned in the Mahabharata and the Gita, refers to three kinds of classic yoga. According to the Yoga Sutra of Patanjali, the purpose of yoga (union) is to lead to a silent mind. This silence is the starting point for the mind to accurately and objectively reflect reality without its own distortions of ego and conditionings that surround us daily and through our lives. Physical yoga does not create the reality of pure spirit, which is above the mind, but only prepares the mind to evolve into to it. This is done by assisting in the exchange of a mind full of thoughts and desires, to a still mind that may then access the next level of thoughtless awareness and spiritual attainment. However, this depends on where the attention is. The great masters have aligned themselves with the knowledge of attainment through their teachings and deep traditions. This transition from human being to spiritual being is established through introspection, detachment and release of the earthly conditionings while using the subtle system of Chakras and their principals of dharma to connect to and guide to our deeper awareness.

The universe within is a beautiful interconnecting network of nerves and sensory organs that decodes the outside physical world. There is also a subtle system of Nadis and centers of energy (Chakras), which monitor our physical, intellectual, emotional and spiritual energy. Depending on our state of spiritual alignment, we can connect to the universal collective of love and divine light energy through understanding this subtle universe within and how it connects to the divine.

The path to self-realization (true yoga) or union is to gradually move inward to experience the balance and purity of divine love at the eternal center of our consciousness. One cannot evolve spiritually through the (left side) Pingala Nadi—moon side/past/emotions—nor can we evolve through the (right side) Ida Nadi—sun side/future/planning. Nor can we evolve through books or our mental intellect. To evolve spiritually we must find peace and balance in the center or present moment so the Kundalini can rise up through the center path of evolution (Susmina Nadi) and establish the true yoga and connection to the universal light consciousness.

As one passes through the limitations of the lower levels of self, ego and attachments and balances the attention, then the 'Sahasrara' or 7th chakra will awaken to nirvana and self-realization will be experienced. At this stage one knows we are all part of the universal light of divine consciousness, and awakens to the subtle aspects of the divine, deities and angels.

Chakra

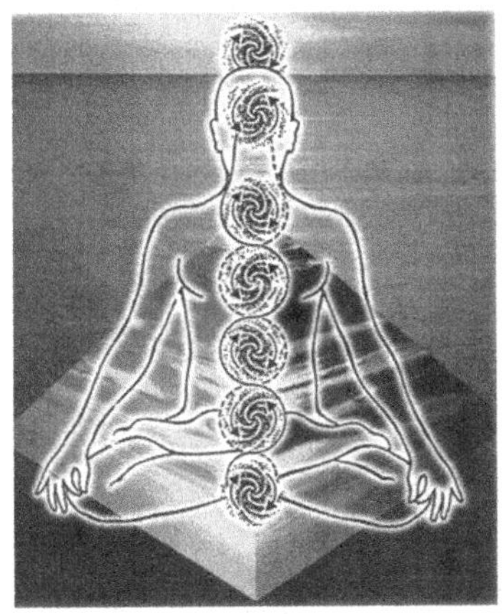

The name Chakra comes from the Sanskrit word meaning "spinning wheel". There are 12 Chakras, 7 of the physical body and another 5 above, that allow ascension to the higher dimensional planes as we evolve beyond the 3rd dimension.

These spinning energy wheels rotate at a divine frequency, acting as the transducer of the pure universal divine love (light) energy (God) as it enters and merges through the human physical form. This divine energy moves through the chakra system manifesting into the physical body through the meridians known as Nadis. These Nadis also correspond to the energy meridians used in the ancient Chinese medicine traditions. Each chakra is designed to supervise and maintain the perfect operation of the spiritual and physical bodily systems under its control. This purification is done by spinning in pure or positive vibrations, and spinning out impure or negative ones. Each chakra also imbibes a different quality and aspect of the divine (Deity) as it spins and vibrates in tune with the divine frequency of universal pure love and the dharma. An enlightened being will manifest the blessings of the divine power with all the Chakras spinning in harmony and in tune with the universal vibration of pure divine love. As the person advances their spiritual aspirations through meditation and light work, the vibration of the chakra will change to a higher frequency creating a pure light energy or white light aura. This enlightened state was manifest within the great saints, masters and sages like the Christ consciousness of Jesus and the great Buddha.

Contrarily, the "un-dharmic" life creates blockages and karmic residue debt and this imbalance causes disorders to manifest as the Chakras spin out of balance and out of the divine frequency that vibrate with the universal "OM". This creates the "hell" within as the residue of negative actions is taken on as karma or vibrational residue, and will affect our frequency when we pass from the human physical form, into the ethereal state of spirit.

Our Chakras also correlate directly to the Mother Earth's energy vortexes and grids that appear around the earth and through the universe. Places like Sedona Arizona and pyramid centers are some of the grids and portals of the universal consciousness that connect to the Earth. It is all interconnected, from the microcosm of the cell of the body, to the macrocosm of the universes; it is all one life force. Just as the body has bacteria and virus infections that affect the body, the universe also has lower evolved life forms that affect its flow. So as 2012 approaches we should look at the earth from a galactic point of view, and how in our current state of evolution, we affect other planets and life forms on a vibrational level.

Genesis 28:12 – Jacob's Ladder

"And he dreamed and behold a ladder set up on the earth, and the top of it reached to heaven: and behold the angels of God ascending and descending on it."

1. Earth: Mooladhara 1st chakra/base

2. Enlightened: Sahasrara 7th chakra/crown enlightened

3. Heaven: 8 – 12 chakras

4. Jacob's Ladder: the chakras and levels of consciousness to which we ascend

5. The Angels: the deities and angels that come to help us along the way through our mantras and affirmations.

* It is believed the above is a direct reference to the subtle chakra system.

Kundalini

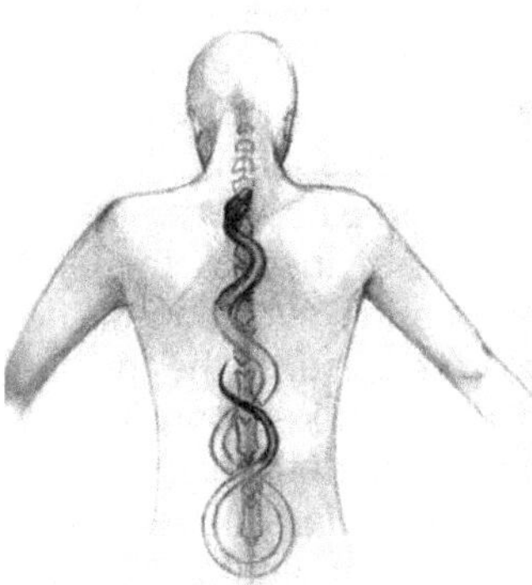

John 3:3 - *"Jesus answered and said unto him, Verily, verily, I say unto thee, Except a man be born again, he CANNOT see the kingdom of God."*

John 3:5 – *" Jesus answered, Verily, verily, I say unto thee, Except a man be born of water AND of the Spirit, he CANNOT enter into the kingdom of God."*

Gnostic Gospel of Thomas *'The Holy Spirit is My Mother'.*

"The Kingdom of God is within you' (Luke 17:21)."

The mother Kundalini is known as the "coiled" sleeping serpent *(Sanskrit)* that resides in the triangular sacrum bone in the base of the spine. This residual divine power *(holy ghost)* is the germinating power of the seed of the evolutionary spiritual being. This primordial cosmic Shakti energy is in every individual and will eventually rise up through the Sushumna Nadi *(center channel)* through advanced meditation yoga. As it rises, the Kundalini awakens each successive chakra. Nirvikalpa Samadhi (nirvana enlightenment) comes as it pierces through the Sahasrara chakra to the enlightened state. Enlightenment is attained when this energy connects through the central channel, piercing through each energy center (chakra) and emerges through the top of the head (fontanel bone area) to the divine light consciousness. This is felt as a peaceful "fountain" of the divine all knowing awareness and coolness.

The Kundalini is interconnected with the universal feminine power of Adi Shakti. This power represents 1/3 of the holy trinity *(Father, Son, Holy Spirit)* that resides within us and the universal planes of the divinity. Our mother Kundalini is part of our subtle autonomous spiritual body that feeds the Chakras and Nadis this divine spiritual love and compassion of the Parum Chitana (God realm). The degree of pure divine light energy we can absorb depends directly on the condition of our Chakras and subtle system receiving it. The awakening of our mother Kundalini will awaken the divine connection to the universal divine knowledge that is vibrating in the Akashic ethers, but is only the beginning. To manifest and integrate this spiritual energy, careful purification and strengthening of the mind, body and spirit must be part of the process. Using the divine protocols, mantras and affirmations in this book will help. The desire and surrendering through pure love, humility and identifying the ego are also the key to spiritual growth and attainment of self-realization.

Swastika

This symbol was misused during the recent times of Nazi Germany. The swastika is really an ancient sacred geometric spiritual symbol, representing the spinning chakra and Shri Ganesha (Deity) whose aspects or qualities reside within the first chakra. The two crosses that make up the symbol represent the two forms of the creator God Brahma—one facing right represents the evolution of the universe and one facing left and it represents the involution of the universe. It is also seen as pointing in all four directions (north, east, south and west) , which indicates stability and grounded ness. It also represents the "spinning" of the chakra as it spins faster via a dharmic life the blessings of the chakra manifest. If it slows down due to anti-god activities or negative thoughts, words or actions, then problems manifest physically and spiritually, often with illness and disease as the first symptom.

Nadis

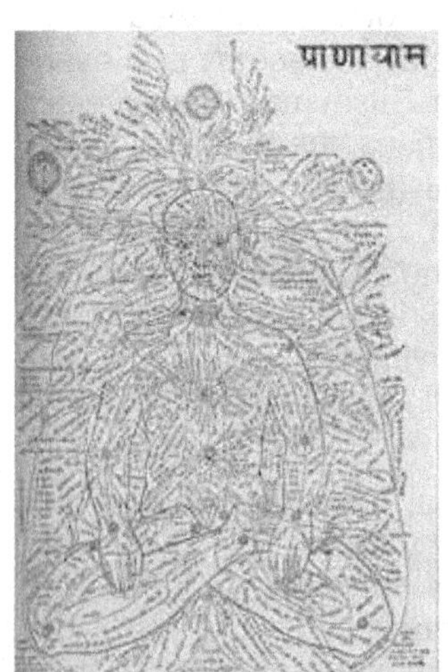

The foundation and theory behind Thai massage and chi in the Chinese culture is the premise that its most basic level, all of life is energy. This energy called Prana in Sanskrit exists in many forms, from the extremely gross levels to the infinitely subtle levels, as all physical and spiritual life interplays within these energies. In the human body these energies flow along a network of channels or lines (Nadis and meridians). In the Vedic yoga tradition there are 72,000 Nadis. Each has a specific function and energy that it deals with on a physical or spiritual level. The three main energetic channels are the Ida Nadi (left side) and Pingala nadi (right side), which run on either side of the spine. Metaphorically they represent (male) Shiva and (female) Parvati, yin and yang, and the Sun and the Moon aspects. There is also the Sushumna Nadi, the center channel of our evolution and the gateway to heaven or the universal light consciousness, that is accessible though our Kundalini awakening, coming 2012 transformation, devotion to dharma and right knowledge. (*See chakra chart*)

Ego

Mahat - means the great, **Ahamkara** - means the ego..

To dissolve the ego, we say:

Om Twameva Sakshat Shri Nirvichara Sakshat

Shri Adi Shakti Maha Devi Namoh Namah

Om Twameva Sakshat Shri Mahat Ahamkara Sakshat

Shri Adi Shakti Shri Maha Devi Namoh Namah

Emotions—Calming

By raising the vibration of our right or left side, we become balanced and can then feel our emotions *"Manas Shakti".* Our emotions become enlightened as we see the pure divine love in all things including our self and the universal light consciousness.

As we view our emotions (left side/ **moon**/feminine) as a detached witness during meditation, they dissolve as we witness control of them, and through this controlling of our emotions our enlightened and powerful being will manifest the balance.

Reduce your breathing and exhale deeply out through the mouth. Then wait for awhile and inhale deeply through the nose. Try and keep the attention on the emotions and proceed with the mantra.

Om Twameva Sakshat Shri Kalki Sakshat

Shri Sahasrara Swamini Moksha Pradayini Parvati

Shri Kundalini Maha Devi Namoh Namah

Havan—Cleansing—Fire

In Vedic/Hindu traditions, fire is a central element in the Yajna *(Sanskrit)* ceremony, with Agni "fire" as dissolver of the problems or negativity attacking one's world. During the Havan ceremony *(sacrificial fire),* objects such as fruits, honey, or problems written on paper are put into the sacred fire. Any evil spirits around you or inside you get burned off in the sacred fire. It is believed that this sacrifice will bring health, happiness, luck and prosperity. It is a deep form of cleansing one's inner spiritual being as well as one's surroundings, home and family. Proper protocols should be observed.

Foot Soaking

Foot soaking is an ancient technique using the water and salt of the earth to cleans ones inner being. It is best done in the evening. Put the feet into a bowl of warm water, salt is added to the water to represent the earth element. In this way we use all the elements, fire *(with the candle),* air, water and earth. The element of water rinses away, and salt *(earth element)* sucks or absorbs away negativity.

Light a candle and burn some incense. Raise your Kundalini, and put your self in bandhan. Give a bandhan *(clock-wise direction)* to the salt water in the foot soaker. The water should be to your ankles. Place your feet in the salt water. Take Shri Ganesha's mantra. Sit for 10 to 15 minutes in the water. Rinse and dry the feet. And throw the water down the toilet. Wash your hands and sit for another meditation. To close your meditation raise your Kundalini and give yourself a bandhan.

Shoe Beating

This is an ancient 'cleansing' technique of Islam, used by Sufis to offer negativity or evil to the Mother Earth. First we draw a circle on the ground with the index finger and symbolically writing into the circle, something that is of concern. Then removing ones left shoe, the circle is 'beaten' gently with the heel of the shoe. This in no way guarantees an outcome to the problem but is a way of surrendering it to Mother Earth, to be dealt with.

'But Jesus stooped down and wrote on the ground with his finger, as though he did not hear."

Bhajans

Singing divine music or Indian bhajan can be very beneficial as they evolved from pure essence of the "OM" (creation). Music is a subtle form of sacred geometry and has a way of carrying the divine vibrations through the ethers and manifesting them. Music that has a divine focus will carry the vibrations that have the greatest impact on the subtle system. As the Kundalini awakens to the vibrations, the tone frequency and notes will vibrate the chakras and its connection to the Audi Shakti power of creation.

Listening to Indian Raggs during meditation can also be helpful to achieve thoughtlessness, as the vibrations have a direct impact on out attention. Not only do certain notes and sounds relate directly to the chakras, but also certain Raggs and Indian instrument tunings correspond directly to the different Chakras and deities. This correlation can help open, cure and balance the chakras and our subtle system, as well as help us focus our meditation into a thoughtless state.

Chakras	Indian Scale	Western
Sahasrara	Ni	Tea
Agnya	Dha	La
Vishuddhi	Pa	So
Anahata	Ma	Fah
Nabhi	Ga	Me
Swadisthan	Re	Rae
Mooladhara	Sa	Doe

Some notes on the Indian tuning scale are slightly different from the western scale.

Aum—OM

The AMEN, is the same WORD used in John's Gospel. The AUM "OM" is the integrated power of the Adi Shakti (Holy Spirit) expressed in Shri Ganesha at Mooladhara Chakra; its manifestation is the aspect of Lord Jesus Christ at Agnya Chakra.

"**A**" Mahakali energy; Ida Nadi—Left sympathetic nervous system. Aspect of "**tamo guna".** Its quality is Desire/Existence.

"**U**" Mahasaraswati energy; Pingala Nadi—Right sympathetic nervous system. Aspect of **"rajo guna".** Its quality is Action/Creation.

"**M**" Mahalakshmi energy Sushumna Nadi—Parasympathetic nervous system. Aspect of **"satwa guna".** Its quality is Evolution/ Awareness.

To meditate with mantras, first sit with palms upward, allowing thoughts to flow in and out with out attaching to them. As you progress to the state of Kundalini awakening you will begin to feel sensations such as tingling, numbness, slight heat and you may feel the Chakras within your fingers. These sensations will tell you where the Chakras blockages are that stem from past lives or current situations and actions.

As you deepen in your meditations you will begin to feel coolness on your hands. This represents the cool breeze of the holy ghost (Adi Shakti). This also means that the chakras have cleared and that Kundalini is rising unimpeded into the state of self-realization. The process can be helped along by the clearing elements of earth, fire, water and air through various ancient cleansing treatments such as burning camphor, shoe beating, foot soaking to name just a few.

Gunas

The three Gunas – are inherent qualities or attributes in which the nature of all things is said to be limited: Satwa (purity, goodness, truth), Rajo (activity, passion, desire) and Tamo (ignorance, darkness, inertia) beyond the Gunas is the collective light of love consciousness.

Puja

A Puja is essentially a spiritual and symbolic offering of ourselves, our thoughts, desires, actions and things to the divine light consciousness to show our humility, devotion and surrender. This allows the subtle aspects of our light frequency to deepen to the levels of the light consciousness. The Puja has a definite protocol, form and structure instilled over the ages. Its

meaning derives from "pu" means "purusha" *(Sanskrit)* the Cosmic man, and "ja" means "janma", to arise or wake up. To allow the blessings and awaken the deity, the vibrations *(life breath)* are offered to the essence of the deity through desire and devotion during the Puja ceremony. A spiritual Puja is a very powerful way to cleanse our surroundings, and ourselves since the Puja awakens the deity and manifests its love and power, destroying negativity while leaving a resonance of beautiful vibrations.

From a spiritual perspective a Puja ceremony should not be conducted for personal means but to express our love, devotion and surrender to the divine light of universal consciousness. The Puja is also a deeper formal way of doing meditation to imbibe the qualities of the deity or the divine while declaring one's surrender and faith to the universal love and divine light.

Symbolically the Puja will represent one of the various deities, or goddesses like Shri Lakshmi or Shri Ganesha in particular. It will consist of an earthen or a metal pot containing water or rice, with leaves of generally five specific

species in its mouth and a bowl of rice, flowers and coconut at its top. The pot represents Mother Earth, the flowers represent the ornamentation, the rice in the bowl represents either the material wealth or the powers of the goddess or both, and the coconut represents the divine consciousness.

Kumkum and turmeric powder: Red is the color of Shri Ganesha. The red powder also stands for our emotions or for our inner wisdom. The turmeric powder stands for our inner purity and on the negative side, for our inner pride and egoism.

Prasad: When we offer our ignorance to the divine, it is suffused with knowledge and light. The word "Prasad" is a combination of two words, "pra" + "sad"—that which is near life and truth. The food that is offered to the divine is a symbolic representation of the gross human body into which the worship the divine breathes new life and new light. When we share the Prasad with others, we share the love, discretion and knowledge we collectively gained during the Puja.

Be Your Own "Guru"

As we search the vast plethora of spiritual guidebooks, it is important, that one first finds truth within. It is from this place we can become our own guru and master, and empower the light that guides our spiritual evolution. Too many times we look for spiritual answers of guidance from others instead of going inward, and connecting to the source of our light.

Part of the problem preventing our assent to higher consciousness has been the attachment to the idol, or symbols of idol worship. These consist of false gurus or teachings, dogmatic religious beliefs, and even some of our movie or sports stars. What ever divides or distracts us from our direct connection to the divine light consciousness is anti-God. When we shift our attention to third party idols or gurus instead of going inward, we lose touch with our own discretion and our connection to the divine consciousness. Our spirit is part of the universal light consciousness; so we must trust and develop this connection.

There really is no fast food or quick way to spirituality, we will never find our truth by looking into someone else's mind or reading their books. Although in the beginning it is nice to formulate an understanding based on many opinions, however, we then need to go inward. In the western world we hear of so many masters, but who are the masters? A fee paid, earning a certificate will not create a spiritual master. Just as wearing a Mercedes Benz logo around your neck does not make you a car. So which Gurus do we trust, and do they really understand the reality of spirit? Or are they just money or power orientated companies, looking to take your innocence and confuse you, based on their own confused reality.

The truth is you are the light, you are beautiful, and you are your own Guru and Master. You do not need to follow, as you have the key to the light you seek. Just be wise enough to turn it on, and empower yourself.

108 Names

In Sanskrit numerology, the number 108 has a universal vibration and deep spiritual significance as it corresponds to the sacred geometric laws of creation and sustenance. The Indian Subcontinent rosary has a set of 108 mantra counts. Since ancient times 108 has been a sacred geometric number to the Indian as well as many other spiritual belief systems. The Indians were excellent mathematicians and 108 was thought to have special numerological significance. Also the Sanskrit alphabet has 54 letters, each with a masculine and feminine aspect—Shiva and Shakti. (54 times 2 is 108). Saying a set of mantras 108 times creates vibration.

Maha Devi—Divine Mother Goddess

The Maha Devi is known as the Divine Mother or Audi Shakti, the primordial power of creation. Maha Devi means goddess, and the goddess has many aspects or forms. Adi means "primordial" and Shakti is the "power". So Adi Shakti means primordial power of God. At the beginning of time only these two aspects existed: God and his Shakti power. With endless love she created whole universes, which are nothing but a beautiful cloak that Adi Shakti created to make Shiva visible.

She is the "Mother Goddess," the one who dwells in the center of the galaxy—the power of the creation or mother of all. Unlike what some doctrine may say, the omnipresent Devi has not incarnated in the human form. Seems money or power orientated groups seeking to control followers have wrongfully stated that she exists in human form. Her most familiar mythological forms are the ferocious aspects such as Durga and Kali, or the benevolent, such as Parvati. In the aspect of Parvati, she is the feminine aspect of the holy trinity—Shri Shiva being the masculine or Father, the god of destruction and regeneration—and Shri Ganesha, the son and remover of obstacles.

Maha Devi is also the mother of all life on Earth—the gentle divine aspect of nature and life bringing rain and protecting against disease. In reality all are one, and one is all because the light is formless, creation and evolution is both destruction and regeneration.

The Prayer to the Divine Mother—*Humility*

Japo Jalpah Shilpam Sakalamapi Mudravirachana
Gathi Pradakshinya-kramana-mashana dyahuti vidhih
Pranam sanveshah sukhama-khilamatmarpana-drusha
Saparyaparyas-tava bhavatu yanme vilasitam

Through the sight of Self surrender let my prattle become recitation of Your name; the movement of my limbs, gestures of Your worships; my walk, perambulation around You; my food, sacrificial offering to You; my lying down, prostration to You; whatever I do for my pleasure, let it become transformed into an act of worship to You.

Prayer to the Maha Devi

Vishwe-shwari twam Paripasi Vishwam
Vishwatmika dharayaseeti vishwam.
Vishwesh-vandya bhavatee bhavanti
Vishwa-shraya ye twayi bhakti namraha.
Queen of the Universe, You are its guardian.
In the form of the Universe, You are its receptacle.
You are worshipped by the Lords of the Universe.
Those who are devoted to You themselves become supporters of the Universe.
Prana-tanam praseeda twam devi Vishwarti-harini.
Trailokya vasina-meedye lokanam varada bhawa.
O Maha Devi, the remover of the afflictions of Universe,
be pleased to us who are prostrating on Your feet.
O Maha Devi, who are worthy of all praise by the dwellers
of three worlds, grant boons to all the people.

Aarti (*Song of praise to the Divine Mother)*

The **Aarti** is an auspicious part of the ancient Vedic fire ceremony or the "homa" coded in the Vedas, Agamas and Dharma and Grihya Shastras *(Sanskrit)* as a rite of passage in Puja and other ceremonies.

Generally, one or more wicks made of cotton or thin cloth strip, is soaked in ghee or camphor, lighted and offered to the deity during singing. This is done at the end of a Puja and it is sung collectively while the fire ritual is being performed.

CHORUS

Sab ko dua dena, Ma	Mother, give blessings to all
Sab ko dua dena	Mother, give blessings to all
Jai Nirmala Maha Devi	Salutations Pure Great Goddess
Jai Nirmala Maha Devi	Salutations Pure Great Goddess
Dil me sada rehena	Always dwell in our hearts
Ma sab ko dua dena	Mother, give blessings to all.

VERSES

Jag me sankat, Karan
Kitane liye Avtar, Ma

Kitane liye Avtar
Vishwa me Teri mahima
Vishwa me Teri mahima
Too Ganga Yamuna
Ma sab ko dua dena
Jo bhi sharan me aya
Sukh hi mila us ko, Ma
Sukh hi mila us ko
Bhait ke dil me O Ma
Bhait ke dil me O Ma
Laut ke na jana
Ma sab ko dua dena
Manav me Avtar ke
Kar diya ujiyaala, Ma
Kar diya ujiyara
Kalyug me maya hai
Kalyug me maya hai
Fir bhi pehechaana

Ma sab ko dua dena
Sant jano ki dharti
Hai Bharat Mata, Ma
Hai Bharat, Mata
Is dharti par ake
Is dharti par ake
Dukh se door karana
Ma sab ko dua dena
Jab dilme aye tab
Madhoo sangeet sun lo Ma
Madhoo sangeet sun lo
Hoye sake jo sewa
Hoye sake jo sewa
Hamse kara lena
Ma sab ko dua dena

Whenever the world was in danger
Mother, You have always
incarnated
On this earth in different forms
Your Grace is all over the world
You are Ganga, You are Yamuna
Mother, give blessings to all.

Whoever surrenders himself to You
Mother, gets complete satisfaction
Once You have entered our hearts
Do not go away, Mother
Mother, give blessings to all.

By incarnating in human form
You have enlightened
Our lives, Mother
In spite of the illusions
Of the Kali Yuga
We have been able to recognize
You
Mother, give blessings to all.
The land of all the saints
Is Mother India
As You have incarnated
In this land
Please take away our sorrows
Mother, give blessings to all.

Whenever You so wish
We can listen to
The sweet music
Whatever service
You wish us to do
Kindly ask us to do it
Mother, give blessings to all.

Meditation—Mantras

Mantras have been handed down from ancient times, from the Star Teachers as a way to access the divine light consciousness and aspects of creation through the Sanskrit words or names, while sitting in meditation.

To meditate, first sit with palms upward and keep attention loose and easy allowing thoughts to flow in and out with out attaching to them. When you become more subtle toward the meditation the Kundalini will awaken and you will begin to feel sensations – tingling, numbness, slight heat – you may feel the Chakras within your fingers. These sensations will tell you where the Chakras blockages are that stem from past lives or current situations and actions.

As you deepen in your meditations you will start to feel coolness on your hands. This represents the cool breeze of the holy ghost *(Adi Shakti).* This also means that the Chakras have cleared and that Kundalini is rising unimpeded. The process can be helped along by the elements of earth, fire, water and air through various ancient cleansing treatments such as burning camphor, shoe beating, and foot soaking to name just a few.

Meditation

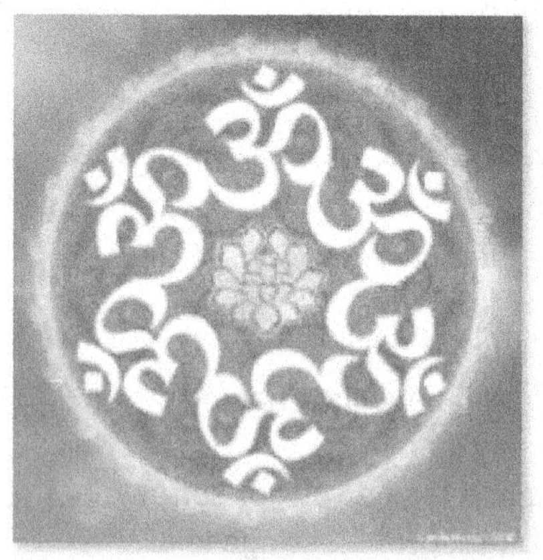

Meditation is a discipline where one attempts to go beyond the reactive, "thinking" mind and into a deeper state of spiritual awareness.

Meditation is established on three base levels:

(1) **Alpha** *beginner*—attention on objects, etc.

(2) **Beta** *more advanced*—attention on the inner being.

(3) **Theta** *the self-realization, enlightened state*—where one connects to the all knowing, divine light consciousness becoming thoughtlessly aware.

All levels involve turning attention inward and finding the peace and balance in ones life.

One should also try to meditate in the morning and evening as they have different vibration potencies. It is best during the sunrise as we face east to welcome the new day and the earthly mother, and her seven angels into our heart and life. At sunset we meditate facing west as we welcome the heavenly father, and his seven angels into our heart and dreams.

To Meditate

First we should sit in silence for a few minutes, and allow all the thoughts of the day to dissipate, if they refuse just ask them to leave and say "not now". After we settle, put your right hand (action) on our heart, in the heart resides the Spirit and energy of the universal light consciousness. From our heart we should ask the Divine Light Consciousness to imbibe us and then spread out to the whole world. We are connected to the Divine and whatever we desire will happen if we have full confidence from within our self.

With eyes closed and palms facing upward we then start our meditation.

1. Put your right hand in the upper part of your abdomen on the left hand side, the centre of your Dharma.

Here we say—

Let me be the light through my dharmic life, through my righteousness. Let people see the Dharma by which my enlightenment has become my power and my pure desire to ascend.

2. Take your right hand in the lower portion of your abdomen, of the stomach on the left hand side. The centre of pure knowledge (VOID). Here we will understand Divine Law, and what really is Kundalini and the Charkas. So let the attention be more on the divine love than on all the mundane human conditionings and drama.

3. Put your right hand on the upper part of your abdomen and close your eyes. Mother Kundalini has given me the awareness to become my own Guru and master. Say the affirmation.

Let there be no neglect.

Let there be dignity in my character.

Let there be wisdom in my behavior.

Let there be compassion and Love for all things from the cell of the body, to mother earth, to the universal light consciousness.

Let me not show my ego, but have a deep divine knowledge about humility and Love.

4. Raise your right hand place it on your heart. Here we expand and encompass the whole Universe with my Love, and every moment we should imbibe the beauty of God's divine pure love.

I am the spirit, I am beyond this intellect, this ego and the drama of life and I am the spirit.

5. Place your right hand on the left Vishuddhi between the neck and the shoulder.

I will not indulge the falsehood.

I will not escape my faults but face them.

I will not try to find fault with others, but in my own wisdom forgive.

Let my pure love become so great that I understand all life is my family, all is one.

Let the feeling that I am part and parcel of the whole imbibe my entire being and attention.

6. Your right hand on your forehead, say:

Divine Mother Kundalini I forgive everyone, I forgive myself.

7. Put your right hand on the backside of your head and say here:

All I do: I do without ego, I do without attachment, and I do without fear, because I am in the attention of the divine light consciousness, the heavenly father, and the earthly mother, and all the angels of divine light.

8. Put your hand on the crown of your head and say:

Please guide me to the light, let me become the light, let me share the light.

Mantras

Through the study of Cymantics and sound vibration, we can understand the foundation of the mantra's power projecting desire into reality.

In Sanskrit, "manana" means to meditate. The OM is the first, and universal Mantra of creation, and also represents the universal tonal frequency to which our Mother Earth (nature) vibrates. Every planet, galaxy and star system, in fact, every single life entity has a vibrational frequency. The Earth frequency of 136.1Hz, is also the frequency of ~OM~. In recent brainwave research, this cosmic note or OM frequency, helped meditation achieve the desired "Theta" brainwave states quickly.

The translation of this OM or Earth frequency into the Sanskrit Mantra evolved by way of the ancient Rishi and Indian Sages, through the ancient Vedic traditions of India. Mantras are a way to connect with the universal light consciousness, through recreating the divine tonal aspects that reside within and outside our human form. Mantras represent our subtle connection or key to all creative forces, including the deities and the divine aspects of our Mother Earth, Heavenly Father, primordial masters, and the Adi Shakti power. It is also a customary practice within Buddhism, Sikhism and Jainism.

A Mantra is a word or tone spoken or sung in meditation. It is the re-creation of a spiritual tone "OM" or an extension of words that have a divine connotation creating the vibration and connection that has a direct effect on the inner spiritual Chakras and physical being. When a soul meditates and chants a mantra, he/she is first imbibing the spiritual energy for the specific purpose or chakra, for which the mantra is intended.

Mantras add to the vibration awareness by recreating the tonal sound of creation within. This is done by chanting the spiritual sound or mantra that allows different levels of divine connection. For this reason, great emphasis is put on correct pronunciation *(resulting in ancient development of a science of phonetics in India)* and understanding the meaning of the mantra, as the qualities and blessings are manifested through the current meaning and pronunciation. Pure desire to evolve ones spiritual ascent is also important to attaining this awakening—second is humility and controlling the ego. It is also important to know that wrong pronunciation or misuse of the sacred mantras without understanding divine protocols is not useful. Daily mantras/affirmations can be used to divert the mind from basic instinctual desires or material attachments such as OM—*"I am a pure love and awareness".*

Mantras are most effective while sitting in meditation. By using the Sanskrit names we are invoking the vibration of the name or tone that has a specific goal and connection to the divine aspects passed down from ancient times. The seeker usually absorbs these mantras by focusing on a specific chakra or deity that will manifest the results desired. So when a realized soul or seeker meditates and says a mantra, he/she is manifesting the spiritual energy for the specific purpose or chakra the mantra is intended.

Mantras—The Affirmations

There are two types of Mantras, each are used differently:

1—The Affirmation

2—Poem of Praise

The Affirmation

The Affirmation is the act of affirming or asserting your humility and pure desire, through a prayer or phrase. This will imbibe the humanity that allows the innocence to manifest, and as this takes place the gateway (Agnya Chakra) opens the Sahasrara Chakra to your spiritual enlightenment or spiritual assent to the Light Consciousness.

To open the Chakra or when the residing deity of the Chakra recedes, it is because the qualities of that Chakra do not maintain themselves without constant attention and spiritual nourishment. The Affirmation is used to bring our humility to the pure essence so the qualities return and imbibe us with the vibration of the divine light.

LEFT SIDE

1—**Mooladhara**

Shri Maha Devi, by Your Grace, I am the powerful innocence of a child.

2—**Swadisthan**

Shri Maha Devi, by Your Grace, I am the creative knowledge.

3—**Nabhi**

Shri Maha Devi, by Your Grace, I am satisfied, I am peace.

Shri Maha Devi, by Your Grace, I am a giving person.

3a—**Void**

Shri Maha Devi, am I my own guru/master?

Shri Maha Devi, by Your Grace, I am my own guru/master.

4—**Heart**

Shri Mother Kundalini, am I the Spirit?

Shri Mother Kundalini, by Your Grace, I am the Spirit.

Shri Mother Kundalini, by Your Grace, please forgive me for any mistakes against my Spirit.

Shri Mother Kundalini, by Your Grace, I am the instrument of divine love.

5—**Vishuddhi**

Shri Maha Devi, I am not guilty, as I am the Spirit, How can I be guilty?

6—**Agnya**

Shri Maha Devi, by Your Grace, please forgive my discretion.

7—**Right Sahasrara**

Shri Maha Devi, by Your Grace, I am protected from all the challenges to my ascent.

8—**Whole left side**

Shri Maha Devi, by Your Grace, I am fortunate to be in the attention of the Holy Spirit.

RIGHT SIDE

1—**Mooladhara**

Shri Maha Devi, verily You are the Killer of devils.

2—**Swadisthan**

Shri Maha Devi, I do nothing. Verily You are the Doer.

3—**Nabhi**

Shri Maha Devi, verily you are the spiritual dignity within me. You solve my money/family worries and take care of my well-being.

3a—**Void**

Shri Maha Devi, verily you are my Guru/Master.

4—**Heart**

Shri Parvati, verily you are the responsibility in me.

Shri Parvati, verily you are the boundaries of good conduct and the benevolence of a good father.

5—**Vishuddhi**

Shri Maha Devi, verily You are the sweet expression of my words and deeds.

6—**Agnya**

Shri Maha Devi, I forgive everyone and I forgive myself.

Shri Maha Devi, by Your Grace, please keep me in your attention.

7—**Left Sahasrara**

Shri Maha Devi, verily you defeat all the challenges to ascent.

Shri Maha Devi, verily you are the Holy Spirit, Shri Audi Shakti, and Maha Kundalini.

The Poem of Praise

These Sanskrit verses are said in praise of the residing Deities, thus giving sustenance and energy to those centers. The qualities of the Deities manifest themselves in everyday life spontaneously, bringing you towards an integration of all the qualities of the Divine. Sanskrit is the language of the light and is used to help the Kundalini rise. Sanskrit derives its sound vibrations of the universal OM.

Aum Twameva Sakshat, Shri__ ***Chakra / Deitie*** __Sakshat,

Shri Adi Shakti Parvati,

Shri Maha Devi Namoh Namah

LEFT SIDE

1. Mooladhara	Shri Ganesha
2. Swadisthan	Shri Nirmala Vidya
3. Nabhi	Shri Gruha Lakshmi
	Shri Hazarat-Ali Fatima
3a Void	Adi Guru Dattatreya
4. Heart	Shiva Parvati
5. Vishuddhi	Vishnumaya
6. Agnya	Mahavira

CENTER Channel

1. Mooladhara	Shri Ganesha
1a Mooladhara	Shri Ganesha Gauri (Sacrum Bone)
	Shri Kundalini Mata
2. Swadisthan	Shri Bhramadeva Saraswati
3. Nabhi	Shri Laxmi Narayana
3a Void	Adi Guru Dattatreya
4. Heart	Durga Mata / Shri Jagadamba

5. Vishuddhi	Shri Radha Krishna
6. Agnya	Shri Jesus Mary
(Front)	Shri Maha Kartikeya
(Back)	Shri Maha Ganesha

RIGHT SIDE

1. Mooladhara	Shri Kartikeya
2. Swadisthan	Shri Nirmala Chitta
3. Nabhi	Shri Raja Lakshmi
3a Void	Adi Guru Dattatreya
4. Heart	Sita Rama
5. Vishuddi	Yeshoda
6. Agnya	Buddha
7. Vishuddhi	Yeshoda

8. **SAHASRARA**

Om Twameva Sakshat Shri Mahalaxmi Mahasaraswati Mahakali Trigunatmika Kundalini Sakshat Shri Adi Shakti Shri Maha Devi Namoh Namah

Om Twameva Sakshat Shri Kalki Sakshat Shri Adi Shakti Shri Maha Devi Namoh Namah

Om Twameva Sakshat Shri Kalki Sakshat Shri Sahasrara Swamini Moksha Pradayini Shri Maha Devi Namoh Namah

Nadis—Channels

(I) Ida Nadi	*Whole Left Side* **Mahakali / Bhairava**
(II) Pingala Nadi	*Whole Right side* **Mahasaraswati / Hanumana**
(III) Shushumna Nadi	*The Centre* **Mahalakshmi / Ganesha**

Meditation Mantras for clearing the Chakras

To raise the Kundalini, we can invoke the different aspects of the Divine (Deities), which resonate within each Chakra.

The basic form is as follows:

Om Twameva Sakshat ________ Sakshat, Shri Adi Shakti Parvati Shri Maha Devi Namoh Namah

Substitute the name of the Deity related to the chakra you wish to clear.

THE DEITIES	THE CHAKRA	MANIFESTATION
Shri Ganesha	Left - Mooladhara Chakra	Innocence, wisdom
Shri Kartikeya	Right - Mooladhara	Valor, knowledge
Shri Gauri Kundalini	Mooladhara	Seat of Kundalini, purity
Shri Brahma Granthi Vibedhini	Brahma Granthi	Material attachment
Shri Brahmadeva-Saraswati	Swadhistan	Creativity
Shri Nirmala Vidya	Left Swadhistan	Pure knowledge
Shri Hazrat Ali Fatima	Right Swadhistan	Creative action
Shri Laxhmi-Vishnu	Nabhi	Sustenance
Shri Gruha Laxhmi	Left Nabhi	Household matter
Shri Shesha Laxmana	Right Nabhi	Liver attention
Shri Raja Lakshmi	Right Nabhi	Liver, attention
Shri Adi Guru Dattrateya	Void	Guru principle
Shri Jagadamba	Center Heart	Sense of security
Shri Shiva-Parvati	Left Heart	Mother's place—existence
Shri Sita-Rama	Right Heart	Father's place—Behavior
Shri Vishnu Granthi Vibehdini	Vishnu Granthi	Beginning of Ego
Shri Radha-Krishna	Vishuddi	Collectivity
Shri Sarva Mantra Siddhi	Vishuddi	Collectivity
Shri Vishnumaya	Left Vishuddhi	Self-esteem
Shri Yeshoda	Right Vishuddhi	Respect for others
Shri Vittala Rukmini	Right Vishuddhi	Respect for others
Shri Hamsa Chakra Swamini	Hamsa Chakra	Discrimination
Shri Ekadesha Rudra	11 destructive powers of Kalki—faith in God	
Shri Jesus-Mary	Agnya The Lord's Prayer	Forgiveness
Shri Mahavira	Left Agnya	Superego—conditioning
Shri Buddha	Right Agnya	Ego
Shri Maha Ganesha		
Shri Maha Bhairava		
Shri Maha Hiranya Garbha	Back Agnya	
Shri Mahakali-Bhairava	Left Side—Ida Nadi:	Emotion
Shri Mahasaraswati-Hanumana	Right Side—Pingala Nadi	Physical & mental activity

Sahasrara Mantra

The Sahasrara Chakra is a thousand petal Lotus manifesting on the physical nerves under the surface of the head. It is also the integration of all the lower Chakras fusing their powers and rising up for our enlightenment onto the realm of the universal light consciousness. When one reaches enlightenment the qualities of all the Chakras manifest on the crown of the head, looking like dancing flames or the halo of ancient Christian depictions of Jesus.

Om Twameva Sakshat Shri Mahalaxshmi Mahasaraswati

Mahakali Trigunatmika Kundalini Sakshat Shri Adi Shakti

Shri Maha Devi Namoh Namah

Om Twameva Sakshat Shri Kalki Sakshat

Shri Adi Shakti Shri Maha Devi Namoh Namah

Om Twameva Sakshat Shri Kalki Sakshat

Shri Sahasrara Swamini Moksha Pradayini

Shri Maha Devi Namoh Namah

Morning Prayer

May I on this day, be all I can be

May I on this day, be the truth I will say

May I on this day, be part of the whole

And may my thoughts be of a realized soul

May I on this day, be the Love for all life

Maha Devi, imbibe all my heart and my mind.

1—Mooladhara Chakra

Shri Ganesha

Shri Ganesha—Hubble Telescope

Shri Ganesha

The essence or qualities of eternal innocence and wisdom manifest through the aspect of Shri Ganesha in the first chakra *(Mooladhara)*. His essence is the personification of innocence and wisdom. He removes obstacles to our evolution and bestows eternal wisdom and good fortune. Metaphorically Shri Ganesha is depicted as the son of Shri Parvati and Shri Shiva *(holy trinity)* in Vedic Mythology and is often shown with an open hand, palms upturned, sometimes holding a gift granting favors to his devotees. His vehicle is a rat or a mouse, as these creatures symbolically represent their ability to gnaw through obstacles. The combination of the elephant and the rat or mouse ensures that all obstacles, regardless of size, are removed so one can achieve the higher spiritual path without hindrance of the material realms. Shri Ganesha contains the entire matter of all the universes and all mind as part of the universal light consciousness that guides and protects.

The mantra of **Shri Ganesha** dissolves all obstacles, as the ego becomes the last hurdle to attaining balance.

Om Twameva Sakshat Shri Ganesha Sakshat

Shri Adi Shakti Parvati Namoh Namah

Symbols of Shri Ganesha

Swastika

The swastika - a sign of auspiciousness, a lucky cross-associated with the good fortunes given by Shri Ganesha. It is also representing the spinning "chakra" and blessing received when a dharmic life of innocence is achieved.

Noose

The noose, usually held in Ganesha's left hand, is unlike the more warring weapons of the other Deities. It is a gentle implement, used to capture and then hold obstacles or difficulties, to direct us along the right path much as a rider guides his steed by the use of the bridle and reins.

Modaka

The modaka is a sweet, round cake made of rice and sugar, and offered to Ganesha, The modaka is looked upon as the sweetest of all things sweet: as Siddhi, the gladdening fulfillment or joy hidden within everything.

Tusk

The single broken tusk held in Ganesha's fourth hand is considered the symbol of sacrifice. For the elephant the tusks are beauty and pride and strength. But, in order to save the Mahabharata, Ganesha broke His own tusk. Thus teaching us the noble principle of personal sacrifice."

How To Awaken—Shri Ganesha—Within

Prayer

Shri Ganesha, I am going to be worthy of your love,

Please make me innocent, as a child

Please give me wisdom of self, and universal Divine Light Consciousness.

Ganesha Atharva Sheersha—*Sanskrit Mantra*

Ganapathi Atharva Sheersha - is a part of Atharvana Veda. It is an Upanishad and universally is considered the greatest and most effective prayer addressed to Shri Ganesha. This is also called Gana Upanishad or Ganapthi Seersha Upanishad.

Om Namaste Ganapataye, Twameva Pratyaksham Tattwamasi,

Twameva Kevalam Kartasi, Twameva Kevalam Dhartasi,

Twameva Kevalam Hartasi, Twameva Sarvam Khalvidam Brahmasi,

Twam Sakshat Atmasi Nityam,

Ritam Vachmi Satyam Vachmi, Ava twam Mam, Ava Vaktaram,

Ava Shrotaram, Ava Dataram, Ava Dhataram, Ava noo Chanam.

Ava Shishyam, Ava Pash chat tat, Ava Puras tat,

Avot tarat tat, Ava Dakshinat tat, Ava Chor Dhvat tat,

Ava Dharat tat, Sarvato Mam, Pahi Pahi Saman tat.

Twam Vang mayas, Twam Chin mayah,

Twam ananda mayas, Twam Brahma mayah,
Twam Sat chit ananda dvitiyosi, Twam Pratyaksham Brahmasi,
Twam Gyana mayo Vigyana mayosi, Sarvam Jagadidam,
Twatto Jayate, Sarvam Jagadidam twat tas tish thati,
Sarvam Jagadidam, Twayi Laya me shyati,
Sarvam Jagadidam, Twayi Pratyeti,
Twam Bhoomi rapo nalo nilo Nabhah, Twam Chatvari Vak Padani,
Twam Guna traya teetah, Twam Deha traya teetah,
Twam Kala traya teetah,
Twam Moola dhara sthitosi Nityam, Twam Shakti trayat makah,
Twam Yogino Dhyayanti Nityam, Twam Brahma, Twam Vishnus,
Twam Rudras, Twam Indras Twam Agnis, Twam Vayus, Twam Sooryas,
Twam Chandramas, Twam Brahma bhoor bhuvah Swarom,
Ganadim Poorva much charya Varna dim Tada nan taram,
Anus varah Para tarah, Ardhendu lasitam Tare na Ruddham,
Etat tava Manuswa roopam, Gakarah Poorva roopam,
Akaro Madhyama roopam, Anuswarash chantya roopam,
Bindu ru tara roopam, Nada Sandha nam, Sanhita Sandhih,
Saisha Ganesha Vidya, Ganaka Rishihi, Nich rid Gayatri Chandah,
Ganapatir Devata, Om Gam Ganapataye Namah.
Eka Dantaya Vidmahe.Vakra Tundaya Dheemahi,
Tanno Dantih Prachodayat,
Ekadantam Chatur hastam Pasham ankush dharinam,
Radam Cha Varadam Hastair bi bhranam Mooshak dhvajam,
Raktam Lambodaram Shoorpa karnakam rakta vasasam,
Rakta gandhanu liptangam Rakta pushpaihi Supoojitam,
Bhaktanu Kampitam, Devam jagat Karanama chyutam.
Aavir bhootam Cha Shristyadau Prakritehe Purushat param,
Evam Dhya yati Yo Nityam Sa Yogi Yoginam Varah.

Namo Vratapataye, Namo Ganapataye, Namaha Pramatha Pataye,
Namaste Astu, Lambodaraya ekadantaya,
Vighna Nashine, Shiva sutaya Shree, Varada moortaye Namah.

Sakshat Shri Audi Shakti Shri Parvati Shri Maha Devi Namo Namah

Ganesha Atharva Sheersha—*Translation*

OM. Salutations to Ganapati. You are verily the (Primordial) principle. Only you are the doer. Only you are the supporter of the Earth. Only you are the remover of obstacles. You are verily the Brahman. You are verily the eternal Self. From the front, from back-side, from north, from south, from above and from below: protect me from all sides.

You are in the literature, you are in the Consciousness, You are the Bliss.

You are one with the Brahman. You are the absolute Truth-Consciousness-Bliss (Sat-Chit-Ananda). You are all knowledge. You are the recognition. The entire world has originated from you and it is sustained by you; it ends in you and you manifest as the world.

You are the earth, water, air and sky. You are the four parts of speech (para, pashyati, madhyama, vaikhari).

You are beyond the three Gunas (satwa, raja, tama). You are beyond the three times (present, future, past). You are always present at Mooladhara. You are within the three powers (Mahalaxshmi, Mahasaraswati, Mahakali). Yogis always meditate upon you. You are Brahma, Vishnu, Rudra (Shiva), Indra, Agni (God of fire), Vayu (wind God), the Sun, the Moon and the three Lokas (terrestrial, celestial, atmospheric).

Uttering Gana, followed first by varna (syllable), then by the nasal sound. Your form is sporting the half moon and star. G (Gakar) is the first form. A (Akar) is the middle form and the nasal sound is the last form. The Bindu is on top. The sound, thus made, may be meditated on for the knowledge of all Vedas. It is Ganesha Vidya. We want to have the knowledge of the God with one tusk. We meditate upon the God with the curled up trunk. May he stimulate our intellect.

He has one tusk, four arms and is holding a noose and goad. With one hand He is blessing. He has a mouse as His vehicle. He is red in complexion, has a big belly and ears like winnowing fans. He wears red clothes and smears red colored fragrant paste on His body.

He is worshipped with red flowers. He is the God who has compassion for His devotees and is said to be the cause of the world. He manifests before the creation from supreme Prakriti and Purusha. He, the greatest of all Yogis, is eternally worshipped by the Yogis.

Obeisance to the Lord of assemblage (Vrata-pati). Obeisance to the Lord of Ganas (Gana-pati). Obeisance to the Master of Cupid. Obeisance to the big bellied God; the remover of obstacles; the Son of Shiva.

The 12 Names of Shri Ganesha—*Sanskrit*

It is said the one who says, or even listens to these twelve names,
At the beginning of learning, marriages, entrance and exit,
in battles and at times of difficulty, faces no hurdle.

Sum-ukha	having good face
Eka-danta	having one tusk
Kap-ila	eternal
Gaja-karnaka	having elephant's ears
Lam-bodar	big-bellied
Vi-kata	huge
Vig-hnanasha	destroyer of obstacles
Gana-dhip	leader of Ganas
Dhoom-raketu	grey-bannered
Gana-dhyaksha	chief of Ganas
Bhala-chandra	sporting moon on forehead
Ga-jananah	elephant-faced

Nirvighnamastu—*Palm Leaf Manuscript (Sanskrit)*

Sumukhashch Aikadantashcha Kapilo Gajakarnakah
Lambodarshcha Vikato Vighnanasho Ganadhipah
Dhoomraketur Ganadhyaksho Bhalachandro Gajananah
Dwadaishitani namaniyah pathet shrunu yadapi
Vidyarambhe vivahecha praveshe nirgame tatha
Sangrame sankate chaiva vighnastasya najayate

Aum, OM—The Prayer

Let our ears only hear that which is true;
Let our eyes only see that which is pure;
Let our beings only praise that which is Divine;
And let those who listen hear not the voice but the wisdom of divine love.

The Prayer

Salutation to Shri Ganesh, Sakshat Shri Jesus
Sakshat Shri Maha Devi Namoh Namah.

It is You who is the beginning of all the beginnings.
It is You who is the doer of all deeds which have been done,
are being done and will be done.
It is You who supports all things that are supported.
It is You who protects all things that are protected.
It is You who is the complete, all-pervading Spirit. God's Divine energy.

Speak Only Truth

Let the presence, awakened by Mother Kundalini in me, speak;
Let the presence, awakened by Mother Kundalini in me, listen;
Let the presence, awakened by Mother Kundalini in me, bless;
Let the presence, awakened by Mother Kundalini in me, protect;
Let the presence, awakened by Mother Kundalini in me, Love.

Mother Kundalini is the feminine—Audi Shakti power of creation reflected within. Mother Kundalni you are the essence of all the Sacred Literature and Holy Words, and you are the Energy that understands the Holy Words; You are the Divine combination of complete Truth, complete Happiness and complete Energy; And you are beyond thought and ego;

You are the connection to all knowledge, and you are the use to which the Knowledge is put. You exist until the end of all things, and after the end of all things, You are; You create the end of all things, and after the end of all things, You remain;

MAHA DEVI you are the Universal Mother and you are the Earthly Mother, you are all, because all is one.

You are the Water, You are the Fire,

You are the Air, and You are the space above the Air;

You are the Gunas; and You are beyond the Gunas;

You are the Body; and You are beyond the Body;

You are the Essence of Time; and You are beyond Time;

You and exist at the Mooladhara Chakra and beyond,

You are the Spirit; and you are beyond the Spirit;

And those who would join the light consciousness, meditate upon You.

You are Brahman, Vishnu, Rudra;

You are Indra, Agni, Vayu;

You are the Sun at noon; You are the Full Moon; Through all of these, and more,

You are the all-pervading energy of innocence and wisdom.

You are the Divine servant who humbly stoops to wash the feet of saints.

You are all things; you are the key to the Akashic libraries and of all the scriptures, where Truth is told;

You are the Crescent Moon;

You are the Stars; and,

You are beyond the Stars; All things, from tiny cel to Universe, is You.

You are where the sound of Om begins ;

You are the silence between the sounds;

You are the rhythm of all music and all prayers; This is the knowledge of Shri Ganesh, and,

You, share all that is, and all that is divine in Shri Ganesh, the master of all Knowledge.

You are the Goddess of creation, life and love.

AUM GAM Ganapataye

Ganesha To Your powers, let all surrender; Let the left side of memory and the right side of action surrender to You and let enlightenment prevail.

Your first tooth you have, and four-hands; one holding a rope, the second a goad, the third is raised in blessing and the fourth offers sustenance.

Your banner is that of a humble mouse. You have long ears and are clothed in red; red decorates you and you are worshipped with red flowers.

You have compassion for those who love you, and it is for those who love you that you manifest as the eternal child on this Earth. You are the force that creates, the energy that pervades and the Spirit that protects. Those who seek union with the divine light pray through you: Those who seek union with divine light worship you.

AUM GAM Nirmal Jesusya

To Your powers, Aum Jesus, let all surrender;

Let the left side of memory and the right side of action surrender to you and let your enlightenment prevail.

You are the Word that was the beginning; the alfa as Jesus

You are the Word that will be the ending. the omega as kalki

You are he who was born of a Virgin, and lived on the cross;

You are he who absorbs all sins, and who showed death is life again;

You are God in Man, and You are worshipped with red flowers.

You have compassion for those who love you, and it is for those who love you that you came to this Earth, from the realm of the light.

You are the force that creates, the energy that pervades and the Spirit that protects. Those who seek union with God love you.

Those who seek union with God worship your qualities.

Shri Ganesha, Salutations to You.

Shri Jesus, Salutations to You.

He who is the beginning of all worship, Salutations to You.

He who destroys all the powers of evil, Salutations to You.

Sakshat, Son of Lord Shiva, who is unending blessings, Salutations to You.

Sakshat, Son of Mary, who is unending Love,

Salutations to You. Sakshat, Maha Devi, who is unending Joy,

Salutations to You.

Sakshat Shri Adi Shakti Maha Devi Namoh Namah

Aarti—To Shri Ganesha

Sukha karta dukha harta varta vighnachi

Noorvi poorvi prem krupa jayachi

Sarvangi sunder oti shendurachi

Kanthi jhalke mal mukta falanchi

Refrain

Jai Deva Jai Deva
Jai mangala murti
Darshan matre man kamana purti
Jai Deva Jai Deva...

Ratna kachita fara tuza Gauri Kumara
Chandanachi uti kumkum keshara
Hiray jadita mukuta shoba tobara
Roon jhunti noopooray charni ghagariya

Refrain

Lambodar pitambar fanivar vandana
Sarela soda vakra tunda trinayana
Das ram acha vatpahe sadana
Sankashti pavave nirvani rakshave survar vandana

The Mantras for Shri Ganesha

Om Svaha
Om Shrim Svaha
Om Shrim Hrim Svaha
Om Shrim Hrim Klim Svaha
Om Shrim Hrim Klim Glaum Svaha
Om Shrim Hrim Klim Glaum Gam Svaha
Om Shrim Hrim Klim Glaum Ityantah Gam Svaha
Om Vara Varada Ityantah Svaha
Garvajanam Me Vasam Ityanto Svaha
Anaya Svaha Itantah
Aim Hrim Klim Chamundaya Vije Namaha

The 108 Names of Shri Ganesha

Om Vinayakaya Namaha	Adoration to the Peerless One.
Om Vighnarajaya Namaha	Adoration to the Ruler of Obstacles.
Gauriputraya	Adoration to the Son of Gauri.
Ganeshvaraya	Adoration to the Lord of Categories.
Skandagrajaya	Adoration to the First-born, Skanda's elder.
Avyayaya	Adoration to the Inexhaustible One.
Putaya	Adoration to the Pure One.
Dakshaya	Adoration to the Skilful One.
Adhyakshaya	Adoration to Him who presides.
Dvijapriyaya	Adoration to Him who is fond of the twice born.
Agnigarbhachide	Adoration to Him who contains fire within.
Indrashripradaya	Adoration to the Bestower of Power to Indra.
Vanipradaya	Adoration to the Bestower of Speech.
Avyayaya	Adoration to the Inexhaustible One.
Sarvasiddhipradaya	Adoration to the Bestower of All Fulfilment.
Sharvatanayaya	Adoration to the Son of Shiva.
Sharvaripriyaya	Adoration to Him who is fond of night.
Sarvatmakaya	Adoration to Srishtikartre Adoration to the Creator.
Divyaya	Adoration to the Resplendent One.
Anekarchitaya	Adoration to Him who is worshipped by multitude.
Shivaya	Adoration to the Auspicious One.
Shuddhaya	Adoration to the Pure One.
Buddhipriyaya	Adoration to Him who is fond of Intelligence.
Shantaya	Adoration to the Peaceful One.
Brahmacharine	Adoration to Him who is celibate.
Gajananaya	Adoration to Him who has an elephant's face.
Dvaimatreyaya	Adoration to Him who has two Mothers.
Munistutyaya	Adoration to Him who is praised by sages.
Bhaktavighnavinashanaya	Adoration to the Destroyer of Devotee's obstacles.
Ekadantaya	Adoration to Him who has one tusk.

Chaturbahave	Adoration to Him who has four arms.
Chaturaya	Adoration to the Ingenious One.
Shaktisamyutaya	Adoration to the Powerful One.
Lambodaraya	Adoration to Him who has a large belly.
Shurpakarnaya	Adoration to Him whose ears are like winnowing fans.
Haraye	Adoration to Him who is lion like.
Brahmaviduttamaya	Adoration to the foremost knower of Brahman.
Kalaya	Adoration to the Embodiment of Time.
Grahapataye	Adoration to the Lord of Planets.
Kamine	Adoration to Him who is Love.
Somasuryagnilochanaya	Adoration to Him whose eyes are the Sun & the Moon.
Pashankushadharaya	Adoration to Him who wields the noose and goad.
Chandaya	Adoration to Him whose actions are rhythmical.
Gunatitaya	Adoration to Him who transcends qualities
Niranjanaya	Adoration to Him who is without blemish.
Akalmashaya	Adoration to Him who is without impurity.
Svayamsiddhaya	Adoration to Him who achieved fulfillment by Himself.
Siddharchitapadambujaya	Adoration to Him whose lotus feet sages worship.
Bijapuraphalasaktay	Adoration to Him who is fond of pomegranates.
Varadaya	Adoration to the Bestower of Boons.
Shashvataya	Adoration to the Unchanging One.
Krutine	Adoration to Him who works incessantly.
Dvijapriyaya	Adoration to Him who is fond of the Twice-born.
Vitabhayaya	Adoration to Him who is free from fear.
Gadine	Adoration to Him who wields the mace.
Chakrine	Adoration to Him who wields the discus.
Ikshuchapadhrite	Adoration to Him who holds the surgar cane bow.

Shridaya	Adoration to the Bestower of Wealth.
Ajaya	Adoration to the Unborn One.
Utpalakaraya	Adoration to Him who holds the blue lotus blossom.
Shripataye	Adoration to the Lord of Wealth.
Stutiharshitaya	Adoration to Him who rejoices in praise.
Kuladribhettre	Adoration to Him who supports the Mountain ranges.
Jatilaya	Adoration to the Intricate One.
Kalikalmashanashanaya	Adoration to the Destroyer of Kali's Impurity.
Chandrachudamanye	Adoration to Him who wears a Moon on His Head.
Kantaya	Adoration to the Beloved One.
Papaharine	Adoration to the Destroyer of Wickedness.
Samahitaya	Adoration to the Attentive One.
Ashritaya	Adoration to Him who is our refuge.
Shrikaraya	Adoration to Him who manifests prosperity
Saumyaya	Adoration to the Pleasant One.
Bhaktavanchitadayakaya	Adoration to the Grantor of Devotee's desires.
Shantaya	Adoration to the Peaceful One.
Kaivalyasukhadaya	Adoration to the Bestower of Absolute Happiness.
Sachidanandavigrahaya	Adoration to Him whose form is Existence, Knowledge and Bliss.
Jnanine	Adoration to the Wise One.
Dayayutaya	Adoration to Him who is full of compassion
Dantaya	Adoration to Him who has self-control.
Brahmadveshavivarjitaya	Adoration to Him who is free from aversion to the Supreme.
Pramattadaityabhayadaya	Adoration to Him who is feared by power intoxicated men.
Shrikanthaya	Adoration to Him who has a beautiful throat
Vibhudeshvaraya	Adoration to the Lord of the Wise.
Ramarchitaya	Adoration to the God worshipped by Rama.

Vidhaye	Adoration to the Controller of Destiny.
Nagarajayajnopavitavate	Adoration to Him who wears a cobra as a sacred thread.
Sthulakanthaya	Adoration to Him who has a stout neck.
Svayamkartre	Adoration to Him who acts independently.
Samaghoshapriyaya	Adoration to Him who is fond of the
Sound of Sama Veda Parasmai	Adoration to Him for whom there is no Other.
Sthulatundaya	Adoration to Him who has a stout trunk.
Agranye	Adoration to the First-Born.
Dhiraya	Adoration to the Courageous One.
Vagishaya	Adoration to the Lord of Speech.
Siddhidayakaya	Adoration to the Bestower of Fulfilment.
Durvabilvapriyaya	Adoration to Him who is fond of Durva and Bilva.
Avyaktamurtaye	Adoration to the Manifestation of the Unmanifest.
Adbhutamurtimate	Adoration to the Wondrous Form.
Shailendratanujotsanga	Adoration to Him who is fond of playing
Khelanotsukamanasaya	His Mother Parvati, daughter of the Mountain Lord.
Svalavanyasudhasarajita	Adoration to Him who is a vast ocean of sweetness more charming than God of Love.
Samastajagadadharaya	Adoration to the Supporter of All the Worlds.
Mayine	Adoration to the Source of Illusory Power.
Mushikavahanaya	Adoration to Him who rides the mouse.
Hrushtaya	Adoration to the Rapturous One.
Tushtaya	Adoration to the Content One.
Prasannatmane	Adoration to the Benign One.
Sarvasiddhipradayakaya	Adoration to the Bestower of All Fulfillment.

Sakshat Shri Parvati Shri Adi Shakti Maha Devi Namoh Namah

The 108 Names of Lord Ganesha—*English*

Wakra Tunda Mahakaya Suryakoti Sammaprabha
Nirvighnam Kuru Me Deva Shuba Karyeshu Sarvada

You are the One to be worshipped first.
Obeisance to You again and again.
You are the Word that was in the beginning.
'Obeisance to you..
You are the Omkara
You are the source of life.
You are the source of security.
You are worshipped with red flowers.
You are adored by yogis and yoginis.
You are the Support of the root and the Support of the fruit.
You are auspiciousness and the bestower of auspiciousness.
You are wisdom and the bestower of wisdom.
You are innocence and the bestower of innocence.
You make Holy what evil had soiled.
You build anew what was destroyed.
You resurrect the innocence that was lost.
You are the Lord of Chastity.
You are the bestower of the inner paradise.
You are the refuge of all.
You have compassion for Your devotees.
You are the giver of satisfaction and fulfillment.
You are the beloved Son of Mahagauri.
You are the greatest pupil of Mahasaraswati.
You are the guardian of Mahalakshmi.
You are listened to by Adi Kundalini.
You are manifested in the four heads of Brahmadeva.
You are the foremost disciple of Shiva.
You are the glory of Mahavishnu.
You are the bond of Love between Rama and His brothers.
You lead the dance of Krishna's Gopis.
You are Jesus the Child and Christ the King.

You fill the nets of Jesus' disciples.
You reside in all the Deities. All the Deities reside in you, all are one
You are the house of Yoga.
You are the substance of the Adi Guru.
You become the Adi Guru to reveal Your Mother.
You only know how to worship Your Mother.
You only know Your Mother.
You are the Joy of Your Mother.
You live on the complete blessings of Your Mother.
You live in the present which is the presence of God.
You are the foundation of the Sangha.
You are the body of Dharma.
You are the essence of Buddha.
You are the humility and innocence of the child.
You are the Primordial Friend.
You create the sphere of Yoga.
You are the honesty of Yoga.
You are the eldest Brother of the Yogis.
You bestow the Shakti of chastity upon the Yogis.
You are pleased by humility.
You are pleased by simplicity.
You grant the Knowledge of pure Love.
You grant the Love of pure Knowledge.
You are beyond grasp.
You are beyond temptations.
You are beyond imagination.
You challenge, defeat and punish negativity.
You watch the gates of hell.
You open and close the gates of hell.
That which is not within You is hell.
You are the Lord of the ganas.
You grant the subtlety of discretion.
You remove all the obstacles.
You bless the sanctity of the marriage union.

You call on this earth the realized souls.

You are the dignity of childhood eternal.

You are the Lord of Maharashtra.

You are complete and perfect.

You do not tolerate fanaticism, especially in Sahaja Yogis.

You play and see the play.

You are magnetic and fascinating.

You are the Beloved One.

You are the quality, that makes Love enchanting.

You are the power of all Bandhans.

You are the Savior of our attention.

You have a prominent belly expressing contentment.

You are fond of Kusha grass which is Mother Earth's green saree.

You are fond of Laddhus, because You are the essence of sweetness.

You are fond of dancing for Your Mother's delight.

You fan Your ears to make the Chaitanya blow.

You have one tusk to lift us out of Samsara.

You hold many weapons for the doom of evil doers.

You are the guardian of the Sanctum Sanctorium.

You shine like a thousand Suns.

You rule over a galaxy of lotuses.

You bestow upon the seekers the power to become lotuses.

You are the remembrance of God within all seekers.

You sustain the hope for God during the quest.

You destroy the impurity of Kali Yuga.

You are the bestower of boons.

You are the bestower of absolute happiness.

You gave an infinitesimal fraction of Your power to Manmatha and he conquered the world.

You give to Love its power of attraction.

You are the purity of Love immaculate.

You are the Love that soothes, nourishes and elevates to God.

You are the Love by which we recognize God.

You are the vessel of sacred adoration.

You are lost in the Goddess' darshan.

You bring the Yogi to the Goddess darshan.

You grant the darshan of the form and the formless.

You grant the darshan of Shri Nirguna.

You are the master of protocol of Adi Shakti Maha Devi.

You are the foremost knower of Adi Shakti Maha Devi.

You witness the awesome greatness of Adi Shakti Maha Devi.

You allow the Divine Mother to feel Her Motherhood.

You allow the Divine Father to enjoy Her creation.

You allow the Devoted Yogis to melt into You.

You are the Owner of God just as the child owns his Mother.

You are fond of playing with Your Mother Maha Devi in the snowy regions of the Sahasrara Chakra / Himalaya Mountains of this earthy realm.

Sakshat Shri Adi Shakti Maha Devi Namoh Namah

The 113 Names of Shri Ganesha

Satvatman	He whose Atman expresses Truth.
Satvasagara	He is the ocean of Truth.
Satvavidhe	He knows pure Vidya.
Satva Sakshina	He sees the essence.
Satva Sajaya	He who meditates on the essences.
Amaradhipaya	He who is the eternal Lord.
Bhutakrete	He is the one who creates the past.
Bhutaprete	Salutations to Him who slays the past.
Bhutatman	He is the essence of the past.
Bhutasambhavana	He incarnates as the past.
Bhutabhava	He is the emotions of all that is so far created.
Bhava	He is the emotion.
Bhutavide	He is the expert in all Vidyas so far.
Bhutakarana	He is the cause of all.
Bhuta Sakshina	He is the within of all created.
Prabhuta	He enlightens all that is created.
Bhutanangparamagata	He is the one who takes all that is created beyond.

Bhutasangavidhatmane	He is the one who resides with all that is created.
Bhutashankara	He is the Shankara of all that is created.
Mahanatha	He is the Great Master.
Adi Natha	Primordial Master.
Maheshware	He is the greatest God.
Sarvabhutanirvasatman	He resides in every Spirit.
Bhutashankarparmashina	He kills all that is human i.e. heat due to Sympathetic activity.
Sarvatman	He resides in all the Atmans.
Sarvakritih	The one who encompasses all.
Sarva	He is Everything.
Sarvajna	He is all Knowledge.
Sarvanirnaya	He is the Judgment of everyone.
Sarvasakshina	He is the Witness of everything.
Brihanive	He is the Sun.
Sarvavide	He is the Knower of all Knowledge
Sarvamangala	He is All that is auspicious.
Shanta	He is Peaceful.
Satya	He is Truth.
Samaya	He is with the Maya.
Purna	He is Complete.
Ekakine	He is Alone.
Kamalapati	He is Vishnu.
Rama	He is Rama.
Ramapriya	Rama is very fond of Him.
Viram	He is the full stop.
Ramakarana	He is the cause of Rama.
Shuddha	He is of pure heart.
Ananta	He is Eternal.
Paramaprete	He who achieves ultimate means.
Hamsa	He witnesses pranava. He is discrimination.
Vibhave	He is the Lord of the whole Universe.
Prabhave	He is the enlightenment of all that has been created.

Pralaya	He is the destroyer of creation.
Siddhatmane	He is a Realized Soul.
Paramatman	He is the Highest Spirit.
Siddanangparamagata	He is the One who takes us to the highest state.
Siddhi Siddha	He is the Siddhi and the Siddha.
Ananda	He is joy.
Vijvaraya	He never gets heated.
Mahathaha	His arms are very strong.
Vaholandanavardina	He is the one who gives the greatest joy.
Avyakta Purusha	He is not manifested.
Prajna	He is enlightened awareness.
Parijna	He is beyond all awareness.
Parama Druthishe	He is the one who cares for the emancipation of others.
Buddha	Salutations to the Knower.
Pandita	He is very learned.
Viswatman	He is the Spirit of the whole Universe.
Pranava	He is the one who is **OM**.
Pranavatita	He is beyond Pranava.
Shankaratman	He is the Spirit of Shankara.
Paramaya	He is beyond the Maya.
Devanamparamagata	He takes the Devas to the Parama State.
Achita	He is beyond attention.
Chaitanya	He is the flow of awareness.
Chaitanavikrama	He conquers the hero.
Parabrahmane	He is beyond Brahma.
Param Jyotis	He is the highest light.
Param Dhamne	He is the highest abode.
Param Tapasye	He is the greatest of those who do penances.
Paramsutra	He is the highest thread.
Paramtantra	He is the highest mechanism.
Kshetrajna	He is the Knower of the field.
Loka Pala	He who looks after the people.
Gunatmane	He is the Spirit of the three gunas.

Anantaguna Sampanna	He is of unlimited virtues.
Yajna	He is a fire that burns off and gives auspiciousness.
Hiranyagarbha	He is the Creator.
Garbha	He is the Womb of the Mother.
Surhada	He is a good friend.
Paramananda	He is the highest Joy.
Satyananda	He is the highest Joy of Truth.
Chidtananda	He is the highest Joy of the attention.
Suryamandalmadya	He who resides in the centre of ego.
Janaka	He is the Father of Sita.
Mantravirya	He is the Essence of mantra.
Mantrabija	He is the Seed of mantra.
Shastravirya	He is the Essence of the scriptures.
Ekaiva	He is the One.
Nishkala	He is complete without any phases.
Nirantar	He is Eternal.
Sureshwara	He is God of all the Gods.
Yantrakrute	He is the Creator of yantra.
Yantrine	He is the engineer of yantra.
Yantravide	He is the Knowledge of yantra.
Yantrarudraparajita	He defeats all that comes in.
Yantramata	He is the Way of yantra.
Yantrakara	He resides in and sustains the Kundalini.
Brahmayona	He is the essence of Brahma.
Vishwayona	He is the power.
Guruvai	Salutations to our Guru.
Bramana	He is Brahma.
Trivikrama	He is the conqueror of the three worlds.
Sahasrambayonibhava	Born out of Sahasrara of his Mother.
Rudra	He is the destructive power over enemies of the spirit.
Hrudayastha	He resides in the heart.

Sakshat Shri Parvati Shri Adi Shakti Maha Devi Namoh Namah

The 108 Names of Shri Kartikeya

Skandaya	(Hail Skanda) Vanquisher of mighty foes.
Guhaya	Praise be to the mighty Lord, He who abides in the hearts of devotees true.
Shanmukhaya	Praise be to the six-faced one.
Bala Nethrasutaya	Praise be to the Son of the three-eyed Shiva
Prabave	Praise be to the Lord supreme.
Pingalaya	Praise be to the golden-hued one.
Krittikasunave	Hail to the Son of the starry maids.
Shikhi Vahanaya	Hail to the rider on the peacock.
Dwadashbhujaya	Hail to the Lord with the twelve hands.
Dwadashnithraya	Hail to the Lord with twelve eyes.
Shaktidharaye	Hail to the wielder of the lance.
Pisidasprapancha Naya	Praise be to the destroyer of the asuras.
Tarakasura Samharine	Praise be to the destroyer of Tarakasura.
Rakshopala Vimarthanaya	Praise be to the victor over the asuric forces
Mathaya	Praise be to the Lord of felicity.
Pramathaya	Praise be to the Lord of Bliss.
Unmathaya	Hail, oh passionate One.
Sura Sainya Surakshakaya	Hail, savior of the devas.
Devasenapataye	Hail, commander of the heavenly hosts.
Pragnaye	Hail, Lord of widwom.
Kripalave	Hail, compassionate One.
Bhaktavatsalaya	Lover of devout ones, praise be to Thee.
Umasuthaya	Son of Uma, praise be to Thee.
Saktidharaya	Oh, mighty Lord, praise be to Thee.
Kumaraya	Lord of eternal youth, praise be to Thee.
Krauncha Taranaye	He who rent as under the krauncha mount, Praise be to Thee.
Senanye	Praise be to the Army chief.
Agnijanmane	To the effulgence of fire, all hail.
Visakhaye	To Him who shone on the astral visaka, All hail.
Sankarathmajaye	Thou, son of Sankara, all hail.

Sivaswamine	Thou, Preceptor of Shiva, all hail.
Ganaswamine	Oh Lord of the Ganas, all hail.
Sarva Swamine	Oh Lord God Almighty, all hail.
Sanathanaya	Oh Lord eternal, praise be to Thee.
Anantashaktaye	Thou, potent Lord, praise be to Thee.
Akshopiyaye	Unsullied by arrows art Thou, praise be to Thee.
Parvathipriya Nandanaya	Thou, beloved of Parvati, praise be to Thee.
Ganga Suthaya	On, son of Goddess Ganga, praise be to Thee.
Sarod buthaya	Hail, Thou who did nestle in the Saravanai Lake.
Pavakatmajaya	Hail, Thou who are born of fire.
Abhuthaya	Hail, Thou, the Unborn Lord.
Agnigarbhaya	Hail, Thou who didst sustain the fire.
Sarmigarbhaya	Hail, Thou who didst arise out of the Vanni flame.
Visvarethase	Thou, Glory of the absolute Paramsiva, all hail.
Surarigne	Oh, Subduer of the foes of the devas, all hail.
Hiranyavarnaya	Thou, respondent One, all hail.
Subhakruthe	Thou, auspicious One, all hail.
Vasumathe	Oh, Splendor of the Vasus, all hail.
Vadaveshaprathe	Praise be to Thee, a Lover of celibacy.
Trumbaye	Praise be to Thee, oh Peerless One.
Prajrumbaye	Praise be to Thee, Auspicious One.
Ujrumbaye	Praise be to the Invincible One.
Kamalasana Samstaya	Praise be to the Lord extolled by Brahma.
Ekavarnaya	The One Word art Thou, all hail.
Dvivarnaye	In Two art Thou, all hail.
Trivarnaye	Thou are the Three, all hail.
Chaturvarnaye	In Four art Thou, all hail.
Panchavarnaye	In Five Letters art Thou
Prajapathaye	Father of all Creation, all hail.
Booshane	Thou, Luminous Sun, all hail.
Kapasthaye	Thou, Effulgence Divine, all hail.
Kahanaye	Thou, Omniscient One, all hail.

Chandra Varnaye	Thou, Radiance of the Moon, praise be to Thee.
Kalatharaye	Thou who adorns the Crescent, praise be to Thee.
Maya Tharaye	Energy art Thou, praise be to Thee.
Maha Mayine	Great Delusion too, art Thou, praise be to Thee.
Kaivalyaya	Everlasting Joy of Attainment, praise be to Thee.
Sahatatmakaya	Thou who art all pervading, all hail.
Visvayonaye	Source of all existence, all hail.
Ameyatmane	Oh Supreme Splendor, all hail.
Tejonithaye	Illumination Divine, all hail.
Anamayaya	Savior of all ills, all hail.
Parameshtine	Thou are Immaculate, Lord, all hail.
Gurave	Oh, Matchless Guru, praise be to Thee.
Para Brahmane	Thou, Transcendent One, praise be to Thee.
Veda Karpaye	The Quintessence of the Vedas art Thou, praise be to Thee.
Pulinthakanya Parthre	Praise be to the Lord of Vali.
Mahasarasvataprathaye	Praise be to the Source or Gnosis.
Asritha Kiladatre	Praise be to Him who showers Grace on those who seek His solace.
Soraknaye	Praise be to Him who annihilates those who steal.
Roganashanaye	Praise be to the Divine Healer.
Ananta Murthaye	Praise be Thine whose Forms are endless.
Anandaye	Praise be Thine, oh Thou Infinite Bliss.
Sigandikrutha Gedanaye	Praise be Thine, oh Thou, Lord of the Peacock Banner.
Dambaye	Praise be to Thee, oh Lover of Gay Exuberance.
Parama Dambaye	Praise be to Thee, Oh Symbol of Superb Liveliness.
Maha Dambaye	Praise be to Thee, Oh Lord of Lofty Magnificence.

Vrsha Kapaye	Thou, who art the Culmination of all Dharma, hail.
Karanopathadehaye	Thou, who designed Embodiment for a Cause, all hail.
Karanathita Vikrahaye	Form transcending casual experience, all hail.
Aneeswaraya	Oh, Eternal, Peerless Plentitude.
Amrthaye	Oh, Everlasting Nectar, all hail.
Pranaye	Thou, Life of Life, praise be unto Thee.
Pranatharaye	Thou, Support of all beings, praise be unto Thee.
Paravaraye	Oh, Sovereign Goodness, praise unto Thee.
Vrithakhandare	Praise unto Thee, who subjugates all hostile forces.
Viraknaye	Thou, Vanquisher of heroic opponents, Praise unto Thee.
Raktashyamagalaye	Thou art Love and of Crimson Beauty, praise unto Thee.
Loka Gurave	Oh, Universal Teacher, praise unto Thee.
Supingalaye	Distilled Sweetness, all praise to Thee.
Mahadhe	Oh, Consummation of Glory, all praise to Thee.
Subrahmanyaye	We Praise Thee, oh Effulgent Radiance.
Guha Priyaye	We Praise Thee, oh Dweller in the Cove of Hearts.
Brahman Yaye	We Praise Thee, Luminous Wisdom Serene.
Brahmana Priyaye	We Praise Thee, Beloved of seers.
Sarveswaraye	We Praise Thee, Sovereign Lord Almighty.
Akshaye Bala Prathaye	We Praise Thee, oh Bestower of Beneficence Ineffable.
Nishkalankaye	We Praise Thee, Faultless Brilliance.

Sakshat Shri Adi Shakti Shri Maha Devi Namoh Namah

2—*Swadisthana Chakra*

SHRI SARASWATI

Gayatri Mantras—*Center Swadisthan Chakra*

Gayatri is the mother-creator of the Vedas, the foremost mantra in Hindu belief and inspires wisdom. Its meaning: *"May the Almighty God Illuminati our intellect to lead us along the righteous path".*

The mantra is also a prayer to the *"giver of light and life"* - the sun (savitur).

OM Bhooh, OM bhuvah, OM Swah, OM Mah,
OM Janah, OM Tapah, OM Satyam,
OM Tatsavitruvarenyam, Bhargo Devasya Dhi Mahi,
Dhiyoyonah Prachodayat, Om Apo Jyotirasomritam,
Brahma Bhoor Bhuvah Swarom.

Shri Brahmadeva Saraswati—21 Names

Creativity Pure Knowledge

Om Shri Buddhi Namah
Om Shri Maha Ahamkara Namah
Om Shri Surya Namah
Om Shri Chandra Namah

Om Shri Tattwa Swamini Namah
Om Shri Vayu Tattwa Swamini Namah
Om Shri Tejas Tattwa Swamini Namah
Om Shri Apa Tattwa Swamini Namah
Om Shri Prhtvhi Tattwa Swamini Namah
Om Shri Aksha Tattwa Iswari Namah
Om Shri Aneela Tattwa Iswari Namah
Om Shri Tejo Tattwa Iswari Namah
Om Shri Jala Tattwa Iswari Namah
Om Shri Bhoomi Tattwa Iswari Namah

Om Shri Hiranyagarbhaye Namah
Om Shri Pancha Tanmatrasye Namah
Om Shri Pancha Bhuteshuye Namah

Om Shri Vishwa Namah
Om Shri Taijasatmika Namah
Om Shri Prajnatmika Namah
Om Shri Turya Namah

Sakshat Shri Adi Shakti Shri Maha Devi Namoh Namah

Prayer to Shri Adi Bhoomi Devi

Divine aspect of Mother Earth

OM Sakshat Shri Bhoomi Devi Namoh Namah.

Upon You Beloved Mother Earth

We stand at this the crossroads of humankinds destiny.

Only through Your kind Love of Your children are we here now.

You have graciously sustained us thus far.

You have given us food, water, clothing and shelter.

'O' Beloved Mother Earth, with our heads bowed we thank You.

And with our heads bowed we come humbly to You asking further sustenance and strength for the many long days ahead as this age ends.

'O' Beloved Mother Earth, now that we have grown a little and stand firmer each day, we pray to You to help clear the way as we begin to march forwards.

We long for the cleansing of all lands, so that upon You, beloved Mother Earth, the righteous may return to their Divine home. We hope to be many.

'O' Beloved Mother Earth, give us patience as we search for our brothers and sisters. Give us detachment from all distractions. Give us perseverance in our task.

'O' Beloved Mother Earth, most of all, help us, as Your seas cleanse the shores, to clean our hearts, so that we may desire only that which is right.

'O' Beloved Mother Earth, support us so that we may soon stand upon You in great numbers and invoke with one mighty voice the Dance of Lord of divine love and light.

'O' Beloved Mother Earth, we pray to the seven angels that represent your love and grace upon the earth.

These things we most humbly pray for.

Om Sakshat Shri Bhoomi Devi Bolo Shri Bhoomi Devi,

Shri Maha Devi Namoh Namah

3—Nabhi Chakra

Ten Commandments

As one of the primordial masters, Moses received the code of dharma or ten laws, *(10 Commandments)* on Mount Sinai in the southern Sinai Peninsula of Egypt around 1350 BC. It is said these laws were written on stone tablets by the divine and given to Moses so he could take his followers to the next level of their spiritual awareness. They were spiritually destined to escape the enslavement of the Pharaohs and their seed line. Since society was less spiritually evolved during this period—idol worship and slavery was the level of their understanding. The commandments were offered to the masses to encourage a new spiritual awareness, but as Moses tried to de-condition his followers and connect them to their spiritual essence, he was met with resistance and negativity by the powers that be.

As time evolved through the ages the qualities of the Chakras have been gently awakened through the primordial masters or incarnations sent to guide our awakening. This is similar to a child in preschool evolving to high school with different teachers along the way. Each step in our spiritual awareness has been awakened at the beginning of a new age by a divine incarnation. Our evolution correlates directly to the spiritual awakening of the Chakras, now with the Sahasrara chakra opening during the Age of Aquarius (enlightenment).

We are now leaving the Piscean age (water sign) and symbol of the early Christians (fish). Over the past 2200 years the shipping industry and the great armadas controlled communication and trade. Now as we ride the cusp of the Aquarian age (air sign) we see telecommunications, air travel, etc. The great clock of the cosmos correlates to this new age of enlightened awareness as the next step to our spiritual evolution. This evolution of our awareness from the ape-man to the human is complete, and now the transformation into the age of enlightenment has the human being evolving into the realm of the spiritual being or 5th dimension.

Yet, even in today's modern world we still find idol worship and dogmas. Our modern version is through the movie, pop and sports stars or the gurus that line up as avatars—masters using saffron words to promote their "branded" divinity for money, power, control or adoration, which is nothing more than pampering the ego. They take advantage of the seeker's innocence and manipulate them, claiming that the way to the divine is through them. But the only way to the divine is through understanding that we are our own guru and master, responsible for our own evolution. This was the message of Moses and all the great saints and incarnations.

This new awareness coming in the golden Aquarian age will now allow us to evolve and deepen our divine collective discretion and to understand and connect to the true yoga of self and the divine consciousness.

Laws or 10 Commandments of Moses

1 - I am the Lord thy God. Thou shalt not have Gods before me.

(This was a reference to the Idol worship of figures at the time, whereby the connection to the divine directly through the Yoga had been lost.)

2 - Thou shalt not take the name of the Lord thy God in vain.

Respect and Humility

3 - Remember thou keep the Sabbath Day.

Most of the great masters mentioned this as the time to connect with the Divine.

4 - Honor thy Father and thy Mother.

It is the dharma of right conduct

5 - Thou shalt not kill.

It is based on the law of Karma, and cause and effect – for every action there is an equal and opposite reaction.

6 - Thou shalt not commit adultery.

It is the Dharma of right conduct

7 - Thou shalt not steal.

It is the law of Karma

8 - Thou shalt not bear false witness against thy neighbor.

It is against the Vishuddhi Chakra

9 - Thou shalt not covet thy neighbor's wife.

It is the law of Karma and Dharma

10 - Thou shalt not covet thy neighbor's goods.

It is the law of Karma

Prayer to Shri Santaana Lakshmi—*The Giver of Children*

Ayi gaja vahini
Mohini Chakrini
Raga Vivardhini
Gnana maye
Guna gana varadhi
Loka hitaishini
Sapta swara vara gana nute
Sakala surasura
Deva muni swara
Manava vandita
Pada yute.
Jai Jai He Madhusudhana kamini
Santana Lakshmi Shri Maha Devi Palaya Mam.

You are The One who rides on an elephant
You are extremely attractive,
You have the Chakra in Your hand;
You have no anger,
You are full of knowledge,
You are the good-natured one,
You always wish good for the whole world,
You are the seven sounds,
We praise You by singing the seven 'swaras'.
Everybody good and bad,
All the Devas and Munis and also the humans,
They all praise Your Lotus Feet.

Prayer to Shri Raja Lakshmi—*The Giver of Sustenance*

Jaya jaya durgatinasini Kamini
Sarva phala prada, Sastra maye,
Ratha gaja turanga padati Sama vruta
Pari jana mandita Loka nute
Hari Hara Brahma supujita sevita
Thapani nivarini Pada yute
Jai jai He Madhusudhana kamini
Raja Lakshmi Shri Maha Devi Palaya Mam.

Victory to the destroyer of all our miseries!
You are the One who loves us,
You are the Giver of all the fruits of our prayers, chariots, elephants, horses,
Its a total congregation of all the people,
The world bows down to You.
The Lords Vishnu, Shiva and Brahma worship You and serve You.
You lift the sadness of people who are in extreme sorrow,
They come to Your Feet.
Oh, Shri Raja Lakshmi, Thou who Art the
Giver of help & prosperity.
Shri Maha Devi, I bow to Thee,
You rule over me.

The 108 Names of Lord Vishnu

The 108 names are from the Vedic shastras and thus have a definite capacity of sustaining our meditation. Shri Vishnu is known as the All-Pervading essence of all beings, the master of—being beyond—the past, present and future, the creator and destroyer of all existences, one who supports, sustains and governs the Universe and originates and develops all elements within. One who imbibes the love of Maha Devi.

Sayanambudhau Twavaiva Narayanakyam pranatosmi rupam

Om Twameva Sakshat Shri:

Keshavay Namaha	Having all powers
Narayanay Namaha	The refuge of men.
Madhavay Namaha	The honey-like spring.
Govinday Namaha	Lord of the cows.
Vishnuve Namaha	All pervading.
Madhusudanay Namaha	Killer of Madhu.
Trivikramay Namaha	Who measured the world with three steps.
Vamanay Namaha	Incarnated as short man.
Shridharay Namah	Bearing Shrimata on his chest.
Hrishikeshay Namaha	Controlling the senses.
Padmanabhay Namaha	In his nabhi is the cause of universes.
Damodaray Namaha	Attained by disciplines.
Sankarshanay Namaha	Drawing everything together.
Vasudevay Namaha	Residing everywhere (as Maya)
Pradyumnay Namaha	Infinite, enlightened wealth.

Aniruddhay Namaha	Never obstructed nor overcome.
Purushottamay Namaha	Highest among the Purushas.
Aghokshay Namaha	Known by turning inwards.
Narasimhay Namaha	Incarnated as man-lion.
Upendray Namaha	Above Indra.
Achyutay Namaha	Unchanging.
Janardanay Namaha	Oppressor of evil, savior.
Haray Namaha	Remover
Krishnay Namaha	Dark One.
Vishnave Namaha	His splendor pervades the firmament and beyond.
Peshalay Namah	Charming in His darshan, speech, action and mind.
Pushkarakshay Namah	His eyes are like lotuses.
Harine Namaha	Bearing a yellow garb, or, liquidating samsara.
Chakrine Namaha	Master of the discus, the Sudarshana Chakra
Nandakine Namaha	Holding the sword called Nandaka.
Sharngadhanvay Namaha	Having the boy called Sharnga.
Shankhadhrte Namaha	Bearing the conch called Panchajanya.
Gadadharay Namah	Bearing the club called Kaumodaki.
Vanamaline Namah	Wearing the garland called Vaijayanti.
Kuvaleshaya Namaha	Lying on the belly of Shri Shesha.
Garudadhvajay Namah	His flag bears the emblem of Garuda.
Lakshmivan Namah	Shri Lakshmi resides in His chest.
Bhagavan Namaha	He knows the origin and dissolutions Of all beings.
Vaikunthapataye Namaha	Lord of Vaikuntha.
Dharmagup Namaha	He safeguards Dharma.
Dharmadhyakshay Namaha	He presides over Dharma.
Niyantay Namah	He establishes men in their respective functions.

Naikajay Namah	Born many times for the preservation of Dharma.
Svastine Namaha	His nature is auspiciousness.
Sakshine Namaha	The witness.
Satyay Namaha	The Truth.
Dharanidharay Namaha	The support of the earth.
Vyavasthanay Namaha	Everything is based on Him.
Sarvadarshine Namaha	He sees and knows what is done by all creators.
Sarvagyaya Namaha	He is the All and the Knower.
Ghanay Namaha	He is Inscrutable.
Nahushay Namaha	He binds all creatures by His power of Maya
Mahamaya Namaha	Supreme creator of illusions.
Adhokshajay Namaha	Knowledge of Him arises only when the attention goes inward.
Yagyapataye Namaha	The protector, enjoyer and Lord of all sacrifices.
Vegavan Namaha	Endowed with great speed.
Sahishnu Namaha	He bears the duality of cold and heat (Ida, Pingala).
Rakshana Namah	Taking His stand on Sattwa Guna; He protects the 3 worlds.
Dhaneshwara Namaha	The Lord of wealth.
Hiranyanabha Namaha	He whose navel is auspicious like gold.
Sharirabhrt Namaha	Sustenance and food.
Annam Namaha	He causes all beings to eat.
Mukunda Namaha	The one who grants release.
Agrani Namaha	He leads the seekers of salvation to the foremost abode.
Amogha Namaha	He who blesses His worshippers.
Varada Namaha	He bestows the desired boons.
Subhekshana Namaha	Breaking all knots.
Satamgati Namaha	The refuge of the seekers.

Sukhada Namaha	He endows righteous people with happiness.
Vatsala Namaha	He is cherished by His devotees.
Veeraha Namaha	He destroys the various life styles of Kali Yuga.
Prabhu Namaha	Skilled in action.
Amaraprabhu Namaha	The Lord of the immortals.
Suresha Namaha	The Lord of the devas.
Purandara Namaha	He destroys the cities of the enemies Of the devas.
Samitimjaya Namaha	Victorious in war.
Amitavikrama Namaha	Of enormous valor.
Shatrughna Namaha	He kills the enemies of the devas.
Bhima Namaha	Of Him everything is afraid.
Surajaneshvara Namaha	Exceeding in prowess the greatest heroes.
Sampramardana Namaha	He punishes and torments the evil doers.
Bhavana Namaha	The giver of the fruits of action.
Kshetragya Namaha	Knowler of the field.
Sarvayogavinissrta Namaha	Dvoid Lord of all attachments.
Yogeshwara Namaha	Detached Lord of the yogis.
Chala Namaha	He moves in the form of wind.
Vayuvahana Namaha	He makes the wind blow; or, the wind is His vehicle.
Jivana Namaha	In the form of the breath of life.
Sambhava Namaha	Manifesting by His own free will.
Samvatsara Namaha	Standing in the form of time.
Vardhana Namaha	He who makes things to evolve.
Eka Namaha	He is One.
Naika Namaha	He is not only One as He has many forms.
Vasu Namaha	All beings abide in Him.
Ishana Namah	Controller of all things.
Lokadhyaksha Namah	The chief supervisory witness of all

	the world.
Trilokesha Namaha	The Lord of the three worlds.
Jagatswami Namah	The Master of the Universe.
Yugavarta Namaha	He who makes the yugas turn.
Vistara Namaha	He in whom all worlds are expanded.
Vishvarupa Namaha	Form the Totality.
Anantarupa Namaha	Infinite are His forms, or; form of infinity.
Avishista Namaha	The pervasive inner Ruler of all.
Maharddhi Namaha	Whose glory is greatest.
Paryavasthita Namaha	He envelops the Universe pervading it everywhere.
Sthavishtha Namaha	He stands in the great form of Virata.
Mahavishnu Namaha	He who manifested His evolved form as Lord Jesus Christ.
Kalki Namaha	The immaculate Rider of the last days.

Shantakaram Bhujagashayanam Padmanabham Suresham
Vishvadharam Gaganasadrusham Megavarnam Shubhangam
Lakshmi kantam Kamalanayanam Yogibhir Dhyanagamyam Vande
Vishnum Bhava Bhaya Haram Sarvalokaikanatham Amen!
Jai Shri Vishnu!

Nabhi Chakra

The third chakra gives us the sense of complete satisfaction and contentment. It makes us peaceful and generous, and also sustains our spiritual ascent. When enlightened by the Kundalini, it expresses as righteousness and inner sense of morality, and it gives us complete balance at all levels in our life."

The 10 Holy Petals of the Nabhi Chakra

Om twameva Sakshat Shri Adya Lakshmi Namah	Adi Shakti
Om twameva Sakshat Shri Vidya Lakshmi Namah	Knowledge
Om twameva Sakshat Shri Saubhagya Lakshmi Namah	Good Fortune
Om twameva Sakshat Shri Amruta Lakshmi Namah	Grace of Spirit
Om twameva Sakshat Shri Gruhah Lakshmi Namah	Wife
Om twameva Sakshat Shri Rajah Lakshmi Namah	Queen
Om twameva Sakshat Shri Satya Lakshmi Namah	Awareness of Truth
Om twameva Sakshat Shri Bhogya Lakshmi Namah	Enjoyer
Om twameva Sakshat Shri Yoga Lakshmi Namah	Giver of Yoga
Om twameva Sakshat Shri Maha Lakshmi Namah	Power of Evolution

Om Twameva Sakshat Shri Maha Devi
Tvamekum Sharanam Gachami Namo Namah

Shri Audi Guru

The ten incarnations: of Shri Adi Guru, the Primordial Master are: *Raga Janaka, Abraham, Moses, Zarathustra, Confucius, Lao-Tse, Socrates, Mohammed, Guru Nanak, and Shri Sai Baba of Shirdi.*

Shri Adi Guru Dattatreya is recognized as an Avatar or incarnation of the Lord Shiva and as the Adi-Guru *(First Teacher)* of the Adinath Sampradaya of the Nathas.

The first "Lord of Yoga".

The 108 Names of Shri Adi Guru Dattatreya

Sattvaya	Salutations to the one who is Sattva
Sattvabhrtangataya	Salutations to the one who sustains Sattva.
Kamalalayaya	Salutations to the one who is the abode of Lotuses
Hiranyagarbhaya	Salutations to the Golden Egg of Brahma, the Subtle body of the Virata.
Bodhasama Shrayaya	Salutations to the one who is the collective Shelter of awakening.
Nabhavine	Salutations to him who lives in or is the possessor of the navel or Nabhi Chakra.
Dehashunyaya	Salutations to the one who is the Void of the body.
Paramarthadrshe	Salutations to the one who can see the Supreme Goal.
Yantravide	Salutations to the knower of yantras.
Dharadharaya	Salutations to the support of all supports.
Sanatanaya	Salutations to the Seed of Mantras.
Chitkirtibhushanaya	Salutations to the one who is adorned in the glory of attention and awareness.

Chandrasuryagni	Salutations to the one who is not excited or lochanaya agitated.
Antahpurnaya	Salutations to him who is completely fulfilled within.
Bahirpurnaya	Salutations to him who is completely fulfilled without.
Purnatmane ness	Salutations to him who is the Self of full- and fulfillment.
Khagarbhaya	Salutations to the one who is self-contained.
Amararchitaya	Salutations to the immortal one honored and respected.
Gambhiraya	Salutations to him who is deep and profound.
Dayavate	Salutations to him who is possessed of mercy and compassion.
Satya vijnanabhaskaraya	Salutations to him who shines brilliantly with discernment and knowledge.
Sadashivaya	Salutations to the one who shines by his own light.
Shreyaskaya	Salutations to him who makes better.
Ajnanakhandanaya	Salutations to the one who annihilates non-knowledge.
Dhritye	Salutations to the one who is fairness, constancy and contentment.
Dambhadarpamadapa-	Salutations to the remover of hypo critical Pride haya and intoxicated frenzy.
Gunantakaya	Salutations to the remover of the Gunas.
Jvaranashanaya	Salutations to the destroyer of fever and illness.
Bhedavaitandakhana-	Salutations to him who breaks destructive ness danaya and silly arguments.
Nirvasanaya	Salutations to the one who has no Vasanas or entrapping conditionings.

Nirihaya	Salutations to him who is motionless, inactive, desire less and still.
Nirahamkaraya	Salutations to the one who is without ego.
Shokadukhaharaya	Salutations to him who removes anxiety and pain.
Nirashir nirupadhi kaya	Salutations to him who is devoid of the qualities of hopelessness and depression.
Anantavikramaya	Salutations to him who endlessly Conquers and overcomes.
Bhedantakaya	Salutations to him who makes an end of Destruction and splitting.
Munaye	Salutations to him who is the great Muni (sage), the essence of silence.
Mahayogine	Salutations to the great yogi.
Yogabhyasa prakash-	Salutations to him who Illuminatis the repeated anaya practice and discipline of Yoga.
Yogarira darpa-	Salutations to the destroyer of arrogance and nashanaya enemies of Yoga.
Nityamuktaya	Salutations to him who is eternally in Yoga.
Yogaya	Salutations to the one who is Yoga.
Sthanadaya	Salutations to him who gives stability and a place to stay.
Mahanubhavabhavitaya	Salutations to the one who is the becoming of great experience and understanding.
Kamajitay	Salutations to him who has conquered desire, lust and passion.
Shuchirbhutaya	Salutations to him who is most Magnificent and glorious.
Tyagakaranatyagatmane	Salutations to the one who is the Self of abandoning and the cause of abandoning.

Manobuddhivihinatmane	Salutations to him who has abandoned totally both intellect and manas.
Manatmane	Salutations to him who is the Self of the Manas—imaginative desiring quality in man.
Chetanavigatayane	Salutations to the one who has Abandoned and gone beyond thinking awareness.
Aksharamuktaya	Salutations to him who is eternally free and liberated.
Parakramine	Salutations to him who takes the last Absolute step.
Tyagarthasampannaya	Salutations to the one who is perfectly accomplished in the meaning of renunciation.
Tyagavigrahaya	Salutations to him who is the analysis and resolution of renunciation.
Tyagakaranaya	Salutations to him who is the cause of renunciation
Pratyaharaniyojakaya	Salutations to him who causes one to Become attached to withdrawal of the senses.
Pratyakshavaratave	Salutations to him who dawns and becomes light before ones very eyes.
Devanam Paramagataye	Salutations to him who is the supreme goal of the Devas.
Mahadevaya	Salutations to him who is victorious of death dead spirits.
Bhuvanantakaya	Salutations to him who limits and destroys the Universe of Shri Yama.
Papanashanaya	Salutations to him who is the destroyer of sins.
Avadhutaya	Salutations to the one who has come through hell, conquering it.

Madapahaya	Salutations to the one who sustains and removes intoxication.
Mayamuktaya	Salutations to the one who has been freed from Maya.
Chiduttamaya	Salutations to him who is the highest attention.
Kshetrajnaya	Salutations to the knower of the field, Shri Krishna, the Atman or the Spirit.
Ksetragaya	Salutations to the goer into the field.
Ksetraya	Salutations to the one who is the field.
Samsaratamonashanaya	Salutations to him who destroys the Darkness of samsara and transmigration.
Sankamuktasamadhi-	Salutations to him who is Bliss, free from fear mate or alarm.
Patre	Salutations to the protector.
Nityashuddhaya	Salutations to him who is eternal purity.
Balaya	Salutations to the boy, the child.
Brahmacharine	Salutations to the pure and chaste youthful student.
Hrdayasthaya	Salutations to him who is placed in the heart.
Pravartanaya	Salutations to him who is in constant enlightened motion.
Samkalpa Dukkha	Salutations to him who rips apart and destroys Dalanaya the pain of planning.
Jiva Sanjivanaya	Salutations to him who brings living creatures alive.
Layatitaya	Salutations to the one who is beyond dissolution.
Layasyantaya	Salutations to him who flows with dissolution.
Pramukhaya	Salutations to the most excellent one who faces all
Nandine	Salutations to the rejoicer.

Nirabhasaya	Salutations to him who is devoid of false appearances.
Niranjanaya	Salutations to him who is simple, pure, clean, undecorated.
Shraddharthine	Salutations to him who is endowed with meaning, purpose, faith and devotion.
Gosakshine	Salutations to the one who has many eyes.
Nirabhasaya	Salutations to him who is without falseness or deception.
Vishuddhottama-	Salutations to him who is the highest untainted gauravaya purity of the Guru.
Niraharine	Salutations to the one who gives and takesnothing for himself.
Nityabodhaya	Salutations to the one who gives eternal awakening.
Puranaprabhave	Salutations to the ancient Lord, the ancient dawning light.
Sattvabhrte	Salutations to the one who bears and supports that which is essential to existence.
Bhutashankaraya	Salutations to him who is auspicious and beneficent to all beings.
Hamsasakshine	Salutations to the witness, pure and swanlike in his discrimination.
Sattvavide	Salutations to the knower of the essence of existence on sattwa guna.
Vidyavate	Salutations to him who is possessed of Vidya or Knowledge.
Atmanubhava-	Salutations to him who is perfect and excellent sampannaya in his perception of the Atman.
Vishalakshaya	Salutations to him who has mighty, large, powerful eyes.

Dharmavardhanaya	Salutations to him who increases Dharma
Bhoktre	Salutations to the enjoyer.
Bhogyaya	Salutations to him who should be enjoyed
Bhogarthasampannaya	Salutations to the perfected one in the meaning and significance of how to enjoy.
Bhoga Jnana	Salutations to him who Illuminatis the knowledge Prakashanaya of how to enjoy.
Sahajaya	Salutations to him who is spontaneous.
Diptaya	Salutations to the one who blazes with light.
Nirvanaya	Salutations to the one who is Nirvana.
Tattvatma Jnana	Salutations to him who is the ocean of the Sagaraya knowledge of the Tattvas.
Paramanandasagaraya	Salutations to him who is the ocean of supreme Bliss.

Om Twameva Sakshat Shri Dattatreya Sakshat
Shri Maha Devi Twamevam Saranam Gachami Namoh Namah

Guru Mantra

Guru Brahma Guru Vishnu
Guru Devo Maheshwarah
Guru Sakshat Parabrahma
Shri Maha Devi Ma
Tasmai Shri Guruve
Namah

Prayer to—Shri Annapurna

Shri Annapurna - is the Goddess of food and nourishment and is considered as the sustainer of prosperity. In Sanskrit 'Anna' means food and grains and 'Purna' means full or complete.

Nityananda kari Varabhaya kari Saundarya ratnakari
Nirdhootakhila-ghora-papa-nikari pratyaksha-maheshwari
Praleya-chala-vansha-pavanakari kashipuradhishwari
Bhikshamdehi krpavalambana-kari Matanna-purneshwari

Nana-ratna-vichitra-bhooshana kari hemambara dambari
Mukta-hara-vidamba-mana-vilasad-dakshoja Kumbhantari
Kashmiraga-ruvasitang-ruchire kashipuradhishwari
Bhiksham dehi Krpavalambana-kari Matanna-purneshwari

Yogananda kari ripukshaya-kari dharmaika-nishtha kari
Chandrarkanal-bhasamana-lahari trailokya rakshakari
Sarvai-shwarya-kari tapah-phala-kari kashi puradhishwari
Bhiksham dehi krpavalambana-kari matanna-purneshwari

Kailasachala-kanda-ralaya kari Gauri Uma Shankari
Kaumari nigamartha gochara kari Onkara beejakshari
Moksha-dwar-kapata-patanakari kashipuradhishwari
Bhiksham dehi krpavalambana kari matanna-purneshwari

Annapurne Sadapurne Shankar-prana-vallabhe
Jnana vairagya siddhyartham bhiksham dehi cha Parvati
Mata cha Parvati devi pita devo Maheshwarah
Bandhavah Shiva-bhaktashcha Swadesho bhuvanatrayam
Indriyanam adhishthatri bhootanam chakhileshu ya
Bhooteshu satatam tasyai vyapti devyai namo namah
Chitiroopen ya kritsna-metadvyapya sthita jagat
Namastasyai Namastasyai Namastasyai Namo Namah

O Mother Anna—Purnesshwarii

You are the bestower of eternal Bliss, you give boons with one hand and fearlessness with the other, you are the ocean of beauty and the destroyer of all sin, you are verily the supreme Goddess. You have purified the clan of Himalaya (Parvati was the daughter of King Himalaya or Himavan).

Kindly be pleased and give me the alms.

Your hands are bedecked with different ornaments of jewels and diamonds. Your throne has a golden canopy. Your clothes are shining. Necklaces of pearls are adding to your splendor. You have applied saffron, musk, sandal-wood paste and other scented materials to your body which are enhancing your beauty.

O Mother Anna-purneshwari! Be pleased with me and give me the alms.

You are the bestower of the joy of Yoga. You strengthen the allegiance to Dharma. You are the destroyer of enemies. The Resplendence of your being reminds us of the light of the sun, the moon and the fire. You are the protector of "Trailokya" (the earth, heaven and netherworld). You give all prosperity and reward of penances.

O Mother Anna-purneshwari! Be pleased and give me the alms.

You are residing in the caves of Kailasa. You are Gauri, Uma, Shankari (the consort of Shri Shankara) Kaumari (Mother of Kumar, i.e. Karttikeya). It is by your blessings alone that the true meaning of Vedas becomes clear. You are the first letter Om. You are all beejaksharas (Primordial letters. These are the sounds produced when Kundalini pierces chakras). You open the gates of Moksha for your devotees.

O Mother Anna-purneshwari! be pleased and give me the alms.

Shri Adi-Shankaracharaya has further praised the Divine Mother. He says:

> "O Mother you are looking after and guiding those visible and invisible Gods and officials, your belly is the receptacle of entire universe, you are conducting all the play and the drama that is this universe, you are lighting the lamp of knowledge, you are the foundation of all letters from "a" to "Ksha", you give victory to your devotees, you are the ocean of mercy, you are the supreme Goddess who gives food".

He ends the prayer as follows:

> "O Mother Annapurna, you are always complete. You are the beloved of Shri Shankara. Please give me the alms of success in attaining the true knowledge and vairagya."—*complete detachment.*

The Mother—You Are

Twameva mata	You are the Mother
pita twameva	You are the Father
Twameva bandhu	You are the relation,
sakha twameva	You are the Friend
Twameva vidya	You are the technique,
dravinam twameva	You are Mercy
Twameva sarvam,	You are everything,
Mama deva deva	O my God, my God.
Apradh Sahasrani	I must have committed a thousand
Kriyante aharnisham maya	Sins in my life from day to day;
Daso'yam iti mam matwa	Please accept me as Your servant
Kshamaswa Parameshwari	O Mother, forgive me
Kshamaswa Parameshwari	O Mother, forgive me
Kshamaswa Parameshwari	O Mother, forgive me
Aawahanam na janami	I do not know how to invoke You
Na janami tavarchanam	I do not know how to welcome You
Poojam chaiwa na janami	I do not know how to do Your Puja
Kshamya tam Parameshwari	Forgive me, Adi Shakti
Kshamya tam Parameshwari	Forgive me, Adi Shakti
Kshamya tam Parameshwari	Forgive me, ***O S**upreme **O**ne*
Mantrahinam kriyahinam	I have no mantras,
Bhaktihinam Sureshwari	I have done nothing
Yat pujitam Mayadevi	I have no devotion,
	***O G**reat **God**dess*
Pari purnam tadastu me	And yet whatever my prayers have been to You.
	Please fulfill them, through Your Grace.

4—Heart or Anahata Chakra

Shri Rama

RAMAYAHA

The Ramayana took place around 5561 BC. It is about Lord Rama who was born in a royal family and was forced into exile from his kingdom for fourteen years. During this period his wife Sita was kidnapped by the 10-headed king of the demons called Ravana, who was the king of Lanka. Rama with the help of his brother, Lakshman, and an army of monkeys under the leadership of Shri Hanuman, set out and rescued Sita in the great battle.

Spiritually, the Ramayana is about devotion, loyalty, family roles and respect of elders, and the people on Earth who suffered from the demon king Ravana. This evil king terrorizes the people of Earth, especially the religious people by preventing them from performing religious rituals. But Ravana is also a great devotee of the three gods who rule the universe: Brahma the creator, Vishnu the preserve, and Shiva the destroyer—and therefore has their blessings. But the people of the Earth, who suffer from Ravana, rise up to heaven to visit the gods and ask for their help. The gods decide that Lord Vishnu will incarnate as a human being on Earth and destroy Ravana.

So what does all this really mean? Could this be about a ruler from the planet Nibiru put in place by the Anunnaki to rule the Earth beings? This theory is not so far-fetched when we relate it to the Sumerian history which states we were enslaved by these aliens in ages past, or to the gods like Brahma who evolved as light beings from the constellation PLEIADES. But all the answers will be revealed by 2012.

Ramraksha or Rama Kavacha—*Sanskrit Translation*

This spiritual hymn *(affirmation)* is written by Budha-kaushik rishi in ancient times and is a very potent hymn for it wards of evil n fear of mind, also recited when traveling, to get rid of all Perils, obstacles that may be in the way.

In the beginning one should meditate on Shri Rama, putting one's attention on the right heart where the qualities of Shri Rama reside.

The physical description of Lord Rama follows:

His hands are very long, reaching His knees; He is holding a bow and arrow in His hands, sitting on a throne and wearing yellow clothes. His eyes are like a fresh lotus petal and He is happy as He looks at His wife, Sita who is sitting on His left. His skin is the color of a water-filled cloud (light blue). His hair is very long and His body is covered with different ornaments.

1) Lord Rama's character is so vast that we could write 1000 million verses describing it, every word of it capable of destroying the greatest sins of human beings.

2) A wise man should learn this praise of Lord Rama (called Ramrasha) by heart.

3) The qualities of Lord Rama are described as follows: His skin has a light blue color and His eyes are like a lotus, big and joy-giving. In front of Him is Shri Laxmana and His Wife Sita. He is decorated by a crown made of long hair. He has a sword in one hand and a bow and arrow in the other and on His back spare arrows to kill the Rakshasas.

4) May Lord Rama, who is born in the famous line of Raghuraja, protect my head. May Lord Rama, the Son of King Dashratha, protect my forehead.

5) May Lord Rama, Son of Queen Kausalya, protect both my eyes. May Lord Rama, the favorite disciple of Lord Vishwamitra, protect both my ears. May Lord Rama, the protector of the Havan of Lord Vishwamitra, protect my nose. May Lord Rama, who loves His brother Laxmana, protect my mouth.

6) May Lord Rama, who holds all knowledge, protect my tongue. May Lord Rama, who is worshipped by Bharata, protect my throat. May Lord Rama, who possesses all the powerful weapons, protect my shoulders. May Lord Rama, who broke the strong bow during the Swayamvara of Sita, protect both my arms.

7) May Shri Sita's Husband, Lord Rama, protect my hands. May Lord Rama, who won against Parashurama, protect my heart. May Lord Rama, who destroyed the Rakshasa named Khur, protect the centre of my body. May Lord Rama, who gave refuge to Jambvan, protect my navel.

8) May Lord Rama, who is the Lord of Sugriva, protect my waist. May Lord Rama, who is the Lord of Hanumana, protect my groin. May Lord Rama, who is the Destroyer of the lineage of the Rakshasas, protect my thighs.

9) May Lord Rama, who built a bridge over the seas, protect my knees. May Lord Rama, who destroyed the ten-faced Ravanna, protect my calves. May Lord Rama, who gave Rajlakshmi to Bhibishana, protect

my feet. May Lord Rama, who gives joy to everyone, protect my body.

10) Anyone who learns this Rama Kavacha, which is full of the Power of Lord Rama, will live a long life, will be contented and happy, will have sons and will succeed wherever he goes, gifted with humility.

11) Anyone who has the protection of this Rama Kavacha will be saved from the evil spirits of dead people living on the Earth, in the sky or in Hell.

12) Anyone who remembers the name of Lord Rama as Ram.

13) Ramchandra or Rambhadra, never falls prey to sin, will experience all types of well-being and in the end is liberated (i.e. he gets his Self-Realization).

14) This Ramraksha or Ramakavacha is as strong as the iron cage of Lord Indra, hence it is also called Vajrapanjar. The one who recites this Ramraksha triumphs wherever he goes, is blessed and obeyed by all.

15) This Ramraksha was recited by Lord Shiva in the dreams of Sage Buddhakaushika, and he wrote it down in the morning of the following day, exactly as told.

16) Lord Rama is like a beautiful garden of nectar-giving Trees. Lord Rama – who is the Destroyer of all our troubles and worries and who is praised throughout the three lokas (Heaven, Earth and Hell) – is our God Almighty.

17) Lord Rama and His Brother Laxmana, who are the heads of the

18) Raghu dynasty, protect us.

19) Lord Rama and Laxmana are described as follows: Young, handsome, well-built, very strong and courageous. Their eyes are like lotuses and They wear a pitambar. They eat roots and herbs. They have gained mastery over the organs of Their bodies and appear spiritually evolved. They are celibate. They protect all the animals and are great warriors with the bow and arrow. They have destroyed the dynasty of the Rakshasas.

20) May Lord Rama and His Brother Laxmana who have a bow and arrow ready in Their hands and many arrows on their backs walk in front of me on my path to protect me.

21) May Lord Rama, who is always on guard, having a bow and arrow and club, who is always guiding our minds and who, with Laxmana, is omnipresent in the Universe, protect us.

22) One who takes the names of Lord Rama in different forms now.

23) Given gets many blessings from Lord Rama.

24) The different names of Lord Rama are: One who gives joy Son of Dashratha One, Whose servant is Laxmana, Who is strong

Who is a great man, The One who is Purnabrahma (the entire Universe)

Son of Kausalya, Who has very great knowledge, Lord of havanas Puran Purushottam (the ideal human being), Dear one of Shri Sita Who possesses everything, and A warrior without equal.

25) One who praises Lord Rama, having light blue skin, eyes like a lotus, who wears a pitambar, is freed from the bondage of sin and death.

26) Lord Rama, who is the elder brother of Laxmana, the highest of the Raghu dynasty, the husband of Shri Sita, who is very handsome, full of compassion and who is replete with good qualities, who loves brahmanas (realized souls), who is very dharmic, who is the King, lover of Truth, Son of Dashratha, whose skin is fair and whose personality is peaceful, who gives joy to others, who decorates the Raghu dynasty like kum-kum on the forehead and who is the enemy of Ravanna, I bow to you.

27) I bow to the Husband of Shri Sita who is known also as Ram, Rambhadra, Ramchandra, Vedhas, Raghunath and Natha.

28) Oh Lord Rama, who is the elder brother of Bharata, who is merciless in battle, be our protector!

29) I worship the Feet of Lord Rama in my mind.

I praise the Feet of Lord Rama.

I bow at the Feet of Lord Rama.

I surrender at the Feet of Lord Rama.

30) Lord Rama is my Mother and my Father. He is my Lord and my Friend. So also the ever compassionate Lord Rama is everything to me and I do not even know anyone else at all.

31) I bow to Lord Rama on whose right side is Laxmana, and on whose left is King Janaka's daughter Shri Sita.

32) Lord Rama, who gives joy to everybody, who fights courageously on the battlefield, whose eyes are like a lotus, who is the Greatest of the Raghu dynasty and who is the compassionate Lord.; I surrender to Him.

33) Shri Hanumana, who flies in the sky as he wills, who is as swift as the wind, who has mastered and controls his senses and organs, who is the Most Intelligent of all, who is the Chief of the monkeys, who is the Son of the Lord of the wind and who is the messenger of Lord Rama; I surrender to You.

34) Sage Valmiki, who sits on a Tree branch in the form of a cuckoo, chanting "Ram Ram" in a beautiful voice; I bow to you.

35) Lord Rama, who is the Destroyer of all our troubles, who gives us wealth and who gives joy to the people; I bow to You again and again.

36) When we say "Ram Ram" and worship Lord Rama, it makes us detached from worldly problems, makes us the witness, helps us to encounter material well-being and frightens the messengers of Yama (God of death).

37) I worship the Husband of Shri Sita, Lord Rama, who gains always the Victory. I bow to Lord Rama who has killed the army of Rakshasas. I consider no-one greater than Lord Rama and I am His servant. Lord Rama, let my attention be always on Your Being and may You help me to evolve.

38) Shri Shiva tells Shri Parvati "One who takes the Name of Lord Rama and worships Him, with such a person I am pleased". This Praise of Lord Rama is equal to the Vishnusahasranama.

Thus the Ramakavacha written by Sage Buddhakaushika comes to an end and may it be offered at the Feet of Lord Rama in humility.

Shri Rama Jayam

Om Shri Anjaneyaya Namaha

Sarvarishta Nivarakam Subhakaram

Pingakshmakshapaham

Seethanweshanathatparam Kapivaram

Kodindu Soorya Prabham

Lankadweepa Bhayangaram Sakaladham

Sugreevasammanidham Devendradhi

Samastha Devarinudham

Kakustha Dootham Bhaje

Khyatha Sree Rama Dhootha

Pavanuthanupava Pingalaksha Sighavan

Seethasokapahari Dasamugha Vijayee

Laxmana prana datha

Anetha Beshajadre Lavanajala Nidhe

Langane Deekshithoya veera Sreeman Hanuman

Mama Manasivasam Karyasiddhim Thanothu

Buddhir Balam Yaso Dhairyam

Nibayathwamarogatha

Ajadyam Vak Paduthwancha

Hanumath Smranadh Bhavedh

The 108 Names of Shri Rama

Om Shri Ramaya namaha	Pleasing One.
Om Ramabhadraya namaha	Auspicious and Pleasing One.
Om Ramachadraya	Whose countenance is pleasing like the Moon.
Om Saswathaya	Eternal.
Om Rajeevalochanaya	Deer-eyed One.
Om Sreemathe	Glorious.
Om Rajendraya	Like Indra among Kings.
Om Raghupungavaya	Star among the race of the Raghu.
Om Janakivallabhaya	Janki(Sita) is fond of him.
Om Jaithraya	
Om Jithamithraya	One who wins His friends over.
Om Janardhanaya	Lord of the people.
Om Viswamitrapriyaya	Vishwamitra is fond of Him.
Om Dandhaya	One with great Arms.
Om Saranathranathath paraya	One who gives refuge to Orphans.
Om Vallepramadhanadhaya	Giver of great treasures and prosperity
Om Vagmine	The One with sweet speech.
Om Sathyavache	Speaker of Truth.
Om Sathyavikramaya	One who is victorious in the name of Truth.
Om Sathyarrathaya	Imbiber of Truth.
Om Vrathadharaya	Observer of Vows.
Om Sadha Hanumada Srithaya	He who is eternally worshipped by Shri Hanuman.
Om Kousaleyaya	The Famous One.
Om Kharadwansine	The One who lives through hardship.
Om Viradhvnadha	Pandithaya
Om Vibeeshanapari Tratre	
Om Hari Kodanda Khandanaya	The One who broke the bow of Shri Shiva.

Om Saptha Thala-Prabhathre	The One who enlightens the Seven Seas (Chakras).
Om Dasagreeva Siroharaya	The One who defeated the ten-headed demon (Ravana).
Om Thatakanthaya	Giver of life to the dead Vanaras.
Om Vedantasaraya	The One who is the Essence of the Vedas.
Om Vedatmane	The One who is the Spirit of the Vedas.
Om Bhavarogasya	Bheshajaya Healer of diseases.
Om Dooshana Trisiro Hanre	Slayer of Dooshana (demon).
Om Trimoorthaya	Master of the three gunas (left, right and centre).
Om Trigunathmakaya	One whose nature is of the three Gunas.
Om Trivikramaye	He is victorious over the three Gunas.
Om Trilokathmane	The Atma of the three Worlds.
Om Punyacharithra Keertanaya	He who is famous for His Unblemished character.
Om Trilokarakshakaya	Protector of the three Worlds.
Om Dhanwine	He who possesses all the riches.
Om Dandakaranya Kartaya	One who has Strong Arms.
Om Ahalyasopasamanaya	The One who released Ahalaya from the curse.
Om Pitrubhakthaya	He is devoted to His parents.
Om Varapradaya	Giver of boons.
Om Jitendriyaya	Conqueror of the senses.
Om Jitakrodhaya	The One who has conquered Anger.
Om Jitamitraya	One who wins His friends over.
Om Jagadgurave	The Pride of the World.
Om Rikshavanara Sangathine	He who collected the Vanaras (monkeys) as His Army.

Om Chitrakoota Samasrayaya	One who resides in Chitrakoota.
Om Jayanthathranavaradaya	
Om Sumitraputrasevithaya	The One who is served by the Son of Sumitra (Laxmana).
Om Sarvadevadhidevaya	The One who is outstanding among Devas.
Om Mrutavanarajeevanaya	Giver of life to the dead Vanaras.
Om Mayamareechahantre	The Destroyer of the maya of Mareecha (rakshasa).
Om Mahadevaya	Great among Devas.
Om Mahabhujaya	The One with great Arms.
Om Sarvadeva Stuthaya	Praised by all the Devas.
Om Sowmyaya	He who is Soft.
Om Brahmanaya	Realised One.
Om Munisamsthuthaya	He who is praised by all the Saints.
Om Mahayogine	The Mahayogi.
Om Mahodharaya	Big-bellied.
Om Sugreevepsitha Rajyadaya	The One who restored Sugreeva's Kingdom.
Om Sarvapunyadhika Bhalayya	Giver of credit for good deeds.
Om Smritha Sarva Gana Sanaya	Ganas meditate upon Him.
Om Aadhi Purushaya	Primordial One.
Om Parama Purushaya	The Highest Human.
Om Maha Purushaya	Greatest among human beings.
Om Punyodayaya	Giver of credit for all good deeds.
Om Dhaya saraya	He is kind.
Om Purana Purushothamaya	The Greatest of the heroes of legends
Om Smithavakthraya	He who speaks with a smiling face.
Om Mithabashine	Sweet speaking One.
Om Poorvabashine	The First Orator.
Om Raghavaya	From the race of Raghava.
Om Ananda Guna Gambhiraya	Adorned by the quality of joy.
Om Deerodhatha Gunothamaya	He who has the quality of courage.
Om Mayamanushacharithraya	Whose character is full of human Maya.
Om Mahadevadhi-Poojithaya	The One who is worshipped before Shiva.

Om Sethukrithay	He who built the bridge over the Sea.
Om Jithavarasay	Bestower of Victory.
Om Sarvadheerhamayaya	He who contains all the courage.
Om Haraye	He who is Hari Himself.
Om Shyamangaya	He who has a dark body.
Om Sundaraya	Handsome One.
Om Sooraya	Brave and courageous One.
Om Peetha Vasase	He who gains the highest seat.
Om Dhanurdharaya	He who wears a Bow.
Om Sarvayajadhipaya	
Om Yajwane	
Om Jaramaranavarjithaya	He is beyond birth and death.
Om Vibeeshana Prathishtathre	The One who established Vibhishana (brother of Ravana) as a King.
Om Sarvapa Guna Varjithaya	Beyond all gunas.
Om Paramatmane	The Supreme Atma.
Om Parabrahmane	The Supreme Spirit.
Om Satchidananda Vigrahaya	Giver of the state of Satchidananda.
Om Parasmai Jyotishe	He who is the brilliance of Parasa (it is a stone which turns everything into gold).
Om Parasmai Dhamne	He who possesses Parasa.
Om Parakasaya	The One who is height itself.
Om Paratparaya	
Om Paresaya	
Om Paragaya	The Wise One.
Om Paraya	
Om Sarvadevatmakaya	Who is One with all the Devas.
Om Parasmai	The One whose touch turns Everything into Gold.

The 108 Names of Shri Shiva

Shri Shiva is responsible for change, both in the form of death and destruction and in the positive sense of the shedding of old habits.

OM represents the sound of creation, the universe and the three deities of the Hindu trinity, the trimurti ("three images"), of Brahma, Vishnu and Shiva. The vibrations of A-U-M represent the fullness of creation, and the three aspects.

Shiva is the destroyer, his role is viewed as beneficial, since destruction is necessary for creation and destruction can also represent sublimation of the lower physical energies into devotion.

Vishnu incarnates in a form (avatar) in each cycle of time to rescue the universe. He represents the maintenance of balance in the universe; this is done through support of physical and spiritual laws.

Brahma sitting on a lotus indicates that he is always rooted in the ultimate reality, the transcendent aspect remains hidden beneath surface awareness. The four heads of Brahma represent the manifestation of consciousness as mind (manas), intellect (buddhi), ego (ahamkar) and conditioned-consciousness (chit). Thought functions within these aspects, but his consciousness is a transcendent witness to everything.

I AM SHIVA by Adi Shankaracharya

Om, I am neither the mind,
Intelligence, ego, nor 'chitta',
Neither the ears, nor the tongue,
Nor the senses of smell and sight,
Neither ether, nor air,
I am Eternal Bliss and Awareness.
I am Shiva! I am Shiva!
I am neither the 'prana',
Nor the five vital breaths,
Neither the seven elements of the body,
Nor its five sheaths,
Nor hands, nor feet, nor tongue,
Nor other organs of action.
I am Eternal Bliss and Awareness.
I am Shiva! I am Shiva!

Neither fear, greed, nor delusion,
Loathing, nor liking have I,
Nothing of pride, of ego,
Of 'dharma' or Liberation,
Neither desire of the mind,
Nor object for its desiring.
I am Eternal Bliss and Awareness.
I am Shiva! I am Shiva!

Nothing of pleasure and pain,
Of virtue and vice, do I know,
Of mantra, of sacred place,
Of Vedas or Sacrifice,
Neither I am the eater,
The food or the act of eating.
I am Eternal Bliss and Awareness.
I am Shiva! I am Shiva!.

Death or fear, I have none,
Nor any distinction of caste,
Neither father, nor Mother,
Nor even a birth, have I,
Neither friend, nor comrade,
Neither disciple, nor Guru.
I am Eternal Bliss and Awareness.
I am Shiva! I am Shiva!

I have no form or fancy,
The All-pervading am I,

Everywhere I exist,
And yet I am beyond the sense,
Neither salvation am I,
Nor anything to be known.
I am Eternal Bliss and Awareness.
I am Shiva! I am Shiva!
That's what you are. You are Eternal Bliss and Awareness, Consciousness, Pure Consciousness.
Om Shivam Shivakaram Shantam Shivatmanam Shivotamam
Shivamarga Pranetaram Pranatosmi Sadashivam.

Shiva	Pure
Shankara	Compassionate
Swayambu	Born out of Himself
Pashupati	Lord and protector of animals
Kshamakshetra	Field of forgiveness
Priyabhakta	Favorite of the devotees
Kamadeva	God of Love
Sadhusadhya	Achieved easily by the saintly
Hrtpundarikasina	Occupying the lotus of the heart
Jagaddhitaisin	Well wisher of the Universe
Vyaghrakomala	Tender to the tiger
Vatsala	Beloved
Devasuraguru	Preceptor of the Gods and of the Asuras
Shambu	Bestower of blessings
Lokottarasukhalaya	Abode of the most excellent happiness
Sarvasaha	Bearer of everything
Svadhrta	Self-supported
Ekanayaka	Sole Lord
Shrivatsala	The darling of the Goddess
Subhada	Bestower of auspiciousness
Sarvasattvavalambana	Supporter of all living beings
Sarvaripati	Lord of the night
Varada	Bestower of boons
Vayuvahana	Having the wind of vibrations as vehicle
Kamandaludhara	Holding water-pot

Nadhishwara	Lord of the rivers
Prasadasva	Lord of the wind
Sukhanila	Pleasing wind
Nagabhusana	Having serpents for His ornaments
Kailashasikharavasin	Residing on top of Mount Kailash
Trilocana	Three eyed
Pinakapani	Holding the mighty bow
Sramana	Ascetic
Acaleshwara	Lord of the mountain
Vyaghracarmambara	Wearing the tiger hide
Unmattavesa	Having the guise of a mad one
Pretacarin	Going about surrounded by bhoots
Hara	Destroyer
Rudra	Fierce
Bhimaparakrama	Of terrible exploits
Nateshwara	Lord of the dance
Nataraja	King of the dance.
Ishwara	The Lord of spiritual reality
Paramashiva	The great Shri Shiva
Paramatma	The soul of the Cosmos
Parameshwara	The supreme Lord
Vireshwara	The Lord of heroes
Sarveshwara	The Lord of All
Kameshwara	The Lord of Love
Vishwasakshina	The Witness of the Universe
Nityanrtya	Ever dancing
Sarvavasa	Abode of All
Mahayogi	The great Yogi
Sadayogi	Primordial, immutable Yogi
Sadashiva	God the Almighty
Atma	The Self
Ananda	The Joy
Chandramauli	With the moon for His crest jewel
Maheshwara	The great Lord

Sudhapati	Lord of nectar
Amrutapa	Drinker of nectar
Amrutamaya	Full of nectar
Pranatatmaka	Soul of the devotee
Purusha	Divine spiritual Being
Pracchanna	Hidden One
Sukshma	Very subtle
Karnikarapriya	Fond of the pericarp of the lotus
Kavi	The poet
Amoghadanda	Of never failing punishment
Nilakanta	With a blue throat
Jatin	Having matted hair
Pushpalocana	Having flowery eyes
Dhyanadhara	The object of meditation
Brahmandahrt	The Heart of the Universe
Kamashasana	Chastiser of Manmatha
Jitakama	Conqueror of lust
Jitendriya	Conqueror of sense organs
Atindrya	Beyond the scope of sense organs
Nakshatramalin	Having a garland of stars
Anadyanta	Having neither beginning nor end
Atmayoni	The origin of the Self
Nabhoyoni	The origin of the firmament
Karuna Sagara	Ocean of mercy
Sulin	Owner of the trident
Maheshvasa	Having a great bow
Nishkalanka	Spotless
Nityasundara	Ever beautiful
Ardhanarishwara	Whose other half is Shri Parvati
Umapati	The Lord of the Mother
Rasada	The bestower of sweetness
Ugra	Frightful
Mahakala	The great destroyer
Kalakala	The destroyer of death

Vaiyaghra Dhurya	The leader of the nature of the tiger
Satrupramathin	The suppressor of enemies
Sarvacarya	Preceptor of all
Sama	Equanimous
Atmaprasannya	Contented soul
Naranarayanapriya	Fond of Nara and Narayana (Shri Shesha and Shri Vishnu)
Rasajna	The knower of the taste
Bhaktikaya	Whose body is devotion
Lokaviragrani	The leader of the heroes of the world
Cirantana	Eternal life
Vishvambareshwara	Lord of the Earth
Navatman	Born again soul
Navyerusalemeshwa	Lord of the New Jerusalem
Adi Nirmalatma	The Primordial Self.
Yogipriya	Fond of Yogis.

**Sakshat Shri Adi Shakti Shri Parvati - Namoh Namah*

Shri Durga

Shri Durga is an incarnation of Maha Devi or the Mother Goddess, and a unified symbol of all divine forces. She manifested at a time when evil forces threatened the very existence of the ancient Gods. To destroy these demons, all the gods offered their radiance to her creation and each formed part of Durga's body.

The 84 Names of Shri Durga

Kameshvara Stra Nirgadha	She annihilates Bandasura and Sabhandasura Shunyakaya his city with her blazing weapons.
Namah Madhu Kaitabha Hantri Namah	She is the killer of Madhu and Kaitabha
Mahish Asura Gatini Namah	She is the slayer of Mahishasura
Raktabija Vinashini Namah	She is the destroyer of Raktabija
Narak Antaka Namah	She is the killer and destroyer of
NaraRavana Madhini Namah	She is the destruction of Ravana
Rakshasagni Namah	She destroys all the evil forces and rakshasas.
Chandika Namah	She is angry with evil forces.
Ugrachandeshvari Namah	She is Fire, Hailstorm and Fury.
Krodhini Namah	She is the Cosmic Wrath.
Ugraprabha Namah	She is the radiance of Fury.
Chamunda Namah	She is the slayer of Chanda and Munda.

Khadgapalini Namah	She rules by the sword.
Bhasvarasuri Namah	Her blinding radiance destroys the demonic forces.
Shattrumadhini Namah	She is the slayer of the enemies of the Saints.
Ranapandita Namah	She is the Mistress of the science of wars and battles.
Raktadantika Namah	Her sparkling teeth chuckle with Bloody thirst for challenging evil forces.
Raktapriya Namah	She is fond of the blood of demons.
Kurukulavirodhini	Namah she is the confronter of demonic hosts and all the sins of the world.
Daityendramadhini Namah	She is the victorious chief demon slayer.
Nishumbashumbasanhatri	She is the destroyer of Shumba and Namah Nishumba.
Chandi Namah cies and	She is the remover of evil tenden- desires of her devotees.
Mahakali Namah	She is the Great Destroyer.
Papanashini Namah the	She is deeply devoted to cleansing sinful souls.
Shmashanakalika Namah	She presides over the dead and lives in the cremation ground.
Kulishangi Namah	She is the Thunderbolt-bodied.
Dipta Namah	She is the beautiful Mother illunimating the dark paths followed by the seekers.
Ghoradanshtra Namah	She has exceedingly fierce jaws.
Mahadanshtra Namah	She is endowed with Cosmic Jaws.
Vijaya Namah	She establishes triumph over evil.
Tara Namah	She is the Savior of all and redeems all evils.

Suryatmika Namah	She is radiant like the sun.
Rudrani Namah	She is the Spouse of Rudra, removing all opposition to the creation.
Raudri Namah	She is the force of Rudra to abolish all outdated things.
Bhayapaha Namah	She liberates her devotees from fear and doubt.
Rathini Namah	She is chariot-seated and supreme in Battle against the asuric forces.
Samaraprita Namah	She has a deep passion for the wars of life as a whole.
Vegini Namah	She crushes all opposition.
Tarak asura samharini Namah	She is the slayer of Taraka.
Vajrini Namah	She is the Thunderbolt-handed Mother challenging the asuric forces.
Atirama Namah	She is the healing influence.
Shankini Namah	She holds a conch for her battle with the demons.
Chakrini Namah	She is holding Vishnu's Discus for war.
Gadini Namah	She is holding a Mace to crush down the demons.
Padmini Namah	She is the Lotus-holding Mother blessing her devotees in the battle of life.
Shulini Namah	She is the demon-killer holding the Trident.
Parighastra Namah	She is the Club-holding Mother paving the way for fresh creation.
Pashini Namah	She is the Noose-holding terrific Image of the feminine Goddess Mother Mahakali.
Pinakadharini Namah	She is the Bow-holding Mother, the Almighty Force for protecting the Gods and her devotees.
Raktapa Namah	She drinks blood in the cosmic war for Love Asurantka
Namah.	She is dedicated to destroying the demons.

Jayada Namah	She symbolises Good over evil.
Bhishananana Namah	She is Huge-faced, and the Cosmic Might for the disruption of brute force on earth.
Jvalini Namah	She is the Cosmic Blaze, burning the asuras
Durdhyeya Namah	She knows no rest in slaying the asuras.
Bherunda Namah	She awakens a formidable Form for slaying the asuras.
Batubhairavi Namah	She is the all-destroying Vigour of Shiva.
Balabhairavi Namah	She is the child-like Wife of Rudra.
Mahabhairavi Namah	She is the Great Consort of Bhairava.
Vatukabhairavi Namah	
Siddhabhairavi Namah	She is in tune with the Power of Lord Shiva
Kankalabhairavi Namah	
Kalabhairavi Namah	She is the fearful Wife of Shiva.
Kalagnibhairavi Namah	
Yoginibhairavi Namah	She is the Consort of Shiva in the form of Great Yogini.
Shaktibhairavi Namah	She is the Power of Shiva.
Anandabhairavi Namah	She is very joyful being the Wife of the Cosmic Destroyer Shiva.
Martandabhairavi Namah	
Gaurabhairavi Namah	
Smashanabhairavi Namah	She is in the spirit of total Dissolution, symbolized by her Love of the cremation' ground.
Purabhairavi Namah	She is the indwelling Spirit of the Goddess
Tarunabhairavi Namah	She is the youthfully buoyant Mother Kali gone crazy for dissolving the universe in tune with Shiva.
Paramanandabhairavi Namah	She rejoices with Lord Shiva.
Suranandabhairavi Namah	She is deeply in Love with the Gods and Godly nectar.
Gyananandabhairavi Namah	She is joyful at the face of the Cosmic

	Deluge.
Uttamanandabhairavi Namah	She is the ecstatically keen for the dissolution of the worlds in tune with Shiva.
Amritanandabhairavi Namah	She is the enjoyer of the philosophy of cosmic dissolution as Shiva's Wife.
Chakreshvari Namah	She holds Discus for Destroying the asuras.
Rajachakreshvari Namah	She is the Royal Discus-holder, making her devotees fearless.
Vira Namah	She symbolizes the Great Strength.
Sadhakanamsukhakari Namah	She is the Dark Divine Deity, devouringly devoted to the cause of healing the hurt minds of her devotee and thus affording them the Eternal Joy.
Sadhakarivinashini Namah	She is the mighty Mother Mahakali, vowed to slay the disruptive forces which confront her children.
Shukranindakanashini Namah	She is avowed to slay those who Condemn the spirit of Purity.
Sadhakadhivinashini Namah	She is the Love incarnated Mother devoted to destroying the suffering of her devotees.

Aparajita Hymn—In praise of the Devi Mahatmyam (Shri Durga)

Ya Devi sarva buteshu	To the Devi who in all beings
Vishnumayaiti	Shabdita is called Vishnumaya.
Namas tasyai	Salutations to Her,
Namas tasyai	Salutations to Her,
Namas tasyai	Salutations to Her,
Namo namah	Salutations to Her again and again.
Ya Devi sarva buteshu	To the Devi who in all beings
Chetanyata bhidhiyate	is termed as Consciousness.
Namas tasyai	Salutations to Her,
Namas tasyai	Salutations to Her,
Namas tasyai	Salutations to Her,
Namo namah	Salutations again and again.
Ya Devi sarva bhuteshu	To the Devi who abides in all beings
Buddhi rupena Samstithan	the form of intelligence.
Namas tasyai	Salutations to Her,
Namas tasyai	Salutations to Her,
Namas tasyai	Salutations to Her,
Namo namah	Salutations again and again.
Ya Devi sarva bhuteshu	To the Devi who abides in all beings
Nidra rupena Samstithan	the form of sleep
Namas tasyai	Salutations to Her,
Namas tasyai	Salutations to Her,
Namas tasyai	Salutations to Her,
Namo namah	Salutations again and again.
Kshuddha rupena	form of hunger
Chaya rupena	form of reflection
Shakti rupena	form of power
Trishna rupena	form of thirst
Kshanti rupena	form of forgiveness
Jati rupena	form of genius

Lajja rupena	form of modesty
Shanti rupena	form of peace
Shraddha rupena	form of faith
Kanti rupena	form of luster
Lakshmi rupena	form of good fortune
Vritti rupena	form of activity.
Smrti rupena	form of memory
Daya rupena	form of compassion
Tushti rupena	form of contentment
Matr rupena	form of Mother
Bhranti rupena	form of error

Shantakaram	Peaceful in form, reclining on the
Bhujagashayanam	serpent, lotus-navelled Lord of the
Padmanabham Suresham	bearer of the Universe, like
Vishwadharam,	the heavens, the color of dark
Gaganasadrsham	raincluds of auspicious limbs;
Meghawarnam	Beloved of Shri Lakshmi, with lotus
Subhangameyes,	approached by the meditation
Lakshmikantam of Yogis,	praise by the meditation
Kamalanayanam	praise Shri Vishnu, the
Yogeebheerdyanagamyam	remover of the fear of becoming, the
Vande Vishnum Bhava	One Lord of all the worlds.
Bhayaharam	
Sarvalokaikanatham	

The 99 Names of Allah

La Illaha Illa Hah Muhammad Rasulullah

Ar-Rahman	The Beneficent	Al-Muhaymin	The Protector
Ar-Rahim	The Merciful	Al-Aziz	The Mighty
Al-Malik	Sovereign Lord	Al-Jabbar	The Compeller
Al-Quddus	The Holy	Al-Mutakabbir	The Majestic
As-Salam	Source of Peace	Al-Khaliq	The Creator
Al-Mu'min	Guardian of Faith	Al-Bari	The Evolver
Al-Musawwir	The Fashioner	Al-Alim	The All Knowing
Al-Ghaffar	The Forgiver	Al-Qabid	The Constrictor
Al-Qahhar	The Subduer	Al-Basit	The Expander
Al-Wahhab	The Bestower	Al-Khafid	The Abaser
Ar-Razzaq	The Provider	Ar-Rafi	The Exalter
Al-Fattah	The Opener	Al-Mu'izz	The Honorer
Al-Muzill	The Dishonourer	Al-Khabir	The Aware
As-Sami	The All-Hearing	Al-Halim	The Forbearing One
Al-Basir	The All-Seeing	Al-Azim	The Great One
Al-Hakam	The Judge	Al-Ghafur	The All Forgiving
Al-Adl	The Just	Ash-Shakur	The Appreciative
Al-Latif	The Subtle One	Al-Ali	The Most High
Al-Kabir	The Most Great	Ar-Raqib	The Watchful
Al-Hafiz	The Preserver	Al-Mujib	The Responsive
Al-Muqit	The Maintainer	Al-Wasi	The All-Embracing
Al-Hasib	The Reckoner	Al-Hakim	The Wise
Al-Jalil	The Sublime One	Al-Wadud	The Loving
Al-Karim	The Generous One	Al-Majid	Most Glorious One
Al-Ba'ith	The Resurrector	Al-Wali	Protecting Friend
Ash-Shahid	The Witness	Al-Hamid	The Praiseworthy
Al-Haqq	The Truth	Al-Muhsi	The Reckoner
Al-Wakil	The Trustee	Al-Mubdi	The Originator
Al-Qawi	The Most Strong	Al-Mu'id	The Restorer
At-Matin	The Firm One	Al-Muyhi	The Giver of Life
Al-Awwa	The First	At-Tawwab	The Acceptor of Repentance

Al-Akhir	The Last	Al-Muntaqim	The Avenger
Az-Zahir	The Manifest	Al-Afuw	The Pardoner
Al-Batin	The Hidden	Ar-Ra'uf	The Compassionate
Al-Wali	The Governor	Malik-Ul-Mulk	The Eternal Owner of Sovereign.
Al-Muta'ali	The Most Exalted	Dhul-Jalal-Wal	The Lord of Majesty, Ikram and Bounty
Al-Barr	The Source	Al-Muqsit	The Equitable of all Goodness
Al-Mumit	Creator of Death	Al-Ahad	The One
Al-Havy	The Alive	As-Samsad	The Eternal
Al-Qayyum	Self-Subsisting	Al-Qadir	The Able
Al-Wajid	The Finder	Al-Muqtadir	The Powerful
Al-Majid	The Noble	Al-Muqaddim	The Expediter
Al-Wahid	The Unique	Al-Mu'ahkhir	The Delayer
Al-Jame	The Gatherer	Al-Hadi	The Guide
Al-Ghani	The Self-Sufficient	Al-Badi	The Incomparable
Al-Mughni	The Enricher	Al-Baqi	The Everlasting
Al-Mani	The Preventer	Al-Warith	Supreme Inheritor
Ad-Darr	The Distresser	Ar-Rashid	The Guide to the Right Path
An Nafi	The Propitious		
An-Nur	The Light	As-Sabur	The Patient

The 108 Names of the Ganga

Gangastottara-sata-namavali

According to Indian folklore; king Bhagiratha who resided in the Heavens, did Tapasya for many years to bring the river Ganga, down to the Earth this so his ancestors could find salvation from the wicked seer who had cursed them. It was said through the blessings of Shiva, the Ganga descended to the Earth, to make the whole earth pious, fertile and wash away the sins of the humans. The Ganga is more than a river, its a mother of life, a goddess, a spiritual tradition, and so much more.

Ganga	Ganges
Vishnu-padabja-sambhuta	Born from the lotus-like foot of Vishnu
Hara-vallabha	Dear to Hara (Shiva)
Himacalendra-tanaya	Daughter of the Lord of Himalaya
Giri-mandala-gamini	Flowing through the mountain country
Tarakarati-janani	Mother of [the demon] Taraka's enemy (i.e. Karttikeya)
Sagaratmaja-tarika	Liberator of the [60,000] sons of Sagara (who had been burnt to ashes by the angry glance of the sage Kapila).
Saraswati-samayukta	Joined to [the river] Saraswati (said to have flowed underground and joined the Ganges at Allahabad).
Sughosa	Melodious (or: Noisy).
Sindhu-gamini	Flowing to the ocean
Bhagirathi	Pertaining to the saint Bhagiratha (whose prayers brought the Ganges down from Heaven).
Bhagyavati	Happy, fortunate

Bhagiratha-rathanuga	Following the chariot of Bhagiratha (who led the Ganges down to Hell to purify the ashes of Sagara's sons).
Trivikrama-padoddhuta	Falling from the foot of Vishnu
Triloka-patha-gamini	Flowing through the three worlds (i.e.Heaven, earth and the atmosphere or lower Regions).
Ksira-subhra	White as milk.
Bahu-ksira	[A cow] which gives much milk
Ksira-vrksa-samakula	Abounding in [the four] "milk Trees' (i.e. Nyagrodha (Banyan). Udumbara (glamorous fig-Tree), Asvattha (holy-fig-Tree),and adhuka(Bassia Latifolia).
Trilocana-jata-vasini	Dwelling in the matted locks of Shiva.
Rna-traya-vimocini	Releasing from the Three Debts, viz. **(1)** Brahma-carya (study of the Vedas) to the rishis, **(2)** sacrifice and worship to the Gods, **(3)** procreation of a son, to the Manes. Tripurari-siras-cuda The tuft on the head of the enemy of Tripura (Shiva). (Tripura was a triple fortification, built in the sky, air and earth of gold, silver and iron respectively, by Maya for the Asuras, and burnt by Shiva).
Jahnavi	Pertaining to Jahnu (who drank up the Ganges in a rage after it had flooded but relented and allowed it to flow from his ear).
Nata-bhiti-hrt	Carrying away fear.
Avyaya	Imperishable.
Nayanananda-dayini	Affording delight to the eye.
Naga-putrika	Daughter of the mountain.
Niranjana	Not painted with collyrium (i.e. colorless)
Nitya-suddha	Eternally pure.

Nira-jala-pariskrta	Adorned with a net of water.
Savitri	Stimulator
Salila-vasa	Dwelling in water.
Sagarambusa-medhini	Swelling the waters of the ocean.
Ramya	Delightful
Bindu-saras	River made of water-drops
Avyakta	Unmanifest, unevolved
Vrndaraka-samasrita	Resort of the eminent
Uma-sapatni Uma	Having the same husband (i.e. Shiva) as (Parvati).
Subhrangi	Having beautiful limbs (or body).
Shrimati	Beautiful, auspicious, illustrious, etc.
Dhavalambara	Having a dazzling white garment.
Akhandala-vana-vasa	Having Shiva as a forest-dweller (hermit).
Khandendu-krta-sekhara	Having the crescent moon as a crest.
Amrtakara-salila	Whose water is a mine of nectar.
Lila-lamghita-parvata	Leaping over mountains in sport.
Virinci-kalasa-vasa	Dwelling in the water-pot of Brahma (or Vishnu, or Shiva).
Triveni	Triple-braided (i.e. consisting of the waters of three rivers; Ganges, Yamuna and Saraswati).
Trigunatmika	Possessing the three gunas.
Sangataghaugha-samani	Destroying the mass of sins of Sangata.
Sankha-dundubhi-nisvana	Making a noise like a conch-shell and drum.
Bhiti-hrt	Carrying away fear.
Bhagya-janani	Creating happiness.
Bhinna-brahmanda-darpini	Taking pride in the broken egg of Brahma.
Nandini	Happy
Sighra-ga	Swift-flowing
Siddha	Perfect, holy.
Saranya	Yielding shelter, help or protection.

Sasi-sekhara	Moon-crested
Sankari	Belonging to Sankara (Shiva).
Saphari-purna	Full of fish (esp. Cyprinus Saphore a kind of bright little fish that glistens when darting about in shallow water—or carp).
Bharga-murdha-kṛtalaya	Having Bharga's (Shiva's) head as an abode
Bhava-priya	Dear to Bhava (Shiva)
Satya-sandha-priya	Dear to the faithful.
Hamsa-svarupini	Embodied in the forms of swans.
Bhagiratha-suta	Daughter of Bhagiratha
Ananta	Eternal.
Sarac-candra-nibhanana	Resembling the autumn moon.
Om-kara-rupini	Having the appearance of the syllable Om.
Atula	Peerless.
Krida-kallola-karini	Sportively billowing
Svarga-sopana-sarani	Flowing like a staircase to Heaven.
Ambhah-prada	Bestowing water.
Duhkha-hantri	Destroying sorrow.
Santi-santana-karini	Bringing about the continuance of peace.
Darirya-hantr	Destroyer of poverty.
Siva-da	Bestowing happiness.
Samsara-visa-nasini	Destroying the poison of illusion.
Prayaga-nilaya	Having Prayaga (Allahabad) as an abode.
Sita	"Furrow". Name of the eastern branch of the four mythical branches into which the heavenly Ganges is supposed to divide after falling on Mount Meru.
Tapa-traya-vimocini	Releasing from the Three Afflictions.
Saranagata-dinarṭa-paritrana	Protector of the sick and suffering who come to you for refuge.
Sumukti-da	Giving complete [spiritual] emancipation.
Siddhi-yoga-nisevita	Resorted to (for acquisition of magic

	powers).
Papa-hantri	Destroyer of sin.
Pavanangi	Having a pure body.
Parabrahma-svarupini	Embodiment of the Supreme Spirit.
Purna	Full.
Puratana	Ancient.
Punya	Auspicious.
Punya-da	Bestowing merit.
Punya-vahini	Possessing (or producing) merit.
Pulomajarcita	Worshipped by Indrani (wife of Indra).
Puta	Pure.
Puta-tribhuvana	Purifier of the Three Worlds.
Japa	Muttering, whispering.
Jangama	Moving, alive.
Jangamadhara	Support of substratum of what lives or moves.
Jala-rupa	Consisting of water.
Jagad-d-hita	Friend or benefactor of what lives or moves.
Jahnu-putri	Daughter of Jahnu.
Jagan-matr	Mother of Bhisma.
Siddha	Holy.
Ramya	Delightful, beautiful.
Uma-kara-kamala-sanjata	Born from the lotus which dreaded Uma (Parvati)
Anjana-timira-bhanu	A light amid the darkness of ignorance.

OM **Namoh Namah**

5—Vishuddhi Chakra

Shri Krishna

Mahabharata

The Mahabharata is a beautiful epic depiction of a great Indian battle for dharma stated to have occurred in 3139 BC. It was written in a poem of 100,000 verses—the Veda Vyasa, the longest epic poem ever created. It also contains the philosophical treatise, the Bhagavad Gita. This is where the Vedic struggle between the deities of truth and light battle the powers of darkness, division and falsehood. This is relevant to the long lasting battle of human kind, as the forces of the anti-Christ try and prevent spiritual evolution. 2012 is relevant to the battle.

The Bhagavad Gita represents numerous subplots, and interpretations on theology and morals. Shri Krishna not only helps his brother Arjuna understand the basis of social laws of civilization, but the absolute map to understanding the riddle of life, self-discovery and inner fulfillment. This epic relates to many things on many levels, including the battle of the self on the physical and spiritual levels that happened during the last great cycle. It represents the power of detachment and witnessing the drama of life, to prevent one from invoking the law of cause and effect (karma). This battle could also apply to the ancient mythological civilization of Atlantis or even before, or to a battle between alien beings that inhabited Earth long ago.

Bhagavadgita—*10th Chapter*

This is a time where Lord Krsishna sums up and describes the attainment of salvation by the paths of karma. Krishna explains the meaning of renunciation and the effects of the modes of nature on human consciousness and activity. He explains Brahman realization, the glories of the Bhagavad-gita, and the ultimate conclusion of the Gita: the highest path of spirit at the time, is absolute, unconditional loving surrender unto the Lord Divine, which frees one from all sins, brings one to complete enlightenment, and enables one to return to Krishna's eternal spiritual abode. The Lord explains that while on the journey to enlightenment one must offer up and surrender to the pure essence of God.

The Perfection of Renunciation

Verse 1—Arjuna said, O mighty-armed one, I wish to understand the purpose of renunciation [tyaga] and of the renounced order of life [sannyasa], O killer of the Kesi demon, Hrsikesa.

Verse 2—The Supreme Lord said, To give up the results of all activities is called renunciation [tyaga] by the wise. And that state is called the renounced order of life [sannyasa] by great learned men.

Verse 3—Some learned men declare that all kinds of fruitive activities should be given up, but there are yet other sages who maintain that acts of sacrifice, charity and penance should never be abandoned.

Verse 4—O best of the Bharatas, hear from Me now about renunciation. O tiger among men, there are three kinds of renunciation declared in the scriptures.

Verse 5—Acts of sacrifice, charity and penance are not to be given up but should be performed. Indeed, sacrifice, charity and penance purify even the great souls.

Verse 6—All these activities should be performed without any expectation of result. They should be performed as a matter of duty, O son of Prtha. That is My final opinion.

Verse 7—Wherever there is Krsna, the master of all mystics, and wherever there is Arjuna, the supreme archer, there will also certainly be opulence, victory, extraordinary power, and morality. That is my opinion.

The 108 Names of Shri Krishna—Vishuddhi Chakra

"Whenever, O scion of Bharata, Dharma declines and evil prevails, I incarnate Myself."

Bhagavad Gita

No names can describe Him. He cannot be grasped, and He is beyond praise. Salutation, Honor and Glory to Shri Bhagavati, Shri Adi Shakti Parvati the love who Shri Krishna dances in the Heavens with as the universes unfold into the Aquarian Age.

He is Shri Krishna. Praise unto Him for Ever and Ever.

He is worshipped through Christ. Praise unto Him...

He grants permission to become a Yogi.

He accepts the Yogis certified by Lord Jesus Christ.

He accepts the Yagnyas of the noble souls.

He is the Primordial Being.

He is the Ishwara of the Yogis.

He is the God of Yoga.

He is our Ideal in its highest Glory.

He is sublime and the source of sublimity.

He is fully aware of His Divine Powers.

He is the Sakshi (Witness).

He is the axis of the whirling universes.

He holds the strings of the cosmic puppet show.

He is the great Enticer of the three worlds.

He is the Father yet He is the Friend.

He is the revelation of ultimate Fatherhood.

He manifests Shri Sadashiva.

Adi Shakti's creation is for His play.

He is the integrated brain of Divinity.

He was, is and ever shall be.

He is Vishnu the Magnificent.

He is the Yahweh of Moses.

Buddha perceived Him as Nirakara (formless).

He is the Father of Yeshu Krisht.

He is the Akbar of Islam.

He is the Lord God Almighty, all-knowing, all-pervading.

He is the Master of the Aquarian Age.

He gets the Divine work done in Krita Yuga.

He carries the yellow-dusted feet of Radhaji in His heart.

He sees Radhaji in Mother's laughing eyes.

He is the worshipper of Shri Nirmala Viratangana.

He pervades Akasha.

He is the blue Lord of ethereal Infinity.

He is blue for the sake of Shri Mahakali.

For His sake the firmament is blue.

He wears many garlands of moons, suns and stars.

He plays with Mother Surabhi on the Milky Way.

Shri Brahmadeva gave Him His yellow dhoti.

The Sun rises to behold Him.

He grants the Power of total Confidence.

He grants the Power of Decision.

He grants the Power of Detachment.

He grants the Power of Responsibility.

He grants the Power of auspicious Vision.

He grants the Power of Leadership.

He granted abundance to America.

He grants the Power of Plentitude.

He grants the Power to communicate and convince.

He grants Power to Silence.

He grants Power to the Sahaja Collectivity.

He grants the Power to Share.

He grants the Power to Permeate.

He grants the Power to expand Thoughtless Awareness.
He grants the Power of Cosmic Consciousness.
He has the Power to make anyone a king.
He grants and withdraws power to human institutions.
He bears the rings of Saturn on His right finger.
He makes fun of worldly powers.
He shatters the pillars of false dharma.
He is blazing doom for adharma.
He is both Madhuri and Samhara-shakti.
He subdues the serpents of anger, hate and arrogance.
He dislikes frivolity, grossness and plastics.
He is mischievous with individuals.
He incarnates on this earth to re-establish the dharma of innocence.
He restores the lost vision of the Absolute.
All myths are consumed by the fire of His Truth.
He leads His worshippers beyond the Kurukshetra of involvement.
He inspired the saints and sages and leaders of truth.
He is propitiated by the twice born for the salvation of America.
He leads the twice born back to Gokul.
He teaches the twice born
He is adorable and adored by the twice born.
He plays around in frolics, joy and happiness.
The cows of Maharashtra rushed to lick His arms.
He is the incarnation of gentle graciousness.
He melts everyone's hearts in the honey-like spring of His Sweetness.
He drives the chariot of the five senses.
He is the protector of chaste womanhood.
He is fond of the Nirmala bhaktas.
He asked Garuda to answer the call of the Nirmala bhaktas.
He sent Sudarshana Chakra to kill the foes of the Nirmala bhaktas.
He purifies all relationships.
He envelops our sister's chastity in Draupadi's sari.
He adorns our brothers with valor and chivalry.
He is the flute player of collective charisma.

He plays Rasa with the gopis.
He is the friend of the Sudhama yogi.
He makes the Energy circulate through everyone.
He establishes the link with collectivity.
He is the collective Consciousness of the Atma.
He breaks the pitcher, which covers the ego.
He dissolves ego in ether Consciousness.
He dispels superego in witnessing Consciousness.
He feeds the roots of the Tree of Life in the brain.
He enlightens the cells of the brain.
He crowns the Consciousness of the twice born.
He sustains Adi Shakti's throne in the brain.
He is the Lord of inconceivable Majesty.
He is the Witness of His own Bliss.
He rules over the Ocean of Amrut.
He resides at the parting of Adi Shakti's hair.
He leads the play of recognition of Shri Adi Shakti Maha Devi.
He will establish on this earth the dazzling Glory of
Shri Maha Adi Shakti Maha Devi.
He will unite the nations of the earth at the Lotus Feet of Divine love.

Sakshat Shri Adi Shakti Parvati Shri Maha Devi Namoh Namah

The 16 Names of Shri Radha Krishna

Vishuddhi Chakra

Om twameva Sakshat, Shri Radha Krishna Sakshat

Shri Adi Shakti Parvati, Shri Maha Devi Namoh Namah

Shri Radha Krishna	The Supreme Power of the Dark-Blue God, who is of the nature of Truth, Consciousness and Bliss.
Shri Vitthala Rukmini	Shri Radha and Shri Krishna with the right Vishuddi power.
Shri Govidampatih	The Supreme Lord of those who know pure speech.
Shri Gopta	Ruling over all creatures, he protects the world
Shri Govindah	The Lord attained by pure speech
Shri Gopatih	The Lord of the Earth
Shri Americeshwari	The Lord of America
Shri Yeshoda	The foster-Mother of Shri Krishna
Shri Vishnumaya	Shri Krishna's sister as the Maya Shakti
Shri Vainavini Vamsanadaya	The One who is the holder of the flute and the Sweet Sound of the flute-melody.
Shri Viratangata Virata	The Supreme Power of the absolute Cosmic Being.
Shri Bal Krishna	Lord Krishna as a Child.
Shri Sikhandi	The Peacock feather adorns his head.
Narak Antaka	The destroyer of Narakasurna.
Shri Mahanidhih	All being are in him.
Shri Maharadah	The Yogins remain peaceful and happy by plunging in the refreshing waters of his Bliss.

Sakshat Shri Adi Shakti Parvati Shri Maha Devi Namoh Namah

6—*Agnya Chakra – Third Eye*

Buddha—Agnya Chakra

Buddha means "Awakened". He fully comprehended the Four Noble Truths and as he arose from the slumbers of ignorance he is called a Buddha. He is not the dogma associated with his name; he is the pure essence of truth, wisdom and ego without desires.

Since he not only comprehends but also expounds the doctrine and enlightens others, He is called a Samma-Sambuddha *(Fully Enlightened One).* One who is connected to the Universal Light Consciousness.

"Your Reverence will be a deity?"

"No, indeed, brahmin, a deity am I not," replied the Buddha.

"Then Your Reverence will be a God?"

"No indeed, brahmin, a God am I not."

"Then Your Reverence will be a human being?"

"No indeed, brahmin, a human being am I not."

"Who, then will Your Reverence be?"

The Buddha replied that He had destroyed Defilements which conditions rebirth as a God or a human being and added:

> "As a lotus, fair and lovely, By the water is not soiled, By the world am I not soiled; Therefore, brahmin, am I Buddha!"

Prayer for Shri Buddha

Buddham Sharanam gachami

Dhamam sharanam gachami

Sangham sharanam gachami

"Neither fire, nor wind, birth nor death, can erase our good deeds.

Fill your mind with compassion." Buddha

The Four Reliances

First,	rely on the spirit and meaning of the teachings, not on the words;
Second,	rely on the teachings, not on the personality of the teacher;
Third,	rely on real wisdom, not superficial interpretation;
Fourth,	rely on the essence of your pure Wisdom Mind, not on judgmental perceptions.

"We are what we think. All that we are arises with our thoughts.

With our thoughts, we make our world."

"To be idle is a short road to death and to be diligent is a way of life; foolish people are idle, wise people are diligent."

"Let us rise up and be thankful, for if we didn't learn a lot today, at least we learned a little, and if we didn't learn a little, at least we didn't get sick, and if we got sick, at least we didn't die; so, let us all be thankful."

"Pay no attention to the faults of others, things done or left undone by others.

Consider only what by oneself is done or left undone. What we think, we become."

"Holding on to anger is like grasping a hot coal with the intent of throwing it at someone else; you are the one getting burned."

"Do not overrate what you have received, nor envy others."

"He who envies others does not obtain peace of mind."

"An insincere and evil friend is more to be feared than a wild beast; a wild beast may wound your body, but an evil friend will wound your mind."

"Words have the power to both destroy and heal. When words are both true and kind, they can change our world."

"Anger will never disappear so long as thoughts of resentment are cherished in the mind. Anger will disappear just as soon as thoughts of resentment are forgotten."

"Do not dwell in the past, do not dream of the future, concentrate the mind on the present moment."

"Words have the power to both destroy and heal. When words are both true and kind, they can change our world."

"On life's journey Faith is nourishment, Virtuous deeds are a shelter,"

"Wisdom is the light by day and Right mindfulness is the protection by night."

"If a man lives a pure life nothing can destroy him;

If he has conquered greed nothing can limit his freedom."

Buddha

The 51 Names of Mary Maha Lakshmi

Sancta Maria—Benedice nos	Holy Mary—Please bless us
Sancta Der Genitrix	Holy Mother of God
Sancta Virgo Virginium	Holy Virgin of all the Virgins
Mater Christi	Mother of Christ
Mater Divinae Gratiae	Mother of the Divine grace
Mater Purissima	Purest Mother
Mater Castissima	Mother most chaste
Mater Inviolata	Inviolate Mother
Mater Intemerata	Spotless Mother
Mater Amabilis	Lovable Mother
Mater Admirabilis	Admirable Mother
Mater Boni Concilii	Mother of good advice
Mater Creatoris	Mother of the Creator
Mater Salvatoris	Mother of the Redeemer
Virgo Prudentissima	Most wise virgin
Virgo Veneranda	Most venerable virgin
Virgo Praedicanda	Virgin to be preached
Virgo Potens	Mighty Virgin
Virgo Clemens	Compassionate virgin
Virgo Fidelis	Trustworthy virgin
Speculum Justitiae	Mirror of justice
Sedes Sapientiae	Seat of wisdom

Causa Nostra Laetitiae	Source of our joy
Vas Spirituale	Vessel filled with the Holy Spirit
Vas Honorabilis	Vessel of honesty
Vas Insignae	Devotionis Vessel of signal devotion
Rosa Majestica	Majestic rose
Turris Davidica	Tower of David
Turris Eburnea	Tower of ivory
Domus Aurea	Golden house
Foederis Arca	Ark of the Covenant
Janus Caeli	Door of heaven
Stella Matutina	Morning star
Salus Infirmorum	Salvation of the suffering
Refugium Peccatorum	Shelter of the sinners
Consolatrix Afflictorum	Comforter of the distressed
Regina Angelorum	Queen of the angels
Regina Patriarcharum	Queen of the angels
Regina Prophetarum	Queen of the prophets
Regina Apostolorum	Queen of the apostles
Regina Martyrum	Queen of martyrs
Regina Confessorum	Queen of confessors
Regina Virginium	Queen of virgins
Regina Sanctorum Omnium	Queen of all the saints
Regina Sine Labe Originalis	Immaculate Queen Concepta
Regina Sacratissimi Rosarii	Queen of the holy rosary
Regina Pacis	Queen of peace
Regina Amoris	Queen of love
Regina Beatitudinis	Queen of Bliss
Imperatrix Mundi	Empress of the world
Lumen Veritatis	Light of Pure Divine Love

Om Twameva Sakshat Shri Omkara Sakshat
Shri Jesus Mahavishnu Sakshat
Shri Mary Mahalakshmi Sakshat
Shri Adi Shakti Bhagawati
Shri Maha Devi Namoh Namah

JESUS the CHRIST – Agnya Chakra

According to the Qur'an, Jesus' true name was Isa.

Notovich, a Russian scholar, arrived in Kashmir during one of several journeys to the Orient. While visiting as a guest in a Buddhist monastery at the Zoji-la pass, a monk told him of the bhodisattva great saint called "Issa". The remarkable parallels between Issa's life, his teachings, and crucifixion that paralleled Jesus stunned Notovich. Who had lived the simple life of the Essenes and became an enlightened master of the light consciousness and later taught these ideals to his disciples.

For about sixteen years, Jesus traveled through Turkey, Persia and Egypt and finally arrived with Mary to a place near Kashmir. After many years in Kashmir, teaching to an appreciative population who venerated him as a great saint prophet, reformer and saint— he died and was buried in a tomb in Kashmir itself.

The Lord's Prayer

OM - Our heavenly Father, who dwells in the Heavens,
Holy is your name,
Our Kingdom will come, it will be done,
On Earth as it is in Heaven,
Give us this day, our daily bread,
And forgive us our trespasses, and sins
As we forgive those, who trespass and sin against us,
And lead us not into temptation of ego
But deliver us from all evil,
For yours is the Kingdom, of the Power and the Glory,
Forever and ever, OM

Quotes of Jesus

"Ask and it will be given to you; seek and you will find; knock and the door will be opened to you."

"What shall it profit a man if he gains the whole world but loses his soul."

"Do unto others as you would have them do unto you."
(For every action there is an equal and opposite reaction - law of karma)

Luke 18:25—*"It is easier for a camel to pass through the eye of a needle than for a rich man to enter the Kingdom of Heaven"*

Corinthians 5:7—*"For we walk by faith, not by sight."*

"For everyone who exalts himself will be humbled, and he who humbles himself will be exalted."

"Yes I am with you always, until the very end of time"

"Let him who is without sin cast the first stone."

John 3:16—*"For God so loved the World that he gave his only begotten Son"*

(In the holy trinity of the Vedic form Shiva, Ganesha and Parvati imbibe the same aspects of Father, Son and Holy Ghost trinity would that mean Ganesha is the same spiritual principal as Jesus - incarnated)

"The good man brings good things out of the good stored up in his heart, and the evil man brings evil things out of the evil stored up in his heart. For out of the overflow of his heart his mouth speaks."

John 4:4—*"Greater is He that is in you, than he that is in the world."*

"No one lights a lamp and puts it in a place where it will be hidden, or under a bowl. Instead he puts it on its stand, so that those who come in may see the light."

"Love the Lord your God with all your passion and prayer and intelligence. Love others as well as you love yourself."

The 108 Names of Lord Jesus the Christ

Namaste to the Son of His Virgin Mother, who was born to teach us of His father Sadashiva, the Everlasting aspect of God Almighty OM.

He is the Primordial Being, the AUM.

He is Vishnu and the son of Vishnu.

He is Mahavishnu.

He is pure pranava energy.

He contains millions of universes.

He was born in the Primordial Cosmic Egg.

He was conceived in the heart of Shri Parvati / Maha Devi.

The prophets foretold him.

A star in the east heralded him.

The three magi, who were Brahma, Shiva and Vishnu, attended him.

He was born in a stable.

He is the teacher.

He is a friend of the cows.

Cows attended him.

His Father is Shri Krishna.

His Mother is Shri Radha.

He is the savior who burns all our sins with His fire.

He adorns the Agnya Chakra.

He is light.

He is of the nature of sky.

He is fire.

He performed miracles out of His compassion.

He whose cloak was touched.

He is a friend of ascetics.

Families worship him.

He is the Bija Mantras Ham and Ksham.

He is the forgiver.

He allows us to forgive.

He is the Spirit.

He is born of the Spirit.

He who was crucified and resurrected in pure Spirit.

He who rose after three days.

He is peace.

He absorbs all thought.

He abides in the Adi Agnya Chakra.

He who promised The Comforter, who is Shri Maha Devi,

The Holy Spirit.

He who returns as a King.

He is Shri Kalki.

He is the principle of evolution.

He is the support of our evolution.

He is the end of evolution.

He is the evolution from collective subconscious to collective Consciousness.

He is the narrow gate.

He is the way to the Kingdom of Heaven.

He is the silence.

He is Lord Karttikeya.

He is Shri Maha Ganesha.

He is the purity of innocence.

He is continence.

He is generosity.

He is the light in the eyes of Shri Mahalaxshmi.

He is obedient to His Mother.

He is the perfect Yogi.

He is the perfect brother.

He is the embodiment of joy.

He is the embodiment of gentleness.

He spits out the half hearted.

He who condemns all fanatics.

He who is uninterested in riches.

He who gives all riches to his devotees.

He who is pure white.

He is the sacred heart.

He wears a crown of thorns.

He who condemns misery.

He who suffered so that we should enjoy.

He is a child.

He is ever ancient.

He is the Alpha and the Omega.

He who gives the Kingdom of Heaven equally to those who are first or last.

He is ever with us.

He is beyond the Universe.

He is the sign of the cross.

He is above discrimination.

He is the witness.

He is the one who is witnessed.

He who overcomes temptation.

He who exorcizes evil.

He who condemns occult practices.

He is the embodiment of tapas (penance).

He worships His Father.

His Father hallows him.

He whose name is Holy.

He is intelligence.

He is wisdom.

He is perfect humility.

He is angry with materialists.

He destroys ego.

He absorbs superego.

He is the destroyer of desires.

He is the pure power of desire.

His church is the heart.

He has the eleven destroying powers.

He is the destroyer of false prophets.

He is the destroyer of untruth.

He is the destroyer of intolerance.

He is the destroyer of racialism.
He is the destroyer of anger.
He is the herald of the Golden Age.
He is adored by Maha Devi the Mother.
He is praised by our Mother Maha Devi.
Our Mother loves him.
He is the One who is chosen.
He is awakened in all Yogis.
He who rides the white horse at the end of the age.
He is the end of our fears.
He guards the gate of our Mother.
He is the only way to the Kingdom of God.

AUM Shri Mahalakshmi Mahavishnu Sakshat
Shri Mahavirata sakshat Shri Adi Shakti Bhagavati Shri Maha Devi Namoh namah.

The 108 Names of Shri Mahalakshmi

Lakshmi by Raja Ravi Varma.

The aspect of the divine or Goddess of wealth, prosperity, light, wisdom, fortune, fertility, generosity and courage; and the embodiment of beauty, grace and charm.

Shri Mahalakshmi Sakshat! Shri Kamalaksha Nivesita Sakshat!

Shri Dhanadhyaksha Sakshat! Shri Jana Chakra Antaralastha Sakshat!

"Sri Rasthu"

Shri Lakshmi Astothra, Sadha Naamavali

Aum Prakruthyai Namah

Aum Vikruthyai Namah

Aum Vidyaayai Namah

Aum Sarvabhoothahithapradayai Namah

Aum Shraddhayai Namah

Aum Vibhuthyai Namah

Aum Surabhyai Namah

Aum Paramatmikaayai Namah

Aum Vache Namah

Aum Padmalayaayai Namah

Aum Padmaayai Namah

Aum Shuchaye Namah

Aum Swahaayai Namah

Aum Swadhaayai Namah

Aum Sudhaayai Namah

Aum Dhanyaayai Namah

Aum Hiranmaiyai Namah

Aum Lakshmaiyai Namah

Aum Nityapushtayai Namah

Aum Vibhavaryai Namah

Aum Adhithyai Namah

Aum Dheethyai Namah

Aum Deepthaayai Namah

Aum Vasudhaayai Namah

Aum Vasudhaarinyai Namah

Aum Kamalaayai Namah

Aum Kaanthayai Namah

Aum Kaamakshyai Namah

Aum Kamala sambhavaayai Namah

Aum Anugrahapradhaayai Namah Aum Buddhaiyai Namah
Aum Anaghaayai Namah Aum Harivallabhaayai Namah
Aum Ashokaayai Namah Aum Amruthaayai Namah
Aum Deepaayai Namah Aum Lokashoka vinashinyai Namah
Aum Dharmanilayaayai Namah Aum Karunaayai Namah
Aum Lokamatre Namah Aum Padmapriyaayai Namah
Aum Padmahasthaayai Namah Aum Padmakshyai Namah
Aum Padmasundariyai Namah Aum Padmodbhavaayai Namah
Aum Padmamukhyai Namah Aum Padmanabha priyaayai Namah
Aum Ramaayai Namah Aum Padmamalaadharaayai Namah
Aum Deviyai Namah Aum Padminiyai Namah
Aum Padmagandhinyai Namah Aum Punyagandhaayai Namah
Aum Suprasannaayai Namah Aum Prasadabhi mukhyai Namah
Aum Prabhaayai Namah Aum Chandravadhanaayai Namah
Aum Chandraayai Namah Aum Chandrasahodharyai Namah
Aum Chaturbhujaayai Namah Aum Chandrarupaayai Namah
Aum Indiraayai Namah Aum Indhu sheethalaayai Namah
Aum Ahlaadha jananvaya Namah Aum Pushtyai Namah
Aum Shivaayai Namah Aum Shivakariyai Namah
Aum Satyaayai Namah Aum Vimalaayai Namah
Aum Vishwajananyai Namah Aum Dhustyai Namah
Aum Dharidriya naashinyai Namah Aum Preethi Pushkarinyai Namah
Aum Shanathayai Namah Aum Shuklamaalyaambharaayai Namah
Aum Bhaskaryai Namah Aum Bilva nilayaayai Namah
Aum Vararohaayai Namah Aum Yashaswinyai Namah
Aum Vasundharaayai Namah Aum Udhaarangaayai Namah
Aum Harinyai Namah Aum Hemamalinyai Namah
Aum Dhana dhanyakaryai Namah Aum Siddhayai Namah
Aum Sthraina Soumyaayai Namah Aum Shubhapradaayai Namah
Aum Nrubavema gathanandhayai Namah Aum Varalakshmaiyai Namah
Aum Vasupradhaayai Namah Aum Shubhaayai Namah

Aum Hiranya praakaaraayai Namah
Aum Jayaayai Namah
Aum Vishnuvakshah
Aum Vishnupathnyai Namah
Aum Narayana Samashrithayai Namah
Aum Devlakshmi Namah
Aum Navadurgaayai Namah

Aum Samudhra dhanaayayai Namah
Aum Mangalaayai Namah
Sthalasdhithaayai Namah
Aum Prasannaakshyai Namah
Aum Dharidriya Dhwamsinyai Namah
Aum Sarva padhrava nivaarinyai Namah
Aum Mahakaalyai Namah

Aum Brahma-Vishnu-Shivathmikaayai Namah
Aum Thrikaalagyanasampannaayai Namah
Aum Bhuvaneshwaryai Namah
Aum MahaaLakshmi Astothra sadha Namah

Padma Purana—*Sanskrit*

The Lotus-Purana; contains an account of the period when the world was "as a golden lotus (padma). It encompasses five books (khandas) treating of the creation, the earth, heaven (svarga), and patala.

Mother Mahalakshmi

Siddhibuddhiprade Devi Bhuktimukti pradayeni Mantramurte sada Devi Mahalakshmi namostute, Adyantrahite Devi Adyashakte Maheshwari, Yogje yogsambhute Mahalakshmi namastute, Padmasan sthite Devi Parbrahma swarupini

Parmeshi jaganmatr Mahalakshmi namoste Te

O Devi, giver of intelligence and success and of worldly enjoyment and liberation (as well), Thou hast always the Mantras as Thy form,

O Mahalaklshmi, obeisance to Thee.

O Devi, Maheshwari, without a beginning or an end,

O Primeval Energy, born of Yoga,

O Mahalakshmi obeisance to Thee.

O Devi, seated on the lotus, who art the Parabhrama,

the great Lord and Mother of the universe,

O Mahalakshmi, obeisance to Thee.

Shri Hanumana Chalisa

The Chalisa Hymn starts with an invocation to the Guru Dohathe in the form of Hanuman.

Hanuman raises the devotee to his own Shri Guru Charan Saroj Raj, (level of vibration), which is a Nij Manu Mukuru Sudhari, perpetual state of bliss.

Tulsidas States:

"I bow to the Lotus Feet of the Barnaun Raghubar Bimal Jasu,

Divine Guru His Jo Dayaku Phal Chari.

The dust of Feet shall clean the mirror of my mind".

Now I will describe the pure glory of Shri Ram who bestows all the four gifts-Buddhiheen Tanu Janike.

Dharma,	(Virtuousness)
Artha Sumiraun Pavan Kumar,	(Wealth)
Kama,	(Desire)
And Moksha,	(Liberation, Salvation)

I pray to Hanuman to grant me strength, wisdom and knowledge to relieve me of all my sufferings and impurities".

The main body of Hanuman Chalisa, has forty quatrains,

That praise Hanuman's qualities of the head and the heart, used for fulfilling the Divine mission to protect the good and destroying the evil.

7—Sahastrara Chakra

Sahastrara Chakra (crown) - *Connection to the Virata*

Om twameva sakshat_________ Namo Namaha
Shri Sadashiva
Shri Adi Shakti
Shri Lalita Chakra Swamini
Shri Chakra Swamini

The following mantra helps dilatate the "Brahmanadi" as it destroys the obstacle to the door at the mouth of Brahma Nadi (Sushumna channel). It enables one to understand and know the Kundalini energy.

Shri Brahmanadi Swamini

Sahastrara Mantras
Shri Atma Parmatma,
Shri Amruta Dayini,
Shri Ardha Bindu
Shri Bindu
Shri Valaya

Ekadesha Rudra—Omega

Shri Kalki – *The Final Judgment*

The collective Christ or light consciousness (aspect of Ganesha) possesses the Powers of Ekadesha Rudras – Shri Kalki is the destroyer, the second incarnation of Jesus. They are the Alfa and Omega, the beginning and the end. Shri Kalki who is known as the rider on the white horse, and who will ride through the flames on judgment day or the end times of 2012. The flames represent the opening of the Sahasrara chakra and the final judgment of how our vibrations hold up under the pure light of divine light consciousness. The destruction of lower illusions during the 2012 end time is a physical manifestation of the universal powers of the Ekadesha Rudra, that manifests through the deity Shri Kalki and Shri Vishnumya, that control the weather and powers of nature.

With eleven destroying powers Ekadesha Rudra is the final incarnation of the evolving principle of Shri Vishnu. The cure is to develop the divine discretion to give up wrong ideas about God, false teachers and Gurus who lead humanity down the path of false knowledge.

The 11 Ekadesa Rudras

Om Twameva Sakshat Shri Ekadesha Rudra Sakshat
Shri Adi Shakti Maha Devi Namoh namaha

Om Twameva Sakshat Shri Maha Ganesha Namoh namaha
Om Twameva Sakshat Shri Maha Bhairava Namoh namaha
Om Twameva Sakshat Shri Hernia Garbha Namoh namaha

Om Twameva Sakshat Shri Buddha Namoh Nemaha
Om Twameva Sakshat Shri Mahavira Namoh namaha
Om twameva Sakshat Shri Jesus Namoh namaha
Om Twameva Sakshat Shri Lakshmi Narayanam Namoh namaha
Om Twameva Sakshat Shri Shiva Shakti Namoh namaha
Om Twameva Sakshat Shri Karttikeya Namoh namaha

Om Twameva sakshat Shri Maha Hanumana namoh namaha
Om Twameva sakshat Shri Brahmadeva Saraswati namoh namaha

Om Twameva Sakshat Shri Sarva Mantra Siddhi Vibhedini
Sakshat Shri Adi Shakti Maha Devi Namoh Namaha

How to correct problems with the Ekadesha Rudra

1. Establish your innocence. Keep attention /eyes to our Mother Earth (Shri Bhoomi Devi)
2. Cleanse your Void. / if you went to a false guru shoe beat his name on Mother Earth.
3. Put your attention more towards Mother Nature than to other people.
4. Be a witness; stop controlling if you are catching on this centre.
5. Obstinacy catches here.
6. A half-hearted commitment to spiritual growth can cause a problem with the Ekadesha Rudra.
7. The Ekadesha Rudra collects from the left and the right Sympathetic. So the combination of left and or right catch will affect it.

The Kavach of the Devi

Guru Brahma, Guru Vishnu, Guru Devo Maheshwarah

Guru Sakshat Parabrahma, Shri Maha Devi Nirmala Ma.

Tasmai Shri Guruveh Namaha.

Our Sath Guru is The Great Mother.

All Her Shakti and Yogini aspects are available for Her children.

By reading The Kavach of The Devi, we mobilize these powers to purify and Enlighten our Koshas *(our mental, emotional and physical bodies).* Thus by the Power of the Gurumata The Atma becomes The Guru of the body. While reading The Kavach of The Devi one should put one's attention on the aspect or part of the body that is protected. One may also, while reading, pause between the names and silently take the corresponding mantra, for example:

Om Twameva Sakshat, *Shri Chandi* **Namoh Namah**

The Kavach should be read aloud. It washes away the 'catches' and bathes the children in Divine Vibrations. May the wisdom and compassion of our Satguru flow through us and reach the four quarters of the earth.

The protection of Shri Chandi.

Salutations to Shri Ganesha.

Salutations to Shri Saraswati.

Salutations to Shri Guru.

Salutations to the Deity Shri Maha Devi, may there be no obstacle.

Amen. Salutations to Narayan.

Amen. Salutations to Naranaratam, that is, Shri Vishnu.

Amen. Salutations to The Goddess Saraswati. Salutations to Ved-Vyasa, that is, Sage Vyasa, the all knowing.

Now begins the "Kavach" of The Devi.

> The Presiding Sage for Shri Chandi-Kavach is Brahma, the metre is Anushtup. The Presiding Deity is Chamunda; The Main Seed is "Anganyasakta Matar". The Principle is Digbandha Devata. It is recited as part of Sapta-Shati, to please Jagadamba.
>
> Amen. Obeisance to Chandika.

Thus spoke Markandeya:

AUM, O Brahmadeva, please tell me that which is very secret and has not been told by anyone to anybody else and which protects all human beings in this world.

Brahmadeva said: Brahmin, there is Devi Kavach which is most secret and is useful to all beings. Please listen to that, O Great Sage.

The following nine names, have been created by the Great Soul Brahmadeva himself.

Durga is known by these names:

First,	Shailaputri	Daughter of the King of Himalayas,
Second,	Brahmacharini	One Who observes the state of Celibacy,
Third,	Chandraganta	One Who bears the Moon around Her neck,
Fourth,	Kooshmanda	Whose Void contains the Universe
Fifth,	Skandamata	Who gave birth to Karttikeya,
Sixth,	Katyayani	Who incarnated to help the Devas,
Seventh,	Kalaratri	Who is even the destroyer of Kali,
Eighth,	Mahagauri	One Who made great penances,
Ninth,	Siddhidatri	One Who grants Moksha.

Those of you whom are frightened, who have been surrounded by the enemies on the Battle field, or are burning in fire, or being at an impassable place, would face no Calamity, and would never have grief, sorrow, fear, or evil, if they surrender to Durga.

Those who remember you with great devotion indeed have prosperity.

Undoubtedly, O Goddess of The Gods, You protect those who remember you.

The Goddess Chamunda sits on a corpse, Varahi rides on a buffalo, Aindri is Mounted on an elephant and Vaishnavi on a condor.

Maheshwari is riding on a bull, the vehicle of Kaumari is the peacock, Lakshmi, the Beloved of Shri Vishnu is seated in a lotus and is also holding a lotus in Her Hand.

The Goddess Ishwari, of white complexion, is riding on a bull and Brahmi, Who is Bedecked with all ornaments is seated on a swan.

All the mothers are endowed with Yoga and are adorned with different ornaments and jewels.

All the Goddesses are seen mounted in chariots and very angry. They are wielding conch, discus, mace, plough, club, javelin, axe, noose, barbed dart, trident, bow and arrows. These Goddesses are wielding their weapons for destroying the bodies of demons, for the protection of Their devotees and for the benefit of The Gods.

Salutations to You, O Goddess, of very dreadful appearance, of frightening valor, of tremendous strength and energy, the destroyer of the worst fears.

O Devi, it is difficult to have even a glance at You. You increase the fears of Your enemies, please come to my rescue. May Goddess Aindri protect me from the east. Agni Devata (Goddess of Fire) from the south-east, Varahi (Shakti of Vishnu in the form of the boar) from the south, Khadgadharini (Wielder of the sword) from the south-west, Varuni (The Shakti of Varuna the rain God) from the west and Mrgavahini, (whose vehicle is the deer) may protect me from the north-west.

The Goddess Kaumari (The Shakti of Kumar, that is, Karttikeya) protect me from the north and Goddess Shooladharini from the north-east, Brahmani, (The Shakti of Brahma) from above and Vaishnavi (Shakti of Vishnu) from below, protect me.

Thus Goddess Chamunda, Who sits on a corpse, protects me from all the ten directions. May Goddess Jaya protect me from the front and Vijaya from the rear; Ajita from the left and Aparajita from the right. Goddess Dyotini may protect the top-knot and Uma may sit on my head and protect it.

May I be protected by Maladhari on the forehead. Yashaswini on the eye-brows, Trinetra between the eye-brows, Yamaghanta on the nose, Shankini on both the eyes, Dwaravasini on the ears, may Kalika protect my cheeks and Shankari the roots of the ears.

May I be protected by Sugandha-nose, Charchika-lip, Amrtakala-lower lip, Saraswati-tongue, Kaumari-teeth, Chandika-throat, Chitra-ghanta-sound box, Mahamaya-crown of the head, Kamakshi-chin, Sarvamangala-speech, Bhadrakali-neck, Dhanurdhari-back.

May Neelagreeva protect the outer part of my throat and Nalakoobari-windpipe, may Khadgini protect my shoulders and Vajra-dharini protect my arms.

May Devi Dandini protect both my hands, Ambika-fingers, Shooleshwari my nails and may Kuleshwari protect my belly.

May I be protected, by Mahadevi-breast, Shuladharini-abdomen, Lalita Devi-heart, Kamini-navel, Guhyeshwari-hidden parts, Pootana-kamika-reproductive organs, Mahishavahini-rectum.

May Goddess Bhagavati protect my waist, Vindhyavasini-knees and the wish-fulfilling Mahabala may protect my hips.

May Narasinhi protect my ankles. May Taijasi protect my feet, may Shri protect my toes. May Talavasini protect the soles of my feet.

May Danshtrakarali protect my nails, Urdhvakeshini-hair, Kauberi-pores, Vagishwari-skin.

May Goddess Parvati protect blood, marrow of the bones, fat and bone; Goddess Kalaratri-intestines, Mukuteshwari-bile and liver.

May Padmavati protect the Chakras, Choodamani-phlegm (or longs), Jwala-mukhi lustre of the nails and Abhedya-all the joints.

Brahmani-semen, Chhatreshwari the shadow of my body, Dharmadharini-ego, superego and intellect (buddhi).

Vajrahasta-pran, apan, vyan, udan, saman (five vital breaths). Kalyana-shobhana-pranas (life force).

May Yogini protect the sense organs, that is, the faculties of tasting, seeing, smelling, hearing and touching.

May Narayni protect satwa, raja and tamo gunas. Varahi-the life, Vaishnavi-dharma, Lakshmi-success and fame, Chakrini-wealth and knowledge. Indrani-relatives, Chandika-cattle, Mahalakshmi-children and Bhairavi-spouse.

Supatha may protect my journey and Kshemakari my way. Mahalakshmi may protect me in the king's courts and Vijaya everywhere.

O Goddess Jayanti, any place that has not been mentioned in the Kavach and has thus remained unprotected, may be protected by you.

One should invariably cover oneself with this Kavacha (by reading) wherever one goes and should not walk even a step without it if one desires Auspiciousness. Then one is successful everywhere and all one's desires are fulfilled and that person enjoys great prosperity on the earth.

The person who covers himself with Kavach becomes fearless, is never defeated in the battle and becomes worthy of being worshipped in the three worlds.

One who reads with faith every day thrice (morning, afternoon and evening), the 'Kavacha' of the Devi, which is inaccessible even to the Gods, receives the Divine arts, is undefeated in the three worlds, lives for a hundred years and is free from accidental death.

All diseases, like boils, scars, etc. are finished. Moveable (scorpions and snakes) and immovable (other) poisons cannot affect him.

All those, who cast magical spells, by mantras or yantras, on others for evil purposes, all bhoots, goblins, malevolent beings moving on the earth and in the sky, all those who mesmerize others, all female goblins, all yakshas and gandharvas are destroyed just by the sight of the person having Kavach in his Heart.

That person receives more and more respect and prowess. On the earth he rises in prosperity and fame by reading the Kavacha and Saptashati.

His progeny would live as long as the earth is rich with mountains and forests. By the grace of Mahamaya, he would attain the highest place, that is inaccessible even to the Gods and is eternally blissful in the company of Lord Shiva.

Namaste

Prayer to Mahasaraswati

Ya Kundenu Tushara	You are decorated
Hara Dhavala	With the snow white Garland
Ya Shubra Vastra Vruta	You wear a white sari
Ya Vina Vara Danda	You hold a veena in your hand
	Mandita Kara
Ya Shweta Padmasana	You reside in a white lotus
Ya Brahma Chuta Shankara	You are praised by all the Deities
	including Shri
	Shiva, Shri Vishnu and Shri Brahma
Prabhritibhir	You are adored by devotees
Devai Sada Vandita	
Samampatu Saraswati	
Bhagavati	Protect us
Nishesha jadyapaha	Destroy the ignorance.

The Negativity Destroying Mantras

Shri Shattru Mardini	
Shri Ambika Devi	
Shri Madhusudanya	
Shri Tarakasura Sambhantri	
Nishumbha Shumba Sanhantri	Destroyer of Shumbha & Nishumba
Shri Durga	Destroyer of the Asuras
Shri Raksakari	Savoir from Raksasas
Shri Rakshasaghni	Slayer of Raksasas
Shri Chamunda	Killer of Chanda & Munda
Shri Madhu Kaitabhahantri	
Shri Nara Kantaka	

The Mantras for the Ida Nadi *(left side)*

Aum Twameva Sakshat, Shri Maha Bhairava sakshat,
Shri Adi Shakti Maha Devi Namoh Namaha.

Aum Shri Siddha Bhairava	Yanamaha
Aum Shri Vatuka Bhairava	Yanamaha
Aum Shri Kamkala Bhairava	Yanamaha
Aum Shri Kala Bhairava	Yanamaha
Aum Shri Kalagni Bhairava	Yanamaha
Aum Shri Yogini Bhairava	Yanamaha
Aum Shri Maha Bhairava	Yanamaha
Aum Shri Shakti Bhairava	Yanamaha
Aum Shri Ananda Bhairava	Yanamaha
Aum Shri Martanda Bhairava	Yanamaha
Aum Shri Gaura Bhairava	Yanamaha

**Aum twameva sakshat, Shri Mahakali sakshat,
Shri Adi Shakti Shri Maha Devi Namoh Namaha.**

The 21 Names of Shri Bhairava—*The Archangel Michael*

Om twameva sakshat Shri Maha Bhairava namoh namaha
Om twameva sakshat Shri Vatuka Bhairava namoh namaha
Om twameva sakshat Shri Siddha Bhairava namoh namaha
Om twameva sakshat Shri Kankala Bhairava namoh namaha
Om twameva sakshat Shri Kala Bhairava namoh namaha
Om twameva sakshat Shri Kalagni Bhairava namoh namaha
Om twameva sakshat Shri Yogini Bhairava namoh namaha
Om twameva sakshat Shri Shakti Bhairava namoh namaha
Om twameva sakshat Shri Ananda Bhairava namoh namaha
Om twameva sakshat Shri Martanda Bhairava namoh namaha
Om twameva sakshat Shri Gaura Bhairava namoh namaha
Om twameva sakshat Shri Bala Bhairava namoh namaha
Om twameva sakshat Shri Batu Bhairava namoh namaha
Om twameva sakshat Shri Shmashana Bhairava namoh namaha
Om twameva sakshat Shri Pura Bhairava namoh namaha
Om twameva sakshat Shri Taruna Bhairava namoh namaha
Om twameva sakshat Shri Paramananda Bhairava namoh namaha
Om twameva sakshat Shri Surananda Bhairava namoh namaha
Om twameva sakshat Shri Gyanananda Bhairava namoh namaha
Om twameva sakshat Shri Uttamananda Bhairava namoh namaha
Om twameva sakshat Shri Amritananda Bhairava namoh namaha

The 108 Names of Shri Mahakali

Aspect of eternal energy, time and change

We, the "Children of the Light", are bowing to the immaculate desire of divine light consciousness the almighty light of all things.

Om Twameva Sakshat Shri...

Mahakali	The seed energy of God's desire.
Kamadhenu	Wish-fulfilling cow.
Kamaswarupa	Whose form is desire.
Varada	Bestower of boons.
Jagadanandakarini	Cause of the total Bliss of the Universe.
Jagatjivamayi	Total life-force of the Universe.
Vajrakankali	Transforms the human skull into a thunderbolt.
Shanta	Peace.
Sudhasindhunivasini	Dwelling in the cosmic ocean of nectar.
Nidra	Sleep
Tamasi	Generating and presiding over the tamo guna.
Nandini	Pleasing everyone.
Sarvanandaswarupini	Embodying universal joy.
Paramanandarupa	The highest form of Divine Bliss.

Stutya	The most fitted for all adoration and worship.
Padmalaya	Residing in the purest lotus.
Sadapujya	The sacred immutable object of adoration.
Sarvapriyankari	Universal wish-fulfilling Divine Energy.
Sarvamangala	The Auspiciousness of the Cosmos.
Purna	Perfect, complete.
Vilasini	Ocean of joy.
Amogha	Mother whose darshan seldom goes unrewarded.
Bhogawati	The supreme enjoyer of the Universe.
Sukhada	Bestowing perfect happiness on Her devotees.
Nishkama	Desireless
Madhukaitabhahantri	Killer of Madhu and Kaitaba
Mahishasuraghatini	Slayer of Mahishasura
Raktabijavinashini	Destroyer of Raktabija
Narakantaka	Destroyer of Narak.
Ugrachandeshwari	Fire, hailstorm and fury;
Krodhini	Cosmic wrath.
Ugraprabha	Radiance of fury.
Chamunda	Killer of Chanda and Munda
Khadgapalini	She rules by the sword.
Bhaswarasuri	Whose fierce radiance destroys the demonic forces.
Shatrumardini	The Slayer of the enemies of the saints.
Ranapandita	Mastering the science of wars and battles.
Raktadantika	Whose sparkling teeth are red with blood.
Raktapriya	Who is fond of blood.
Kapalini	Holding a skull in Her hand.
Kurukulavirodhini	Confronting demonic hosts and all sins of the world.

Krishnadeha	Dark bodied.
Naramundali	Wearing a garland of human skulls.
Galatrudhirabhushana	Whose clothes are dripping with blood.
Praitanrityaparayana	The Spirit of the cosmic dance of dissolution.
Lolajivha	With Her tongue coming out.
Kundalini	Residual energy of the Holy Spirit.
Nagakanya	The virgin serpent.
Patiwrata	Devoted wife.
Shivasangi	Eternal companion of Shri Shiva.
Visangi	Without any companion.
Bhutapatipriya	Fond of the protector of the bhoots i.e. Shiva.
Pretabhumikritalaya	Dwelling in the land of bhoots and ghosts.
Daityendramathini	The victorious chief demon-slayer.
Chandraswarupini	Of the form and cooling radiance of the moon.
Prasannapadmavadana	Having a bright, smiling lotus-like face.
Smerawakttra	The Divine Mother with smiling countenance.
Sulochana	With such beautiful eyes.
Sudantee	Having marvelous glittering teeth.
Sindurarunamastaka	Who puts the red sindur on Her forehead.
Sukaishi	With magnificent long, dark hair.
Smitahasya	Eternally smiling to Her devotees.
Mahatkucha	Her heavy breasts give milk to the whole Universe.
Priyabashini	Gifted with loving eloquence.
Shubhashini	Her speech is soft and sound.
Muktakaishi	Her disheveled hair grants liberation.
Chandrakotisamaprabha	Shining with the luster of a million moons.
Agadharupini	Whose immeasurable beauty enchants the Universe.
Manohara	Magnetic and fascinating so that She

	wins the hearts.
Manorama	Highest Divine grace and charm to please all.
Vashya	Celestial charmer enticing all in Her web of Love.
Sarvasaundaryanilaya	Home of all beauty.
Rakta	Red is Her color.
Swayambhukusumaprana	She is the life force of the self created flowers.
Swayambhukusumanmada	Intoxicated with the self-created flowers (Chakras).
Shukrapujya	Worshipped as the whiteness of purity.
Shukrastha	Surrounded by a halo of purity and whiteness.
Shukratmika	Soul of purity and sacredness.
Shukranindakanashini	Committed to destroying the foes of holiness.
Nishumbhasumbhasanhartri	Slayer of Shumba and Nishumba.
Vanhimandala Madhyasta	Sitting at the centre of the blazing cosmic fire.
Virjanani	Mother of the brave.
Tripuramalini	Wearing as a trophy the head of the demon Tripura.
Karali	Presiding over the cosmic dissolution.
Pashini	Holding the noose of death.
Ghorarupa	Terrifying form.
Ghoradanshtra	Having fierce jaws.
Chandi	Destroys evil tendencies in Her disciples.
Sumati	Mother of the purest wisdom.
Punyada	Showering virtues.
Tapaswini	Ascetic
Kshama	Forgiveness
Tarangini	Bubbling with life and energy.
Shuddha	Saintly chastity.

Sarvaishwari	Mistress of the Cosmos.
Garishtha	Manifesting Her joy at the sight of Her disciples.
Jayashalini	Royal and victorious
Chintamani	Wish-fulfilling Gem
Advaitabhogini	Enjoyer of non-duality
Yogeshwari	Detached
Bhogadarini	Fulfilled intensity of all pleasures, joy, Bliss.
Bhaktabhawita	Fulfilled by the pure Love of Her disciples.
Sadhakanandasantosha	Fulfilled by the joy of Her disciples.
Bhaktavatsala	Cherishing those who worship Her.
Bhaktanandamayi	Source of the eternal Joy of Her disciples.
Bhaktashankari	Bringing the desires of Her disciples to fruition.
Bhaktisamyukta	Bestower of devotion.
Nishkalanka Pure.	

The Vedas

The Vedas are among the oldest sacred texts of our civilization, it is said that the Rig-Veda was compiled from as early as 1500 BC over a period of several centuries.

According to Hindu and other Indian tradition, the Vedas were not of human origin and were supposed to have been directly revealed, to the ancient Rishi and Sages, thus are called śruti ("what is heard"). There is a strong connection and likelihood that the wisdom, and language (Sanskrit) of the Vedas, was given by the Star Teachers of the Pleiades galaxy. It would also make sense that there is only "one" truth of the light consciousness, the stars, and solar occultism. Seems that different alien "Gods" that came to earth, either promoted this knowledge, or suppressed it—based on the agenda of the teachers (Gods). Once the knowledge was taught and imbibed in the spiritual foundation, there became a strategy by the dark forces (Anunnaki) to suppress and color the knowledge, and to confuse and divide. Thus humankind's suffering began and will continue until the great revealing of 2012 that establishes the Golden Age. Namaste

The Mantras of Virata
Universal Divine Light Consciousness

Om Twameva Sakshat
Shri Gruhalakshmi Kubera Virata Sakshat
Shri Adi Shakti Maha Devi Namoh Namaha

Om Twameva Sakshat
Shri Brahmadeva Vithala Virata Sakshat
Shri Adi Shakti Maha Devi Namoh Namaha

Om Twameva Sakshat
Shri Vishnumaya Virata Sakshat
Shri Adi Shakti Maha Devi Namoh Namaha

Om Twameva Sakshat
Shri Vithala Vishnumaya Virata Sakshat
Shri Adi Shakti Maha Devi Namoh Namaha

Om Twameva Sakshat
Shri Nirananda Sakshat
Shri Adi Shakti Maha Devi Namoh Namaha

Dedication: *This book is dedicated to all the seekers, and teachers of the divine light consciousness, and all the many friends and family that have inspired its truth to be told. I would also like to thank; my beautiful Mother Ellen Carrigan, Anand and Kaelyn Carrigan for allowing Dad to be consumed in his work, my good friend Jim Doig for all his endless help, and Brenda Isherwood a true friend of the spirit, as well as all those not mentioned. I love you all. Namaste*

2012 Events—Timeline Predictions

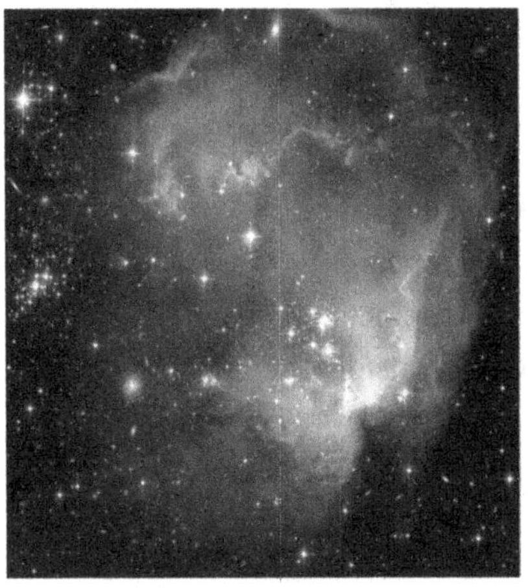

Timeline predictions on the physical events, pre and post 2012, are based on a compilation of all information available to us from scientists, spiritualists, historians and many government and political *whistle blowers*, who risked their lives, jobs, and in some cases, have been killed after revealing classified documents and information.

We do not take what is said lightly, and hope you can see the truth and wisdom behind the message—and, as well, conduct personal research to make your own *informed* decisions.

2010—2011	Natural Disasters Increase
	Illuminati—New World Order
	Deploy Bio Terrorism: H1N1 (Avian Flu Pandemic)
	Initiate selected bombings in US Cities: Incite Fear in Population
	Initiate Marshall Law to quell Civil Unrest: Citizen Detainment—CDF
	Arrival of Anunnaki (Aliens): False Promises & Enslavement
2011—2012	Natural Disasters Increase—Pole Shift—2/3rds of Population could die
	Illuminati—New World Order
	Population Control & Detainment
	World Governments move to underground facilities
	Survivors hunted by Illuminati controlled Government Forces
	Illuminati moves toward Total World Domination
	Battle of Armageddon—Begins: Truth verses Deception
	Illuminati forces rebel: truth uncovered by the dominated and misled
2012—2013	Battle of Armageddon—Continues
	New Age of Humankind Begins (March 2013—Mayan Calendar)
	Survivors look for answers
2014—2017	Battle of Armageddon—Ends
	New Age of Humankind—Begins to Form
	The Foundation of the Golden Age is Laid.

References

Aerial Image—Courtesy to Lucy Pringle, Steve Alexander & Jack Turner

Web Sites:

http://www.timstouse.com/ScienceNews/chilbolton.htm
http://www.lucypringle.co.uk/photos/2009/jun.shtml
http://www.pufoin.com/pufoin_perspective/contact.php
http://www.david-sadler.org/pages/bigQuestions/discIsOurs.htm
http://ourworld.compuserve.com/homepages/dp5/cropcirc1.htm
http://cropcirclemeanings.blogspot.com/
http://www.phils.com.au/cropcircle.htm
http://toraor.net/index.php

Books:

The deepening complexity of crop circles—Eltjo Haselhoff
Crop circles—Colin Andrews, Stephen J. Spignesi
Crop circles—Werner Anderhub, Hans Peter Roth
Crop Circles—Carolyn North, Busty Taylor

Miscellaneous:

[1] Zecharia Sitchin—The 12th Planet, 1976, The Wars of Gods and Men, 1985, Genesis Revisited, 1990, Divine Encounters, 1995, Avon Books, New York.

[2] Laurence Gardner—Genesis of the Grail Kings, Bantam Press, New York, 1999.

[3] Bramley, William—The Gods of Eden, Avon Books, New York, 1989, 1990.

Book in Review

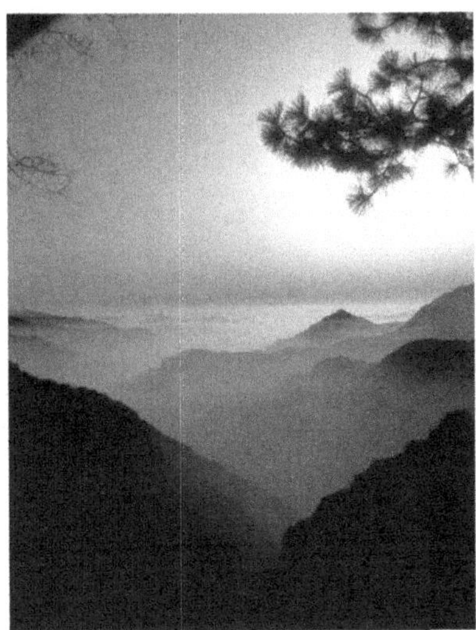

2012 ENLIGHTENED *– by* ***Brad C Carrigan***

2012 ENLIGHTENED encompasses and creates inspiring and beautiful insights into our ancient journey of spiritual ascent—into and beyond modern times. It is a book that masterfully merges the ancient knowledge and wisdom of the past, the 2012 transformation period, and the evolution of the spirit into a deep; but easy to understand; bridge to the coming Golden Age.

At a time of great trials and tribulations within and outside of our realm of comprehension, *2012 Enlightened* presents a refreshing truth and the limitless boundaries of our ascent as a civilization on the brink, and as individuals transforming into the spiritual plane of the 5th dimensional collective light consciousness.

This insightful book is beautifully written and packaged with a powerful blend of 2012 facts, Sanskrit mantras, evocative artwork and design, creating a oneness and clarity that travels beyond our past, present and future journey as evolving spiritual beings. It is a masterpiece of love translated from the light awareness.

Doom & Gloom is a mental concept of fear: that is not our intent or focus in this book. This book is about empowerment—with truth and understanding we become empowered to see what is, and to make decisions, and take responsibility for our knowledge (or lack thereof).

The reality is the media of the world, in most cases, are afraid or controlled by the forces that have been suppressing this truth and knowledge. This does not mean that it does not exist!